TV LAND—*Detroit*

TV LAND
Detroit

Gordon Castelnero

THE UNIVERSITY OF MICHIGAN PRESS Ann Arbor

Copyright © by Gordon Castelnero 2006
All rights reserved
Published in the United States of America by
The University of Michigan Press
Manufactured in the United States of America
⊛ Printed on acid-free paper

2009   2008   2007   2006   4   3   2   1

A CIP catalog record for this book is available from the British Library.

Library of Congress Cataloging-in-Publication Data

Castelnero, Gordon, 1965–
    TV land—Detroit / Gordon Castelnero.
        p.   cm.
    ISBN-13: 978-0-472-03124-5 (pbk. : alk. paper)
    ISBN-10: 0-472-03124-4 (pbk. : alk. paper)
        1. Television broadcasting—Michigan—Detroit—History.   I. Title.

PN1992.3.U5C298   2006
384.5509774'34—dc22   2005028458

Cover illustration © Mack Dobbie

To my parents,
Joseph and Sharon Castelnero
Thank you for a lifetime of
encouragement and support!

Acknowledgments

Of the 123 people who contributed to the completion of this book, my biggest debt of gratitude goes to my friend Larry Dlusky. His incredibly detailed memories of local television in the 1950s and 1960s proved to be one of my most valuable resources. Larry was instrumental in making me sound intelligent when discussing programs that aired well before I was even an idea.

A very special thank you is owed to all of my interviewees for taking the time to reminisce with me about old Detroit TV. All of the stories that appear in this book are the result of their collective memories. Their enthusiastic desire to share personal experiences, photographs, and memorabilia with the public validated all of my reasons for writing this book. In alphabetical order, they are: Neil Addison, Bob Allison, LaWanda Anner, Joe Babiarz, Jerry Booth, Jim Breault, Jim Burgan, Jerry Burke, Art Cervi, Jerry Chiappetta, Ron David, Dave Deming, Lawson Deming, Chuck Derry, John Dew, Dick Dietrich, Sonny Eliot, Jack Flechsig, Errol Fortin, Karlin Fox, Marilyn Fox, Dr. Sonya Friedman, Frank Gadwell, Johnny Ginger, Ed Golick, Deborah Gordon, Scott Gordon, Jerry Hansen, Wally Harrison, John Hilt, Lynda Hirsch, Joe Humeniuk, Jim Humlong, Matt Keelan, John Kelly, Suzy Kennedy, Teri Knapp, Linda Lanci, Henry Maldonado, Carol Marenko, Maureen Mayne, Bob McNea, Tony Micale, Marty Mitton, Chris Montross, Nat Morris, Bill Murray, Ken Muse, Mark Nowotarski, Laurie Oberman, Dr. Alan Pierrot, George Prybyla, Frank Quinn, Dave Riley, Jerry Rimmer, Maurine Robinson, Shaun Robinson, Irv Romig, Art Runyon, Greg Russell, Soupy Sales, Robin Seymour, Erik Smith, Steve Southard, Bob Stackpoole, Chris Stepien, Ellen Stepien, Wayne Stevens, Ron Sweed, Peggy Tibbits, Larry Thompson, Marilyn Turner, Dan Weaver, Mason Weaver, Marv Welch, Mary Wilson, Marci Wojciechowski, and George Young.

Additional recognition goes to the following individuals for their efforts in supplying me with extra photographs, biographical material, coordinating interviews, and other miscellaneous services. Listed alphabetically, they are: Jane Adler, Susan Anastasiou, Larry Baranski, Vivian

Baulch, Marilyn Bond, Gina Brintley, Sue Brooks, Evan Callanan, Dave Carrick, John Claster, Kelley Colello, Mary Rita Deming, Rick Deming, Mack Dobbie, Marty Eddy, Tom Featherstone, Sharon Gates-Rees, Sheryl Helewski, Jerry Hodak, Joanne Hoppe, Gary Howell, Bob Hynes, Dick Kernen, Barb Koster, Rana Kozouz, Bill Laitner, Jan Lovell, Mary Terese Matousek, George Megown, Ruth Miles, Dave Muse, Kathy Ochs, Gail Pebbles, Derek Petro, Kristofer Petruska, Victor Robinson, Rick Saphire, Laura Sebastian, Rudy Simons, Mike Skinner, Wayne Smith, Joe Weaver, Gerry Whitman, and Anthony Zurcher.

Once again, my sincerest thanks to each and every one of you . . . We did it!

Contents

Introduction

Growing up in suburban Detroit during the 1970s, I spent a lot of time parked in front of the television. As part of a wave known as TV's second generation, I was fortunate enough to witness the tail end of what has become a lost art form. Long before the blitz of cable, satellite dishes, prepackaged syndication, infomercials, and reality shows, there existed a brand of pop culture charm that has forever vanished from the airwaves . . . it was known as LOCAL TV!

Back in the days when a hometown television celebrity was someone other than a news anchor, Motor City stations had a host of stars worth showcasing. In the days of my youth alone, I loved waking up to our clowns Bozo and Oopsy. On rainy and wintry afternoons, I reveled in classic B movies with Bill Kennedy and cheesy horror flicks with Sir Graves Ghastly. After the evening news, I'd watch Bob Allison give away more dinners for two at the Roostertail restaurant than the cash jackpot to neighborhood contestants on *Bowling for Dollars*. And when my parents would let me stay up past my bedtime it was a real treat catching the late-night shenanigans of the Ghoul.

Those are just a few of my personal memories, but, going back even farther to television's first generation, Detroit baby boomers grew up with an even larger ensemble of local heroes. Who can forget the likes of such characters as Soupy Sales, Captain Jolly, and Sagebrush Shorty? How about the lovable circus clown Ricky or the Twin Pines magical clown Milky? Who remembers taxiing their tricycles close to the screen to see *Wixie's Wonderland?* Better yet, who was brave enough to travel way beyond the Ishkabow and over the Foo-Fram Sea for fun with *Jingles in Boofland?* And when the music was changing which Motown teens kept in step with the week's hottest records on *Swingin' Time?*

These classic shows and many more belong to a dying breed of home-made talent that's been overshadowed by the popularity and publicity of our sports figures and musicians. Detroit TV played a key role in many of our upbringings, for which it's earned a special fondness in our memories. The emotional attachment our community has to these shows is the main reason why I chose to write this book.

Early in 2004, I was engaged in a nostalgic conversation with a friend. We reminisced about all the wonderfully unique things that have disappeared from Detroit—everything from restaurants to stores to drive-ins, radio stations, and local television shows. It was the part about the TV programs that stuck in my mind. Having worked as an independent television producer, I remembered how much those little local shows inspired me to pursue a career in the media. And because they had such an impact on me I was curious to see just how much they meant to others.

After speaking to a few more individuals, the consensus was the same. Faces lit up with smiles from ear to ear at the mere mention of an old show. It was obvious that someone should do a book to preserve the memory of our television heritage! After all, a number of books have been written that display the richness of Detroit in various contexts: its civic history, architectural wonders, the auto industry, music, and sports. So in late April, with the help of my friend Larry Dlusky (the most trivia-oriented person I know), I began to develop a proposal for a book that would feature 25 of the most popular programs that stand out in people's minds when they think of vintage Detroit TV.

On July 3, 2004, I began the first of what was to become a long but very pleasurable series of interviews. The goal was to tell stories about the shows from the perspective of those who lived them and the fans who loved them! To pull this off, I interviewed 79 people: everyone from the program talent to directors, producers, stagehands, program guests, fans, and relatives of the deceased talent. Why so many? Simply because I wanted the information presented in this publication to be an oral account of Detroit's television history from several viewpoints. Additionally, I think it's much more fascinating to hear what the people involved have to say than to read an outside party's interpretation of events.

Approximately 90 percent of these interviews were conducted in person, with the balance taking place over the telephone. As large as the undertaking was, I saw it as an awesome thrill—a childhood fantasy come true! Not only did I get to meet many of the stars I marveled at as a kid, but in several instances I was a guest in their homes. Most of these folks are still in Michigan, but to interview some of them I traveled as far as New York, Florida, and California. The warm receptions I received from all of them were indeed touching. Their eagerness to relive the "golden age" of Detroit TV was endearing.

Some of the interviews I thought would make wonderful stories in themselves. These included the rainy Saturday afternoon when Trudy Sales served hors d'oeuvres to her husband and me, thus allowing me to have "lunch with Soupy," and the playful banter between John Kelly and Marilyn Turner, which was like having an exclusive front-row seat at an episode of *Kelly & Company*. There were nonstop laughs with Johnny Ginger and the fun of watching Shaun Robinson spring from her *Access Hollywood* chair to demonstrate a dance step she once performed on *The Scene*. I placed my hands inside Boofland puppets Herkimer Dragon and Cecil B. Rabbit and browsed through the personal effects of the late Bill Kennedy at his Palm Beach estate.

Although each interview had its moments, the most precious one for me was when I met Lawson Deming, better known as Sir Graves Ghastly. This 91-year-old man who's now in a wheelchair and breathing with the aid of an oxygen tank, did his best to reprise that unforgettable "neeeyaaahh" laugh we've all grown to love . . . without my asking! Unfortunately, due to his physical condition, he couldn't sustain the long, echoing part of the laugh. He tried three times to no avail. As I was packing up my recorder and preparing to leave, Mr. Deming gave it one final shot. The frustration of not being able to perform the laugh was evident on his face. And, even though the last laugh was no different than the previous ones, bless his heart for trying! On my departure, I shook his hand and said, "Long live Sir Graves Ghastly." Responding like a true showman, he raised his left eyebrow to give me "the eye" . . . that famous Sir Graves stare!

The following pages are filled with countless stories that are humorous, compassionate, inspiring, and above all memorable. This book is a tribute to those we welcomed into our living rooms over the years and whose creative talents we'll forever cherish. Stay tuned to revisit your favorite local shows, brought to you by *TV Land—Detroit!*

Don't Touch That Dial . . .

1

Detroit's Golden Age of Television

When those shows were on, you watched them, you enjoyed them,
and you never thought that someday these would be a part of the
city's history.
—ART CERVI, Bozo the Clown

The year was 1947, World War II had ended a year and a half earlier, and
America was well on its way to embracing the prosperity brought about
by the soldiers who had fought to keep the country free. That same year
Detroit was on the verge of becoming the fourth-largest city in the
nation. Nicknamed the "Motor City" for its booming auto industry,
Detroit also has the honor of being the site of a number of other mile-
stones that affected society worldwide! By the late 1940s, the city was
home to Parke-Davis, Stroh's Brewery, Kowalski Sausages, Sanders
Candy, Vlasic Pickles, Vernors Ginger Ale, Faygo Beverages, the Shrine
Circus, and Kelly Services to name just a few. It witnessed the first traffic
light, the first paved road, the first freeway, and the first snowplow.

And in the ever-changing world of the mass media, WWJ-AM made
history in August 1920 when it became America's first commercial radio
station. More than a decade later, WXYZ-AM's station owner, George
W. Trendle, and his creative staff conceived and broadcast three of
radio's most famous shows: *The Lone Ranger, The Green Hornet,* and
Sergeant Preston of the Yukon. Though many more historic achieve-
ments would emerge in the coming decades, Detroit was a bustling
metropolis in 1947. By March of that year, an exciting new medium was
ready to penetrate the Motor City and become as much of a fixture in
peoples' lives as the automobile . . . it was called television!

Channels 2, 4, and 7. . . Detroit's Other Big Three

With only five of its kind in existence, the *Detroit News* purchased the country's sixth and Michigan's first television station, WWDT, Channel 4. On March 4, 1947, the Detroit station signed on the air, broadcasting a mere 12 hours a week. By May, the station had changed its call letters to match its radio counterpart, WWJ. Being the only TV station in town for the next year and a half, Channel 4 aired the first local newscast, the first sports telecast, and the traditional Thanksgiving Day Parade.

On March 31, 1948, WWJ joined the National Broadcasting Company (NBC) as Michigan's first network affiliate. In October, the station's monopoly on the local market ended when WXYZ (Channel 7) and WJBK (Channel 2) appeared on the very high frequency (VHF) dial with the same call letters as their sister stations in radio. Channel 7 jumped on the American Broadcasting Company's (ABC) bandwagon, while Channel 2 partnered with the Columbia Broadcasting System (CBS). Together, Channels 2, 4, and 7 would parallel the status of Ford, General Motors, and Chrysler as Detroit's other "Big Three"!

Much of the glory of the city's golden age of TV can be attributed to these three stations. Some of the biggest shows and their stars were the brainchildren of men such as WXYZ general manager John Pival, WJBK owner George B. Storer, and WWJ program director Ian Harrower. They introduced children to Soupy Sales, Johnny Ginger, Auntie Dee, Sagebrush Shorty, B'wana Don, Ricky the Clown, Milky, Bozo, Oopsy, Pirate Pete, *Wixie's Wonderland,* and *Romper Room.* They enticed teenagers to dance on *Ed McKenzie's Saturday Party, Detroit Bandstand,* and *Club 1270.* Before there was a Martha Stewart, they drew housewives into fine living with tips from local authorities Edythe Fern Melrose and Carol Duvall. They engaged in drama with shows such as *Police Woman, Mr. Hope,* and *Traffic Court.* And when it was time to kick back and relax with a movie, the names Justice Colt, the Black Spider, Morgus the Magnificent, Rita Bell, and Sir Graves Ghastly lit up the television marquee.

Yes, there was something for everyone on local TV. Even the outdoor enthusiasts and world travelers followed the advice of Mort Neff, Jerry Chiappetta, and George Pierrot. When the "talk show" emerged in the 1970s and 1980s, the Big Three went into action with *Kelly & Company, Sonya,* and a stylized Detroit version of *PM Magazine.* Without question, Channels 2, 4, and 7 have dominated the local airwaves since the dawn of their existence on the television dial.

Channel 9 from across the River

Across the Detroit River in Windsor, Ontario, the Canadian Department of Transport granted CKLW radio a license for television broadcast. Assigned the VHF channel 9, CKLW-TV officially signed on the air with a test pattern on September 16, 1954. From that day forward, Detroit's Canadian neighbor became the breeding ground for some of the city's most popular shows: *Captain Jolly, Jingles in Boofland, Big Time Wrestling,* and *Swingin' Time.* When an unemployed actor named Bill Kennedy arrived from Tinseltown in 1956, CKLW crowned him Detroit's movie king! And when *Romper Room* and *Bozo* left WWJ with nowhere to go, it was Channel 9 that gave them a new home.

In 1974, the Canadian Broadcasting Corporation (CBC) obtained CKLW's license and the following year replaced the old call letters with CBET. Canada's new border protection regulations forced the cancellation of its American programs in 1977, but for more than two decades prior to that the studios on Riverside Drive shipped Detroiters a boatload of entertaining memories from across the river.

Then along Came 56 and Public Television

Three years after the formation of the Educational Television and Radio Center in Ann Arbor, Michigan—the basis for the Public Broadcasting Service (PBS)—WTVS, Channel 56, debuted on the "weaker," ultrahigh frequency band on October 3, 1955, thus becoming the Motor City's first UHF station. Under the direction of National Educational Television (NET) in New York City, WTVS was supplied with educational programs for both children and adults. Although Channel 56 wasn't a major player in Detroit's golden age of television in terms of original productions, it did succeed in introducing impressionable Generation Xers to a new philosophy that was gaining momentum in children's programming from Boston's WGBH in 1969 . . . "Can you tell me how to get, how to get to *Sesame Street?*"

Channels 20, 50, and 62 . . . Who Knew?

Who would have guessed back in the 1960s and 1970s that Detroit's new independent UHF channels would someday become network affiliates?

As Kaiser Broadcasting's WKBD, Channel 50 debuted on January 10, 1965, the small station took a huge chance by becoming the city's first "sports" channel, airing high school, college, and professional sporting events every day of the week . . . long before there was such a thing as the Entertainment and Sports Programming Network, better known as ESPN.

Beginning that summer, Channel 50 sought to diversify its program schedule by adding kid's shows, including the futuristic *Captain Detroit,* and a hard-hitting news magazine hosted by the "people's advocate," Lou Gordon. When CKLW made a bold cost-cutting decision to ax the bulk of its children's shows and movie host Bill Kennedy in the late 1960s, WKBD aggressively snatched up the station's recently unemployed. The gamble paid off over the next decade, as Channel 50 evolved into the most profitable UHF station in the country.

While WKBD was reinventing itself in 1968, another new station, WXON, signed onto Channel 62. A construction permit was issued that year to a station called WJMY for the initiation test patterns on Channel 20; however, WXON later purchased the permit for Channel 20 and relocated its station there in November 1972. Virtually no local programming to speak of originated at Channel 20 in the 1970s except for the bizarre antics of the Ghoul after his departure from WKBD in 1977.

There were a few short-lived productions in the 1980s, one of which was Jim Harper's *Martial Arts Theater,* but unfortunately Channel 20's image as a producing agent didn't surface until the mid-1990s, long after the dissipation of the golden age. However, WXON was the first station in the Motor City to offer subscription television service, the forerunner of cable, with ON-TV in the early 1980s.

Subsequent to WXON's abandonment of Channel 62 in 1972, an African-American-owned radio station on Jefferson Avenue near Downtown Detroit filed an application for a television license. After a three-year wait, in September 1975 WGPR-TV, Channel 62, made history by becoming the first minority-owned television station in America! It paved the way for African Americans to acquire skills and exposure in TV production without any previous experience. In-house programs such as *The Scene* became the premier training ground for many of the city's cameramen, stagehands, producers, and directors. As for on-camera talent, one of the country's top entertainment correspondents, Shaun Robinson of *Access Hollywood,* developed her journalism skills along with a talk show of her own, *Strictly Speaking,* fresh out of college, courtesy of WGPR, Channel 62.

When Detroit's golden age of television fizzled in the mid-1980s, it was hard to imagine that the weakly signaled UHF stations would become network affiliates by the end of the century. First to take the plunge was WKBD when media tycoon Rupert Murdock launched the Fox Broadcasting Company in 1986. Eight years later Detroiters were shocked when WJBK's parent company, Gillette Communications, sold the longtime CBS affiliate to Murdock on December 11, 1994, at the height of his crusade to annex all of the independently owned CBS stations.

With all of the VHF channels spoken for by competing networks, CBS was forced onto the UHF dial in Detroit. Likely prospects for purchase by CBS were thought to be WXON and WKBD, but another surprise was in store for the Motor City when the network bought WGPR, Channel 62, and then revived the old Channel 4 call letters WWJ. Simultaneously, Paramount Pictures and Warner Bros. executed plans to establish television networks of their own: the United Paramount Network (UPN) and the WB. In 1995, WKBD became a UPN affiliate and WXON changed its call letters to WDWB upon its recognition as Detroit's WB. Motown's "Little Three" had finally attained the same network status as the Big Three . . . who knew?

Even though more local channels have popped up on the tube since the mid-1990s, it is the innovative programs from the preceding decades that continue to resonate by striking a sentimental chord that's dear to our hearts. They arrived when the hardships endured during the first half of the twentieth century began to pay off, and they made us proud to be Detroiters!

Characters and Puppets

2

Soupy Sales

I always, as a kid, thought Soupy Sales was the funniest guy on this earth. He always had pies thrown in his face, and at that time I thought that was very hilarious! He was definitely my favorite person on TV.

   —MARY WILSON, Motown legend

Without a doubt, it was *the* most popular and influential show on Detroit TV in the 1950s. A "live" half-hour show that appeared weekdays at noon on WXYZ-TV, Channel 7, had kids literally racing home at lunchtime to eat with their favorite star of the small screen, Soupy Sales. Just ask any baby boomer from Motown, such as Larry Dlusky or Peggy Tibbits, and you'll quickly discover why Soupy's charm is still so fondly remembered by many Metro Detroiters.

Larry Dlusky: "I remember myself and probably other kids would run home from school to watch the show. It was like being in his house . . . he had a table, and that's where lunch would be served . . . and there was a sound effect to go along with different foods. If he bit into a hamburger or cut roast beef, you heard a cow going 'moo!' If he cut into an egg, you'd hear the chicken going, 'ba-bock-bock-bock!' Even foods like Jell-O, if you shook the bowl of Jell-O, you'd hear the sound of a spring, 'boing-boing-boing-boing!' Every food had its little sound effect."

Peggy Tibbits: "I'd come home and watch Soupy Sales every day. I thought he was so funny. Just this young man, and he had a sense of timing . . . funny, zany! He would tell you, 'Tomorrow I'm having tomato soup and a grilled cheese sandwich' . . . and boy, I would just say to my mom, 'Tomorrow I want to have tomato soup and a grilled cheese sand-

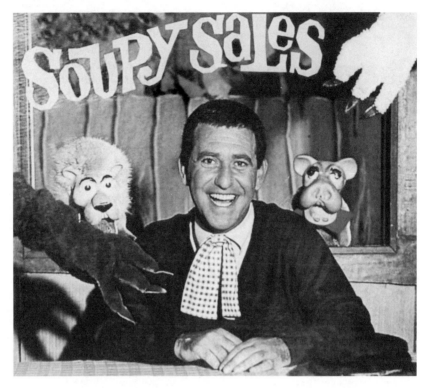

Detroit TV's biggest star with some of his pals on the cover of his first record album. (Courtesy Soupy Sales.)

wich.' And I would want to eat on a TV tray and watch Soupy Sales when I came home."

Originally titled *12 O'clock Comics* for the first couple of years, until it became *Lunch with Soupy* (then renamed as *Breakfast with Soupy* when it was moved to the 8:00 a.m. time slot), the show was the brainchild of WXYZ vice president and general manager, John F. Pival. In 1953, Pival envisioned a children's show that would be a "wraparound" to cartoons such as *Superman* and old silent movies. The program would air at noon, hence the title *12 O'clock Comics,* and would feature its host having lunch with all of the kids at home. But who could carry such a show?

Soupy Comes to Detroit

As fate would have it, the timing was just right for a struggling radio/TV comedian in Cleveland known as Soupy Hines. Born Milton Supman on January 8, 1926, in Franklinton, North Carolina, the fourth son of the

An early publicity photo. (Courtesy Soupy Sales.)

Supmans' was nicknamed "Soupy" as a child by the local kids due to the mistaken belief his last name was Soupman. During his radio days in Ohio, he adopted the name Hines after his sponsor, Hines Soup.

It was at a nightclub gig in Cincinnati that John Pival first laid eyes on the young comic, unaware that one day their paths would cross again. Soupy recalls the circumstances that brought them together for a second time and how a run-through landed him on Pival's new show.

Soupy Sales: "Back in 1953, I was looking to get into a bigger market, so I came to Detroit. I made an appointment to meet with John Pival from WXYZ-TV. Pival was the big wheel; he ran the whole station. I met with him, and we set up to have an audition. When I did the audition, they thought it was the regular audition I wanted to do, it wasn't; it was a rehearsal. But it was fine, and they said, 'Wonderful, we want you to come work.' I said, 'Thank you, I'd like to work in Detroit at WXYZ.'"

Whether it was the brilliance of Soupy's talent or that Pival liked him didn't really matter, the 27-year-old husband and father now had to move to the Motor City. Leaving the family behind temporarily, Soupy headed for Detroit in a car that barely made it and with hardly a dime to spare. Arriving with no more than a couple of shirts, a sport coat, and a pair of slacks, he took up residence in a duplex on Schaefer Road, ready to bet on an insecure future that could go bust anytime. On the flip side, the same risk fell upon the shoulders of John Pival and WXYZ for banking on an unknown comic who'd never hosted a children's show. What if he flopped? What if the show tanked?

It wouldn't be long before all fears subsided, as the gamble paid off in spades. Soupy called Detroit his Mecca, for it was in the Motor City that he established his career, perfected his craft, developed his shtick, and created a cast of unforgettable characters that ultimately traveled beyond the Great Lakes and into the memories of youngsters all over the country. Looking back on his relationship with WXYZ, Soupy commented:

Soupy Sales: "I'd gone to three other stations before I went to XYZ, and they really seemed to be on the ball. I really liked the operation. So it turned out to be wonderful, and I was very happy about that. It was one of those simple things that clicked, and it just worked. I didn't have too much to go on at the beginning, it all came about afterward, but it worked out fine, I must say."

Only one change needed to be made before Soupy could go on the air in Detroit, and that would be his last name. Fearing that Hines would be too closely associated with Heinz Ketchup, Soupy elected to drop the name. For a while, he was just known as "Soupy." But as his popularity grew so did the demand to know this Soupy guy's last name. Without skipping a beat, Pival produced an answer that would last a lifetime, as told by retired WXYZ art director Jack Flechsig.

Jack Flechsig: "John Pival renamed him Sales after Chic Sale, who was a famous silent movie star; movie comic. Pival also was a businessman, and he figured the name Sales would engender business sales that way."

Given a floppy, oversized, checkered bow tie, a black V-necked sweater, and a top hat by the station, Soupy adapted to the costume and created a persona that he believed kids would not only laugh at but identify with as well. He became the ultimate underdog, a simple man who never won at anything and was beaten by everyone: the dogs, the puppets, and anyone who knocked on the door.

On with the Show

As the show got under way in 1953, one by one classic "Soupyisms" began to emerge in a landslide of hilarity. Fans Larry Dlusky and Peggy

Tibbits reminisced about an unlikely dance craze called the Soupy Shuffle.

Larry Dlusky: "Usually when they opened the show, there's this real fast piano music [Bill Snyder's "Flying Fingers"], and then they'd cut to the interior and you'd be hearing the Soupy Shuffle music. The words would be something like, 'Do the Soupy Shuffle, it's a wonderful time . . .' and he'd actually be shuffling from side to side. Then he'd always end up jumping with his legs split like [scissors]. That's what Soupy would be doing until he'd realize, 'Oh, oh, the kids are here . . . hey kids.' And he'd just go into the show from there."

Peggy Tibbits: "Doing the Soupy Shuffle . . . I had to practice, I wanted to do that Soupy Shuffle. I'm sure I could still do it today if I really tried, but I haven't done it in years. The Soupy Shuffle was about as simple as the fifties."

Incidentally, the music used for the Soupy Shuffle was a tune called "It's a Wonderful World." So just where did this little dance come from?

Soupy Sales: "Well, the dance I'd been doing for years. I would do the dance and [when asked] I said, 'Well I call it the Soupy Shuffle.' People went nuts doing the dance, and parents started doing it."

That's right! People of all ages were doing the Soupy Shuffle. In fact, during the fifties the dance was most popular among adolescent teens, who believed if they could do the Shuffle they really had achieved something stupendous!

Of course, the main theme of the show was the lunch. Kids all over the Metro area insisted on eating whatever Soupy was having. There's no telling how many children's dietary habits he changed or how many mothers he may have irked, but one thing's for sure: Soupy did emphasize the importance of a well-balanced lunch . . . a concept that's long gone today.

Soupy Sales: "We had the approval of some group that was cognizant of lunches, and we figured as long as we had milk and basic things it was okay. I'd have a very good lunch . . . that was my lunch for the day."

In the beginning, the stars of the show were the featured cartoons and silent films that Soupy would narrate. Larry Dlusky remembers the humorous way Soupy led the kids into a cartoon.

Larry Dlusky: "Part of what he wore was a big, floppy, bow tie. When he went to announce a cartoon, he would grab the ends of the bow tie and start twisting them like a propeller, and he'd say, 'Contact!' and then he'd go running toward the camera. And then before he'd smash his face into the camera they'd cut to the cartoon."

It didn't take long before Soupy overshadowed the cartoons by becoming a caricature of himself in a sheltered world of pure silliness.

The Cast of Characters

Expanding his creativity, Soupy introduced kids to an ensemble of puppets that quickly spiced up the lunchtime show. The first of these was White Fang, an antagonistic dog whose harsh gibberish was understandable only to Soupy.

Soupy Sales: "White Fang was a creation of mine. I always wanted to have a big dog [called] White Fang. I told them what I wanted as far as the dog was concerned, how I wanted him played and everything like that, and that was it. White Fang was the main one at the beginning."

The idea for White Fang had been born to Soupy years earlier while he was serving in the navy. Stationed aboard the *USS Randall,* he heard a dog growl on a record of the *Hound of the Baskervilles.* Instantly Soupy knew he had found his White Fang! Shortly after the incorporation of the character into the show, an unfortunate incident would change the direction in which White Fang was played.

Originally, the big mean dog wasn't seen at all; he was heard. When Soupy's coveted *Hound of the Baskervilles* record turned up missing, stagehand Clyde Adler began to ad-lib the voice with a rough "rawh-ah-raw-aw-rawh" that was totally laughable.

Jack Flechsig: "Clyde was a very talented guy, and he actually remained the stagehand for a long time and just did occasional bits, and then he finally gave up that part of his job and became a full-time actor for Soupy."

Adler's ingenuity led to banter between White Fang and Soupy that became one of the high points of the show. Soon afterward the wife of engineer Al Magolan cut up an old ladies' coat to make a glove that became the paw of the meanest dog in all of Dee-troit!

In response to a friend's suggestion that White Fang needed a counterpart, Soupy produced Black Tooth, the sweetest dog in all of Dee-troit. He was an exact copy of White Fang but the complete antithesis: a dark paw as opposed to a white one, a soft voice crooning gibberish that only Soupy could translate, and the habit of smothering him with a big, sloppy kiss. During Soupy's latter years in Detroit, a third dog puppet came into existence, Marilyn MonWolf, a sexy movie star with a "mink" paw.

However, the creative juices on the show weren't necessarily limited to Soupy or even Clyde. Such was the case in the evolution of Pookie the Lion. Retired WXYZ director Mason Weaver explains.

Mason Weaver: "Everybody sort of worked on these things, you know. Soupy knew a good thing when he saw it, and when it worked, F-I-N-E . . . that's all he cared about. And he was ready to take ideas from anyone. He might not use them all, but many times he did. Most of the

Pookie interrupts Soupy's lunch. (Courtesy Soupy Sales.)

characters that came to be [were] through people knowing that they could present things to Soupy.

"One of our stagehands was in the next studio over, and they had been doing a commercial over there and used a puppet. But that's how well we knew Soupy, this guy knew Soupy also. He came into the studio, went behind a flat, and came up to the window with this puppet. Soupy's sitting at the table and sees the monitor and he starts doing stuff with the puppet. And the puppet didn't respond just [yet], but wow . . . this worked!"

Soupy Sales: "It was a thing you run into. I ran into Pookie and I said, 'Hey, that'd be great!' One thing followed another as far as creativity [goes], and it was good that way because people grew into liking them like I had developed them."

The name Pookie was derived from a nickname Soupy called his eldest son Tony. However, the actual development of the puppet wouldn't be as easy. Jack Flechsig elaborates.

Jack Flechsig: "There was a morning show on NBC, and Bill Baird, the famous puppeteer, had a puppet called Charlemagne the Lion. And they merchandised that, and we bought one of those puppets. It was a real nice, molded rubber puppet with a mane of hair, and that became Pookie. Clyde performed with that puppet at the window for quite a long time until there was a rumbling about copyright infringement. So Soupy went to New York, and he had a famous sculptor sculpt another Pookie, very similar but different enough to avoid the copyright infringement. It cost him a bundle; it cost him a lot of money. So then he was free to use that puppet all the time."

So what kind of personality belonged to this lovable lion? Larry Dlusky reminisces about one of Pookie's grand entrances.

Larry Dlusky: "A lot of times Pookie wanted a story read to him. Soupy would protest a little bit but eventually would give in to read the story. Sometimes, when Soupy first gave in, Pookie would go down and come back up, and he'd have a hat tilted on his head like Frank Sinatra would wear. And they played that song: 'Fairy tales can come true, it could happen to you . . . if you're young at heart.' Pookie would pantomime to that, and then he'd hand Soupy the book, and that's when Soupy would start reading. As he was reading the story looking at the camera, Pookie would be doing things behind Soupy somewhat sarcastic to Soupy, sometimes acting out what Soupy was reading. And then whenever Soupy would stop and quickly turn around, Pookie would right away have his chin on the windowsill looking at Soupy like he was sitting there, docile, listening to every word Soupy was saying. Then as soon as Soupy turned away he'd be back to his antics again."

From Pookie to Hippy to Willy

Another wonderful attribute of *Lunch with Soupy* was how much character innovation was derived from sheer simplicity. Jack Flechsig ought to know, as he had a hand in Hippy and Willy . . . literally.

Jack Flechsig: "He [Soupy] wanted somebody to play off of Pookie. He wanted another puppet. So we bought another Charlemagne the Lion, I think at a drug store, and I turned him inside out and then pulled his nose in and he looked like a hippopotamus and it became Hippy the Hippo. So there was no fear of copyright infringement there.

"Speaking of simplicity, but it's something I look back on now as quite important, he had a character on his show called Willy the Worm. He was the sickest worm in Dee-troit. Soupy bought Willy at the Downtown Woolworth's dime store for 35 cents. It was a little latex accordion worm that was operated with a bulb in a tube, and when you squeezed the bulb you stick his head out. What he had him do was, he had Willy wish happy birthday to the kids. And the parents would write in or call and tell them when the kid's birthday was and where his present was hidden. The kid whose name was mentioned on the program was an instant celebrity at school. He'd do maybe six or seven at a show.

"This damn little worm was made in some exotic country, and it began to disintegrate by the second day. It was my job to keep him in shape for his appearance every day. So I'd patch him up with rubber cement and cellophane tape and baling wire, [with] anything I could. So I went down to Woolworth's and bought the only other one they had. Still it was almost a daily routine. As soon as Willy was off the set, he'd [Soupy would] rush him over to my drawing board and I'd patch him up and make sure he was ready for his next appearance. I don't know if a thing like that would play today or not."

Also let's not forget Peaches, the girl next door who wanted to marry Soupy. She made occasional appearances near the end of the Detroit run. Any idea who the young girl was? Well, she wasn't a puppet or a paw . . . she was Soupy in drag!

The Clubhouse

When Soupy first appeared on *12 O'clock Comics,* he stood in front of a flat cardboard backdrop that was painted to look like a clubhouse. It wasn't long before he became bored with the flimsiness of the set and decided to expand its dimensions.

Jack Flechsig: "Soupy [had] a very clear idea of what he wanted, what he required in the way of a set. I merely embellished what he described he wanted. He needed a door in the middle of the set to do bits with, and he needed a window . . . a low window for puppets to appear in . . . and he needed a wall with a blackboard on it for words of wisdom and other things. Later we added a potbellied stove and a wall telephone. But he was mainly responsible for the concept; all I did was interpret what he wanted and make it a little more presentable. He knew he wanted knotty pine because that was kind of in fashion then. It was actually quite simple, just a basic set. When we moved to Broadcast House, we rebuilt the set but made it a lot more sturdy because it took a lot of beating and a lot of pratfalls and stuff like that. So we made it rock solid, and it was braced with steel beams to the ceiling . . . so that when he slammed the door the whole set wouldn't shake . . . although that was kind of the charm of it."

Soupy Sales: "Right from the start, it worked out really well because we had people working on the show who were really interested in creating something. I loved them, they were wonderful people. Jack Flechsig was a genius."

The clubhouse for *Lunch with Soupy* soon became a haven of pranks. Sales and his crew stretched the boundaries of that "basic" set as far as their imaginative spirits could take them. They wanted it to be much more than a mere location where the action took place; anything and everything in it had to have a recipe for gags.

Larry Dlusky: "There was a cork in the wall with a sign over it saying, 'Do not touch.' And every once in a while, out of curiosity I guess, he'd pull that cork out and he would immediately get a stream of water shooting in his face or whipped cream coming out of it . . . and he would struggle to get that cork back in the wall."

Jack Flechsig: "He would always have me making pictures on the wall that became animated. One of them was a picture of a crying baby . . . and the baby would be crying, crying, crying, and he would finally get annoyed and go over and turn the picture over and it would be the backside of the baby showing. Or another one would be a steamship sailing along in the water and it would hit an iceberg and sink. The ingenuity of it was the compelling part. He would come up with the basic idea and you were free to interpret it pretty much any way you wanted to. He was so flexible; he could work with anything."

Larry Dlusky: "Every now and then, he goes, 'Let's see what the weather's gonna be like' and he'd go over to the radio. It's one of these big, old-fashioned, Crosley radios, and he'd twist the dial and you'd hear the static in between stations. Then he'd lock into a station and it goes something like, 'There goes a masked horseman on the plains with a hearty 'Hi-ho Silver' and you'd hear the horses hooves, then 'Tune in tomorrow when he learns how to stop!' Then Soupy would roll his eyes to the camera and twist the dial some more, looking for the weather . . . and he'd never get what he was exactly looking for. When he finally got to a weather forecast, 'And now the weather forecast . . .' He goes, 'Oh, good, this is what we wanna hear.' And the guy would say, 'It's gonna be raining cats and dogs this afternoon . . . so, kids, stay inside if you don't want to get bit.' Then [Soupy] would make a disgusted looking face and turn the radio off."

A Knock at the Door—Pies in the Face

Perhaps the most ingenious and certainly the most unpredictable set application was the use of the door. Anytime Soupy met someone at the door all you would see was a pair of hands, and you would hear some sort of comical voice portrayed by Clyde Adler. As in the case with White

Never without a pie in the face! (Courtesy *Detroit Free Press*.)

Fang and Black Tooth, the appearances of visitors at the door were left purely to the imagination of the audience. But not always . . . .

Sometimes if there was commotion outside and Soupy went to investigate, the viewers would catch a glimpse of a ridiculous film clip. Snippets containing celluloid images of such loony scenarios as a man pulling an elephant or circus acrobats on trapezes were inserted to give the illusion that nothing but utter nonsense managed to find its way to Soupy's house. And, as if that wasn't enough, there would be one final smack that hit Soupy square in the face—a pie!

A huge fan of pie fights, Sales adopted the old silent film shtick and made it his own! Originally, meringue pies were used, but they tended to collapse prior to use. After several experiments, pie shells filled with aerosol shaving cream on paper plates became the weapon of choice. To emphasize the impact of the pie hitting the face, a gunshot was added to make what became Soupy's signature bit more unique and funny. Ever wonder who got the honor of slapping him with the pies?

Soupy Sales: "Clyde threw the pies. Pies would come from nowhere . . . I never ducked any of them. Clyde could take your head off throwing them pies!"

Jack Flechsig: "They had the pie fight of the century, I think it was on his last show in Detroit, and he got back at a lot of people that day. They had thousands of shaving cream pies in the studio, and the place was just a shambles when it was through. I understand in New York celebrities were lining up to be on the show to get a pie . . . even Frank Sinatra got one."

Production

Today's high-tech world of instant communication and democratic committees has successfully created an endless amount of paper-pushing bureaucracies, which we've come to accept as the way to get things done. Everything seems so much more complicated than it needs to be with the changing of the times. Jack Flechsig paints a picture of how easy it was to make so much with so little.

Jack Flechsig: "The thing that impresses me now, looking back at Soupy's show, is the simplicity of it. We had no budget to work with at all. Things had to be simple and cheap. He was so prolific, he would just have thousands of ideas that would come as fast as he could talk. We would have a production meeting the day of the show. We had a tiny little office on the fourteenth floor of the Maccabees Building; it was behind the elevators. There was room enough for a desk and five chairs . . . and the chairs would be right up against the wall. We all smoked in those days, and that [room] would just be blue. We'd sit in there for about an hour and plan out the whole show, and then we'd all go off in different directions and do our bit and get the thing ready."

Soupy Sales: "I must say that at XYZ they really were cognizant of the popularity of the show. They wouldn't do anything to ruin it. John Pival was the main man. He was behind everything, and whatever I wanted to do was fine with him."

Words of Wisdom

Like most of the programs from television's golden age, *Lunch with Soupy* had its share of lessons in life to be learned. Soupy called them his "words of wisdom."

Larry Dlusky: "When he was done with lunch, he'd walk over to the blackboard for the words of wisdom. In his words of wisdom, they were some kind of advice to kids . . . some positive reinforcement, like they'd tell them, 'Brush your teeth after every meal and keep your mouth clean.' Then the words of wisdom he'd write down would be a recap of that humorously. Like it might say, 'Be true to your teeth and they won't be false to you.'"

Soupy Sales: "I'd take an idea and write a poem . . . a four-line thing about toys or taking care of yourself or taking your medicine, doing what your mom wants you to do . . . and I did four lines."

Soupy's Humor

Jack Flechsig: "One of the bits that I always remember as being creative [was when] a mouse ran across the floor. [It was] a rubber mouse, [pulled] by a thread . . . and it ran back across and he was getting kind of annoyed with that, so he wanted to catch him. So he gets a mousetrap and he looks in the refrigerator for cheese, but the shelves are bare. Then he turns his pockets inside out—no money. So how to catch this mouse? So he goes to a magazine and he leafs through the magazine and he cuts out a picture of a piece of cheese. He baits the mousetrap with this picture. He puts it down on the floor and continues on with the show. Pretty soon, snap! He goes over there and he picks it up and he caught a 'picture' of a mouse!"

Larry Dlusky: "He would say words, but they wouldn't have the meanings they should have . . . like, 'Show me the bottom of the ocean and I'll show you the prints of whales.' Well, obviously he's not talking about Prince Charles, but that's what prints of whales sounds like. But he's talking about the whales swimming at the bottom of the ocean and making their prints on the bottom of the ocean. So he would do wordplay like that. That I found very, very funny."

Undoubtedly the unique humor of Soupy Sales quickly appealed to a very broad demographic. Local TV buff and webmaster of detroitkidshow.com Ed Golick describes it.

Ed Golick: "He would do some material that kind of went over the heads of little kids. First he had the little kids watching, and then the teenage kids kind of got hooked on it. He did things on about two or three different levels for the little kids and the teenagers, and then the adults started watching the thing. There's a big fallacy that Soupy did blue material on the air. He just didn't do that . . . it basically never happened."

Because *Lunch with Soupy* was attracting a large adult following, John Pival gave Sales a nighttime variety show, *Soupy's On,* almost as fast as the children's program. Competing against local news broadcasts on Channels 2 and 4, Pival believed audiences would tune in to half an hour of Soupy weeknights at eleven rather than the news. Sporting a run almost as long as the daytime show, *Soupy's On* was a late-night success. Also for a short while in 1955 Sales hosted a weekly prime-time program on Wednesday nights called *Soupy's Ranch.* Three shows on the air at once in a major market, what an accomplishment, especially for an individual who two years earlier could barely scratch out a living in Cleveland!

Without the employment of laugh tracks and studio audiences, Soupy relied on his crew for laughter.

Mason Weaver: "One of his biggest deals was getting a response from the camera guys when he did something. If they laughed, he was as happy as could be. He loved it, he just loved it! And he played to the crew."

Soupy Sales: "It's the most important thing in the world to get the reaction of the crew. If they laughed you knew it was funny . . . if they didn't laugh then it wasn't funny. I remember once [in New York] a week or so one time I didn't have anybody laughing. I said, 'What's the problem? Is it the show effects?' They said, 'No, it's funny but they told us not to laugh.' I said, 'Well, this is ridiculous.' I went to the people in charge, and I said, 'I want them laughing. If it's funny, they should laugh.' So, they went back to laughing . . . which is the only thing you can judge anything by—the laughter. If they did that, it proved to me that it was a funny show."

Jokes on Soupy

Most comedians are masters of amusement; regular jokesters who read humor into everything and love to play pranks on others. With that said, how many are willing to be the butt of a joke themselves? And how many can handle interference in their routines? Well, when it came to being the subject of a prank, Soupy Sales proved that he could take it as well as dish it out. Retired WXYZ stage manager Art Runyon remembers how a backstage mishap that caught Soupy off guard became the laugh of the day.

Art Runyon: "I had somebody's comedy routine on, and there was one particular line that was good. Apparently the audio man forgot to kill the pot for the ETs [electrical transcription—the music operator], and it kinda drifted into the next cut. In the meantime, I think Clyde Adler, who did the puppets and also the voice at the door, said something that apparently wasn't exactly what Soupy expected and the next cut on the ET came up with, 'WHY DON'T YOU SHUT UP!' And that broke up Soupy. It was an accident, and he [Soupy] said later, after the show, 'Oh, that was the greatest thing.' He said, 'Don't forget, try that again sometime.'"

Jack Flechsig: "The stagehands were largely responsible for the practical jokes. They were great for that . . . and they used to, instead of apple juice, they'd give him brandy in his glass . . . He'd take a drink and [say, grimacing,] 'Mmm, boy, that's good!'"

Soupy Sales: "They used to put vodka in the orange juice . . . pretty good!"

Jack Flechsig: "About the same time, we seemed to be obsessed with nudity. Soupy got Jell-O as a sponsor. And the first day he was to do a commercial one of the directors brought in a Jell-O mold of a naked lady. We made a Jell-O naked lady, and when he sat down to his lunch they presented him with this Jell-O, and the breasts on it shimmied very realistically and he just broke up with that."

Of course, the Jell-O was a very early foreshadowing of what was to become the ultimate practical joke on Soupy—the infamous naked lady. Many have heard the story about the naked woman who was behind the door when Soupy answered it. Sales has told the story hundreds of times himself. But what most people don't know is that before anyone dared to employ a real woman a centerfold was used. Jack Flechsig recalls how Soupy turned the tables on his prankster.

Jack Flechsig: "They were gonna surprise him, and there wasn't a real woman, there was just a centerfold out of a magazine. There was a knock on the door and Clyde Adler was outside the door . . . Soupy would open the door and Clyde would show him this picture of this centerfold . . . which was pretty risqué in those days. And this was the director of the show, Bill Carruthers; it was his idea to shock Soupy . . . you know, play a big joke on Soupy. Well, Soupy got wind of it [and] didn't say anything. So there's a knock on the door . . . Soupy goes over there and opens it and 'Aahhh' . . . but then he reaches out and grabs the magazine and pulls it in and says, 'Look, kids, what I've got.' But it's a picture of an oil derrick or something. The director, Bill Carruthers, was at the console upstairs; he slid right off of his chair . . . right under the console, and thought his whole career was flashing in front of his eyes because he thought [Soupy] was gonna show us the picture of the naked lady.

"After that, they did use a real woman. They hired a model, and it took him by surprise! He should have known something was coming off because the whole station was pretty much in on it, at least the production staff. The studio was just jammed with people waiting for this to happen."

Retired WXYZ engineer Jim Burgan, who operated camera 1 that day, takes us backstage to meet the mystery woman.

Jim Burgan: "We're doing the show as normal, and the director, Bill Carruthers, said, 'Go behind the set and get the shots when they come up.' I had no idea what the shots were gonna be. Then, in the meantime, they were going on [with the show]; my camera's sitting there, and here comes this young lady with a robe on. She wanders back, stands behind the door, then proceeds to take the robe off . . . she has absolutely nothing on but high heels. And she's preening and primping herself for when he opens the door. She was a very pretty girl, young, dark hair, very slim and very well built. We had a shot there for quite a while, waiting and waiting. When Soupy opened the door, she just stood there and posed. It was a definite surprise!"

Executed perfectly without a hitch, Soupy was shocked to see a nude woman standing behind the door. With camera 1 in position behind the set, he was fooled into believing the girl was live on the air! Like his director before him, it was Soupy's turn to have *his* entire career flash before his eyes . . .

Soupy Sales: "I remember that very well. It scared me to death. I knew the show was going on, so I did all I could to cover it up without ruining the situation."

Jim Burgan: "He worked it as though something exciting was happening back there, but he never let on what it was . . . he was a pro, it just shook him, it was a big shock. They just wanted to shake him up and surprise him . . . and they did! It was the grand marquee."

The Birdbath Club

Larry Dlusky: "Soupy called all of his fans Birdbaths, and that's what we were . . . and we were proud to be called that!"

Soupy Sales: "Well, you look for different things in doing a show, different gimmicks and things. I came up with the thing of 'Birdbath.' I said, 'Birdbath . . . you're a Birdbath' . . . it figures, 'What the hell's he talking about?' And all of a sudden it caught on, and then we started the Birdbath Club. We had memberships, and it was another one of those gimmick things that worked out really wonderful. Because, I think, back in those days you had to have a difference of creating something that people will be talking about and stick with them."

Ed Golick: "He called his production company Birdbath Productions.

Soupy and his Birdbaths, December 1955. (Courtesy Jim
Burgan.)

That's just something he came up with for no rhyme or reason, it just
sounded funny. His sponsor was United Dairies, and you'd send United
Dairies a dime or something and you'd get a card, a membership card, and
you'd get a little button. He'd have these little things at the Fox Theater,
show cartoons and joke around . . . and he would just fill up the Fox Theater. People would be standing outside, wanting to get in. Soupy was the
standard that everyone else tried to live up to, all the other performers."

Public Appearances and the Fans

As part of the promotion for the show, Soupy made numerous public
appearances over the years. Whether it was the Fox Theater, Edgewater

Park, or the Michigan State Fair, fans turned out in droves to see Soupy Sales live in person.

Soupy Sales: "Any time people called, I would do them . . . I would do them sometimes two, three times a week sometimes . . . four times a week sometimes . . . every day sometimes. But in those days it was personal appearances [that] were the main thing, and we never got paid for them, never charged anybody anything for them."

Marv Welch, a fellow comedian and star of another popular WXYZ children's show, *Wixie's Wonderland,* reflects on Soupy's popularity.

Marv Welch: "Soupy and I would go a lot of times on the same show for the charities. I tore the house down and Soupy re-tore the house when he got on. He was very popular back then. Soupy was the top TV star in Detroit at that time."

Channel 7 news anchor Erik Smith shares a fond memory about a Soupy appearance from his childhood.

Erik Smith: "My mom took me to see Soupy Sales at one of his school appearances when I was a youngster. I watched his little show that he did for school kids at Oxford School in Dearborn . . . I'll never forget that. In those days, you never dreamed that one of these days you would be a companion and friend and associate; in the years that passed, Soupy and I shared a wonderful relationship. He was an icon, a figure of towering proportions."

Fans Peggy Tibbits and Larry Dlusky also describe how Sales made a "personal" impression on their lives.

Peggy Tibbits: "My dad [Clare Cummings, also known as Milky the Clown] and Soupy Sales knew each other, and that was to me one of the coolest things ever . . . that my dad knew Soupy Sales and better yet Soupy Sales knew *my* dad! There was some show that they were on together, some live thing, and I sat next to Soupy Sales, as I think my dad was maybe performing. And then Soupy was gonna come on next or something, and I just remember being thrilled because he was the real deal! My dad was not the real deal; he was a dad who got dressed up."

Larry Dlusky: "I was accompanying my grandmother, and I think it was to a doctor's appointment. The doctor was in the Maccabees Building. My grandmother and I were waiting for the elevator to come. I saw [him] coming out of what was either the gift shop or the cafeteria; Soupy Sales came walking up. He was dressed like he would be on his show. He didn't have that big, floppy, top hat on, but he had the V-necked sweater and the bow tie on. Our eyes kind of locked, and he obviously saw me and saw that my eyes got like flying saucers—real wide.

"He walked over to talk to me, you know, took the time to talk to me.

And when I say talk to me, I think I probably did all the talking. I told Soupy I was a member of the Birdbath Club and I had the magic slate that wrote in 'three' colors, I watched his show . . . and he seemed genuinely interested in what I was saying and was talking to me like an equal. That stayed with me the rest of my life—that he took the time to do that."

Soupy Sales: "I was really appreciative of the fans because I had never done a show like that before . . . and doing the show I could tell it was catching on, and I never forgot that with the people."

Lunch Becomes Breakfast

By the late 1950s, *Lunch with Soupy* had evolved into *Breakfast with Soupy*. The show was moved from its noontime slot to eight o'clock in the morning. The familiar lunch sounds of cows and chickens were replaced with marching troops for cereal munching, pig squeals for sausages and a rooster's "cock-a-doodle-doo" for eggs. Soupy comments on the time change and the regret that soon followed.

Soupy Sales: "[The show] was riding high in the noontime, and all of a sudden ABC came up with this set of programs that was going to take place in the afternoon. So we moved to the morning, and after they did it their [ABC's] plan went right into the toilet. The shows bombed . . . but I always started in the morning, so we kept it in the morning. The morning show was pretty good."

Although the breakfast show had a strong start initially, the energy levels were beginning to wane as Soupy's time in Detroit was nearing an end. Art Runyon, who was new to the station at that time, remembers the sentiment of the last days.

Art Runyon: "I started there I think about a week or two after his eleven o'clock show, the adult show, was canceled. And then I did it for the last month or two before he and his director [Bill Carruthers] and [Clyde Adler] went out to Hollywood to do the network show. That was kind of a sad time all the way around. A lot of effort wasn't being put into the show, I mean it was just 'let's just do it and get it over with.' That was kind of sad that way. There was a popular feeling at the time that Channel 7 was Soupy Sales and vice versa. But the vice president/general manager of WXYZ, John F. Pival, the immortal John, didn't see it that way and things went on."

Prior to leaving WXYZ in 1960, Sales struck a deal with ABC to take the local show he had made famous in Detroit for seven prosperous years national. Now a seasoned television professional, Soupy, at age 32, still very young, was ready to conquer America from the entertainment capital of the world, Hollywood.

Soupy Sales: "I looked forward to moving on because I felt I did everything I could do in Detroit. I weighed the idea very carefully and I decided I would move on and I did. It's always very sad to move on anytime, but you have to do it. A few fellas thought I was nuts to leave."

Looking Back

Be it the puppets, the pies, or just plain Soupy himself that mesmerized an entire generation of kids across the country, one fact remains: that goofy little show began in Detroit. Yes, indeed, Soupy Sales lives forever in the hearts of Motown's baby boom generation. And with that in mind here are some afterthoughts about the man and his show.

Jack Flechsig: "When he first came to the station, I thought John Pival had made a terrible mistake. Here was this kid who was zany and we hadn't seen him perform yet, you know, but he was just a kid. In about a week or two, we realized what we had, a real comic genius. He got along with everybody, and everything was a joke. He could turn anything into a joke."

Mason Weaver: "You don't realize you're working with a classic at the time. I mean, it's just a show you do every doggone day. And then later on you realize, wow, this was some kind of show . . . very different than everything else."

Soupy Sales: "I got to do everything I wanted to do on the kid's show. It was creative, and it was definitely innovative!"

Captain Jolly and Poopdeck Paul

As personalities, they were very different. Toby doing Captain Jolly
did it in a German accent and had hand puppets with off-camera
voices that he used quite a bit. Poopdeck Paul personified a sailor;
he dressed in an American navy gob hat, a turtleneck sweater, and
didn't rely on any other characters for the show.
   —NEIL ADDISON, retired director, CKLW-TV

Docked at Windsor's CKLW-TV was a make-believe ship with a cargo of
Popeye cartoons, manned by a crew of two: the skipper, Captain Jolly,
and his first mate, Poopdeck Paul. Washed between the tides of *Popeye
and His Pals,* CKLW radio's morning disc jockey, Toby David, transformed himself into an old German sea captain on weekday evenings,
while Channel 9 weatherman Paul Allen swabbed the decks with fun and
games on the weekends beginning in the late 1950s. Landlubbers Larry
Dlusky and Ed Golick briefly describe a few of the traits belonging to
their favorite television seamen.

   Larry Dlusky: "Captain Jolly was the captain of a ship. As I remember, it was always tied up on the dock, I don't recall seeing him out at
sea."

   Ed Golick: "Poopdeck Paul brought the TV cameras out on the lawn
in front of Riverside Drive and had tag team races and sports; he did
more physical things."

The Man of a Thousand Voices

Born to Lebanese immigrants in 1914, Toby David was inducted into the
circus by his parents, who performed in them. After high school, David
attended Henry Ford College in Highland Park. He married at a young
age and started a family right away with the birth of his eldest son,
Ronald. To quench his burning desire to work in broadcasting, he landed
a job at CKLW radio, sweeping the floors for transportation fare. Barely
earning a livable wage, he was determined to be a success in radio. Former WXYZ director Ron David summarizes the early result of his
father's perseverance.

   Ron David: "Eventually he got his chance to get on the air, and of
course he was a very funny guy with a great imagination. He and Joe
Gentile and Larry Gentile got this radio show at CKLW that was
extremely popular. They would do wild gags and they went on the air

Captain Jolly (Toby David) answering a call on the dock.
(Courtesy Ron David.)

with no script and that show became a tremendous hit. Ultimately he became the number-one morning show [personality] all by himself."

In 1940, David left the Detroit market for New York City, where he appeared on the radio in programs such as soap operas. Soon he left the Big Apple for the nation's capital. During his days in Washington, DC, he became involved in bond rallies with Hollywood stars and the president of the United States. After nearly a six-year absence, Toby David came home to the Motor City, where he quickly reestablished his popularity on WJR in early 1946.

Billed as "The Man of a Thousand Voices," David's first assignment was to appear as *Uncle Toby* every Sunday morning, bringing the comics from the Detroit papers to life. With the accompaniment of an organ, he read the entire comic section in character voices—men, women, children, animals, you name it.

Ron David: "He could do any dialect you can imagine. He became known in New York and Washington for his ability to do all these voices.

Poopdeck Paul (Paul Allen Schultz). (Courtesy CBC Windsor.)

Disney came after him. They wanted him to come out to California and do voice-overs on cartoons. As it turned out, fate steps in; my dad had been using the voices and the dialects so much that he got polyps on his throat. And he was told by his doctor, 'You cannot use your voice that way for a year or you're gonna lose your voice.' So he had to pass up the Disney offer."

Although he lost a chance to work in Hollywood, it didn't stop opportunity from knocking on David's door. He eventually appeared on WWJ radio and television before resuming his morning gig on CKLW radio.

Popeye and His Pals

When CKLW-TV purchased the syndicated cartoon series *Popeye and His Pals* in the late 1950s, Toby David's career was about to get the shot in the arm he'd yearned for his whole life. The *Popeye* package consisted of 237 episodes running three to five minutes each. Stations were free to showcase them utilizing whatever talent they wished to fill the allotted time.

After tasting the flavor of television on WWJ, voicing puppets on *Jolly Man's Circus* and *Willie-Do-It* along with *Comics Come to Life,* a televised version of his WJR radio act, David jumped at the chance to audition in February 1958 as the host of the new *Popeye* show. From his unpublished autobiography in 1983 entitled *The Real Captain Jolly,* he recalled the day he created the treasured captain. His quotes appear courtesy of Ron David.

Toby David: "The station held an open competition among all the performers on the staff for the spot of host of the half-hour show. I fell into the Popeye stride by affecting a captain's cap, a false beard, a German accent, a striped T-shirt and horn-rimmed glasses, which I wore at half-mast on my nose. I resurrected my old sobriquet—Captain Jolly—and beat the competition for the position of host of the show."

Ron David: "The German sea captain was probably one of the easiest [characters] he could sustain and keep the momentum going. So that's really how he chose to be the sea captain. The beard, by the way, started out fake, but he got so tired of putting it on with the spirit gum that he grew a beard. Then he got tired of that because it got so hot and prickly in the summertime, [so] he shaved it off and went back to the fake beard. But finally, in the end, it was a real beard again."

Captain Jolly

Now that David had introduced Captain Jolly to CKLW, the next step was how to present him to the kids at home. His previous experience in broadcasting proved to be invaluable.

Toby David: "To fit the marine theme of the show, I developed a number of dockside characters, using a different voice for each and weaving a little story into each broadcast. Cecil and Stanley were two puppets we used. Also there was Whitey the Mouse, Finny the Fish, Wilhelmina the Whale, and Sylvester the Seal, who did not appear on camera. These were my fishy companions on the show and I supplied a different voice for each as I talked to them."

Ron David: "He did very much like Soupy Sales and the rest of them: menus for the kids and little anecdotes to make kids get the right ideas in life."

Two of the many kids whose mothers let them watch the program, Ed Golick and Larry Dlusky, share a few fond thoughts about the things that made this mariner of the treacherous seas so endearing.

Ed Golick: "He'd always have some different thing going on every day like a continuing story, and I just couldn't wait to see it every day. I just loved Captain Jolly."

Larry Dlusky: "I don't know what Captain Jolly did. He never said if he was a fisherman, he didn't say he was hauling iron ore . . . he was just captain of his ship . . . but he had a lot of stories."

Ed Golick: "Captain Jolly was more of a sketch. I remember once he had the whole half hour of a show revolve around this can that said 'S. O. blank P.' The label had been ripped up, and he thought it was soup. The whole thing wrapped around him trying to find a can opener. When he did find a can opener, he cooked it up, poured it in a bowl and ate it. When he talked, bubbles came out and it turned out to be soap—not soup!"

Larry Dlusky: "What Captain Jolly had the ability to do was give you the feeling that the two of you were together. He would talk with you and he would talk to you—not at you. Captain Jolly had a quiet, soft-spoken manner of talking. He was like a grandfatherly type of figure . . . and I think that was the type of connection he was able to make with the kids. There wasn't this glass screen separating the two of you."

Poopdeck Paul

The weekend edition of *Popeye and His Pals* was decked out with another persona designated for an entirely different audience. With an anchor tattoo painted on his lower right arm and a white gob hat on his head, Paul Allen stood on the waterfront dock looking more like a Popeye fixture than his skipper. Larry Dlusky elaborates.

Larry Dlusky: "The guy that played Poopdeck Paul was more of a muscular guy than Toby David was, so he'd be more energetic. Of course, the name would give him away . . . he was not a captain, he was like one of the grunge workers; he'd be the guy swabbing the deck with a mop."

Retired CKLW director Neil Addison provides a little history about the man known as Poopdeck Paul.

Neil Addison: "His full name was Paul Allen Schultz. He was originally from Kitchener, Ontario. Before he came to CKLW, he had been a morning man in Montreal at one of the larger English-language radio stations there. He used to boast about the fact that he was number one in the ratings there."

Moving to television at CKLW, Allen incorporated his upbeat radio shtick into his weather reports very much the same way Sonny Eliot did at Channel 4. Unlike Captain Jolly, who appealed to the little kids, Poopdeck Paul attracted the older children who weren't watching during the week.

I Yam What I Yam

The successful combination of Captain Jolly during the week and Poopdeck Paul on the weekends paid dividends far beyond CKLW's expectations, as it became one of the most highly rated kid shows in the United States! Toby David explains.

Toby David: "Out of the 260 stations across the nation carrying the show, in 260 different formats, CKLW-TV had the highest rating and largest audience. I felt like the Pied Piper of Hamelin. Everywhere I went, kids recognized me, since the black beard and the glasses at half-mast on my nose were now a part of me. At the Grand Opening of a Shopper's Fair Mall in Toledo, Ohio, ten thousand kids and their parents showed up to say hello to Captain Jolly and to pull that magnificent beard. The following week, another seven thousand showed up with the same intent."

Equaling the masses that turned out at public appearances came boat-loads of mail. As Ron David notes, the captain cherished every one of them.

Ron David: "He did get a lot of fan mail. He's the kind of guy that would not just say, 'take care of that' and have some secretary do it; he would want to read every word of every letter."

Because television was so powerful in reaching out to its audience, children looked to TV stars as heroes, taking everything they said as gospel. To a sponsor, that's a blessing, but, as Captain Jolly fan Larry Dlusky learned (the hard way), you can't always believe what your idols say because, alas, they are human, too.

Larry Dlusky: "He had products he would sponsor. I remember Vernors was a sponsor and Bosco, which was a chocolate syrup; you could eat it on top of ice cream or put it in milk to make chocolate milk. And of course it was the best because Captain Jolly said so! One time he tried to combine them both together with disastrous results.

"There was a drink called the Boston cooler, in which you poured Vernors over vanilla ice cream. If you didn't have vanilla ice cream, they say you could get close to the same thing with half a glass of milk and half a glass of Vernors. This one day Captain Jolly recommended that we take some milk and we take some Vernors and put them together. Then we [should] put in a few teaspoons of Bosco syrup, stir it up, then put in a scoop of vanilla ice cream . . . and 'Oh, we'll have a wonderful taste treat.' Well, I did that . . . and I had one of the worst stomachaches of my life!"

Landlubber's Weekend

On weekends, Poopdeck Paul ran a much looser ship than his commander. While Captain Jolly interacted with puppets, Poopdeck invited the young shipmates at home to join him at the dock to play games for prizes. And in the summertime he frequently hosted the program outside the studio. Poopdeck Paul's style alone changed the format of the show. Ed Golick and Neil Addison look back on how Poopdeck ran *his* ship.

Ed Golick: "I remember that Poopdeck Paul would lip-sync to a record that came out at the time called *Time after Time*. The whole song went on for about two minutes. He didn't do any sketches or comedy bits. Poopdeck Paul was like an emcee; he was a host, and he introduced kids. He had limbo contests; limbo was big at the time."

Neil Addison: "We did go-cart racing in the back parking lot, kids' tap dancing, table tennis, and things of that nature. We even did an ice show one time on the front lawn with the Windsor Figure Skating Club."

So what was the reason for saving all of these goodies till the weekend? Was it a marketing ploy? Budgeting? According to Addison, it was neither.

Neil Addison: "Believe it or not, it had to do with studio facilities. We only had two studios. The larger one was quite busy all week, so Toby had to use the small studio and there wasn't room to do stuff like that. Because Paul was on in the weekend, we were able to utilize the large studio and do the contests."

Yeah, Yeah, Yeah!

Game-oriented contests weren't the only competitions orchestrated by Poopdeck Paul. Fans Greg Russell and Marci Wojciechowski recall the days when the world was captivated by Beatlemania and how Poopdeck Paul saw that as a challenge.

Greg Russell: "In 1964, they would have a Beatles contest every week-end with Poopdeck Paul, where it would be four kids pretending to be the Beatles. Thinking back on that now, I wish somebody had tape of that because it was one of the funniest-looking things in the world."

Marci Wojciechowski: "Little boys about our age would come on with little fake guitars and they were lip-syncing to Beatle songs. Most of them would have the Beatle wigs, and they would have one each week when the Beatles first came out. They lip-synced badly; they didn't sing the songs themselves, but I think the kids really felt special doing that."

Greg Russell: "It was cool, kids of every nationality pretending they were the Beatles on the show. And a lot of times if you couldn't get enough guys your sister would be in it. I remember this one time there were four girl Beatles: Joan, Georgette, Paula, and Ringoto!"

Goodwill to All

In addition to the thousands of children who tuned in to watch Captain Jolly at home and the select group that made it to the studio on Riverside Drive to compete on Poopdeck Paul's show, there was another group of kids who were less fortunate. And it was that group in particular that struck a heartfelt chord in Toby David.

Toby David: "Each year for many years I put on a show in Detroit for leukemia patients and I knew, as I looked out over the audience, that many of those kids wouldn't be there next year. It wasn't easy being 'jolly' under such circumstances, but a performer learns to cope with it."

Ron David: "My dad was a very selfless man, he did a tremendous amount of charity work and he never charged anybody a penny for his time . . . ever! Every single day after he would do his morning show, which was 6:00 to 9:00 a.m., which meant he had to be up at five in the morning or earlier, then he had the Captain Jolly show, which was also live . . . he would always stop by Children's Hospital before he came home and visit the kids. He would come into the house weeping after having been with these very sick kids. Then he would take a nap, and almost every night he had some kind of charity thing or event going on. He was one of those people who just couldn't stop giving."

On a steamy July afternoon in 1961, Toby was pulled over by a traffic cop en route to CKLW. It would be a traffic stop he'd never forget.

Toby David: "The police officer in the car next to me motioned me over to the curb. I wondered what I had done wrong. I knew I hadn't been speeding. 'Captain Jolly,' he said at the window. 'My nephew is dying of leukemia at Grace Hospital and he loves you. Could you give me something that I could give to him, to let him know that you know about him?' 'No,' I answered. The officer looked surprised. 'Which room is he in?' I asked.

"The number he gave me I recognized, for I had been in it a number of times, trying to cheer up those unfortunate kids. The hospital wasn't far out of my way, and I had some time before I was due at the studio. I had my Captain Jolly cap with me and the glasses which drooped on my nose and a few small toys. Blood was caked at the end of the boy's nose, as it does with leukemia victims. The boy's mother and aunt (the policeman's wife) were there. As I played with the boy and gave him one of my pictures and a cap, I noticed they were crying. The nurses were crying . . . and soon, Captain Jolly was too."

Strong to the Finish

Toby David: "Sometimes, when things are going great you have the feeling that 'this is too good to last.' That feeling began to creep over me and to invade my thoughts often late in 1963 and in early 1964. That kid show—the *Popeye* show—was doing very well, holding up in the ratings and fighting off would-be sponsors. But I knew nothing lasts forever. RKO General, one of the big conglomerates in the entertainment and communications field, gained control of CKLW radio and television by buying it in 1964. Their philosophy of entertainment left no room for kid shows."

Ron David: "After many years of success with his Captain Jolly show, RKO General brought in a new general manager. The bulk of all the kiddie show programming at CKLW-TV plus a lot of movies with movie hosts were very inexpensive shows to produce to be commercial carriers. This guy got the big idea that he was gonna save the station a lot of money by getting rid of all this high-priced talent that was on their payroll. So he not only dismissed all the movie hosts but also dismissed all the kiddie show hosts, including my dad. They dropped all that programming, and Channel 50, a new UHF station in Detroit that had been losing money hand over fist, jumped at the opportunity to provide kiddie programming to the Detroit audience and they became the first successful/profitable UHF station in America."

Toby David: "It was no surprise then, when the *Popeye* show met its end on Channel 9. Knowing that there were millions of kids and parents out there who loved Popeye and the show we had created to carry his cartoons, I said the last goodbye to my audience with a lump in my throat almost big enough to choke me."

Out to Sea

After the cancellation of Captain Jolly in the mid-1960s, Toby David took his character to Channel 7, WXYZ, under the name Captain Toby. Both he and Allen reprised their famed show briefly in 1966. An attempt was made to sell their program to ABC that same year, but the network eventually passed. Toby David retired to Mesa, Arizona, where he lived until his sudden death in 1994, one week shy of his eightieth birthday. Paul Allen Schultz passed away at his home in Belle River, Ontario, on September 18, 2000.

And so, even with the passing of the current, the captain's legend still lives on.

Ron David: "Everywhere you go in this town today—throughout Michigan and where there are Michigan transplants—Captain Jolly/Toby David is a magic name to this day."

Jingles in Boofland

I got my tonsils out when I was real little and got really upset that I wasn't gonna be home in time for *Jingles*.
  —ED GOLICK, Webmaster, detroitkidshow.com

Once upon a time, across the river, in a castle far, far away, there frolicked a court jester named Jingles who lived in a mythical kingdom called Boofland. While serving at the whimsical beckoning of the king, Jingles and his puppet pals, Herkimer Dragon and Cecil B. Rabbit, would take the young lads and lasses of Detroit on an hour-long magical excursion of music, comedy, and cartoons every weekday at 5:00 p.m. on CKLW-TV, Channel 9, in the late 1950s and early 1960s.

Appearing between cartoons, mainly Looney Tunes or old Laurel and Hardy shorts, Jingles, played by Jerry Booth, was the straight man whose comical reactions to scenarios had to counterbalance the opposite personalities of his two eccentric cohabitants. Escaping to Boofland required the recitation of four magic words, which were uttered at the beginning of the show by its cocreator and puppeteer, Larry Sands. *Jingles* fan

Jingles (Jerry Booth) with friends Herkimer Dragon (left) and
Cecil B. Rabbit. (Courtesy Matt Keelan.)

Larry Dlusky, along with its star, Jerry Booth, revisit the program's opening ritual.

Larry Dlusky: "Larry Sands, for a children's show, was a very austere,
intimidating-looking person. He was dressed in a dark business suit,
white shirt, and tie, and he had this black beard. It was a nice, well-
trimmed beard, but it made him look very stern. And he had this magic
wand and words he'd say to get us to Boofland."

Jerry Booth: " 'Kowdora Bizzle, Dankora Fizzle . . .' Then there would
be an explosion of some sort and it would fade to a picture of the castle.
Then [Sands] would do this poem . . .

Way beyond the Ishkabow
And over the Foo-Fram Sea
You'll find there's a place called Boofland
Where very soon you'll be.
Boofland is full of surprises
Like dragons and birds and things
And inside a magic castle
Jingles dances, laughs, and sings.

Now if you've been good kids all day long
Here's what has to be done.
Shout 'Jingles' and clap just three times.
Now get ready for fun!

"Then Jingles would dance in from behind the camera somewhere and do a little dance number, then stop the music and start talking."

When Jingles wasn't dancing his way into the castle, he'd often find another humorous way to get there. Such was the case once when he was stranded on the rooftop. After trying to lower himself down by tying handkerchiefs together, he finally gave up and threw down a roped ladder.

A Jester Is Born

While studying business and broadcasting at Millikin University in Decatur, Illinois, Jerry Booth worked for the local television station WTVP. Upon graduation, he accepted a position as a production manager at WSEE-TV in Erie, Pennsylvania. A few months later he received a phone call from his former employer in Decatur, who asked him to come back and host a new children's show. Favoring acting over production management, Booth seized the opportunity to return to the Midwest, where he transformed himself into a unique character of his own creation: Jingles. Larry Dlusky elaborates.

Larry Dlusky: "What separated Jingles from the clown shows was that Jingles was a court jester. He wasn't dressed as a clown, and he had no makeup on his face. He had this court jester suit on with bells all over it, and everywhere he went he would 'jingle.'"

The concept was brilliant. In a demographic dominated by fictitious sailors, cowboys, and clowns, Jerry Booth introduced youngsters to a friendly character they'd never seen or heard of before, the court jester.

Larry Dlusky: "That was a term that I don't think seven-year-old kids would have known. We knew clowns from the circus, but a court jester, well, this is a clown that was at a castle for the entertainment of the king . . . and we learned that from *Jingles*."

Draped in a costume made by his first wife Patty, Jingles was ready to entertain the kids of Decatur every afternoon. Jerry Booth had given the world of children's television a fresh new look into another place and time through the eyes of a medieval clown. Unfortunately, the financial constraints of the small station left no room for imaginative growth, which meant no Boofland, no castle, and no puppets. However, after a year's run as a "solo" act the fate of Jingles was about to take a turn for the better.

Jerry Booth: "The fellow that I worked for in Erie, Pennsylvania, called me and said, 'We're starting a new station in Fort Wayne, Indiana [WPTA], and we want to do that Jingles character and have you do some other on-the-air work.'"

Jerry Booth . . . Meet Larry Sands

Having majored in music at the University of Illinois, Larry Sands worked a radio job for 32 dollars a week in upstate New York before coming to WPTA-TV in Fort Wayne. Retired CKLW-TV director Neil Addison cites a few personal qualities belonging to the future comedic genius.

Neil Addison: "Larry was kind of a caustic personality, but he was a really sharp operator. He really knew his business . . . knew his way around the TV industry . . . a very kind person, too."

In the meantime, Jerry Booth packed his bags and headed to Indiana, unaware that he was about to form a partnership with a man who would elevate his show to heights he'd only dreamed of. Booth comments on the outcome of his meeting with Larry Sands in 1957.

Jerry Booth: "We met when we both showed up at WPTA. Art Hook was the new station manager there; he hired both of us for doing on-the-air work, for producing, announcing, and directing . . . and that's where the 'real' program was born. We sat down and started laying out some ideas for the *Jingles in Boofland* show that started there. We put our heads together and the Boofland set was built there and that's where *Jingles in Boofland* came from. The name, of course, is just a shortening of my own name—the way a kid would pronounce it [Boof]."

With the addition of the Boofland castle for a backdrop, the next expansion was the talent. Jingles would need a few sidekicks. They knew they had to have a dragon since the setting was inside a castle—enter Herkimer Dragon. And, as Sands was a big fan of the Paul Harvey news show—enter Cecil B. Rabbit to round out the cast. Although other characters would eventually debut on the program, Booth and Sands designated Herkimer and Cecil B. as the regular supporting players. With that in mind, what would they look like? More importantly, with a pauper's budget, who was going to make them? Jerry Booth provides the answer.

Jerry Booth: "We went to a person that we heard about in Fort Wayne that worked with papier-mâché and asked him to make us a couple of puppets: a rabbit and a dragon. He made some drawings on a piece of paper, and we said, 'Okay, build them and we'll use 'em.' Those puppets are the ones we used also in Detroit when we moved there."

Over the Foo-Fram Sea

Joining Larry and Jerry in Fort Wayne was another station talent named Don Harris. While Booth pranced in front of the cameras as Jingles, Sands concentrated on working Cecil B. Rabbit, which left Harris as the puppeteer and voice of Herkimer Dragon. As *Jingles in Boofland* gained momentum at WPTA, it also caught the attention of the CKLW-TV sales manager, who was impressed enough to convince his station's brass to purchase the show in 1958.

Coming to the Detroit market, Booth and Sands planned to duplicate the program with a few minor alterations: Jingles's two-toned costume would be revamped, with a striped hat and matching pants made from corduroy, and the Boofland castle would be expanded. With those minor changes intended for the improvement of the show, an unexpected development would persuade the duo to legalize their partnership, as Jerry Booth recounts.

Jerry Booth: "Don Harris did not go to Detroit with us, so it was just Larry and I. We then formed our own company called Sanaboof Productions and began to write the show for CKLW. An interesting sidelight about [Harris] . . . he later became a network news guy and he was in Jonestown when that awful event happened and he actually got shot and killed where the airplane was landing. He was waiting to be taken away and got shot."

Ready to "rock and roll" at CKLW, so to speak, not everyone greeted them with open arms. But as retired CKLW director Matt Keelan remembers, he fell under their spell just like many who had resisted the new pop music scene that was persisting at the time.

Matt Keelan: "What I recall was these two guys coming into the station and we knew they had puppets. My view at that time: I was not into puppets because for the most part puppets had people with strange voices who sounded frustrated. So I wasn't impressed with them when they came in, but once I saw the show, that all changed!"

The Boofland Castle

Just what was so special about this cartoon wraparound show that caught the attention of its young audience? Was it the fairy tale setting? Maybe . . . perhaps . . . Let's ask loyal *Jingles* follower Marci Wojciechowski.

Marci Wojciechowski: "It was a fun show to watch because of the castle, the knights in shining armor type of thing."

And to the many kids like Marci, who were enchanted by the mystique of gallant knights, castles, and kings, the *Jingles* set had to be as believable as the CKLW crew could make it . . . at least to a child. Jerry Booth and Matt Keelan explain how the illusion was executed and guarded.

Jerry Booth: "It was basically a parapet and an archway with some different set pieces like the treasure chest, which was a huge piece that we used for a lot of things. The one, of course, in Detroit/Windsor was designed by one of the stagehands there; he built it and kept adding onto it when we could squeeze some more money out of the budget."

Matt Keelan: "In those days, they only had nine-foot flats. One of the problems for the director was trying to keep the cameraman from shooting over the top of the flat, which would destroy the idea of the set. They used a boom mic, and they were always trying to keep the boom mic out of the set. Everything in those days was taboo. It wasn't like nowadays, where they show cameras on their set and all that; this stuff was supposed to be a mystery."

Jerry Booth: "We never had an audience in the studio . . . we didn't want to give away the fantasy."

Cecil B. Rabbit and Herkimer Dragon

As mentioned, Jingles had two puppet companions: Cecil B. Rabbit, a pompous, baggy-eyed, red-nosed, white rabbit with a black mustache; and Herkimer Dragon, a docile, 17-foot, gleaming green, buck-toothed simpleton.

Taking a cue from Disney, Sands and Booth wanted to introduce an element of fear into their ongoing fable by establishing an egotistical antagonist. The honor went to . . .

Neil Addison: "Cecil B. Rabbit was a takeoff on Paul Harvey, a network newscaster who had quite an unusual voice. The puppet talked just like Paul Harvey. And Paul Harvey always had a thing where he'd go from one news story to another, 'Paaaage one . . .' then the news story and 'Paaaage two . . .' and away he'd go. That's what the rabbit did on the *Jingles* show; it was the same thing."

Jerry Booth: "Cecil B. always had to have an entrance. His first entrance was his newscast, which was exactly like how Paul Harvey started . . . 'Good evening Booflandians, stand by for . . . NEWS!' Sometimes the news would lead into the special event he was doing that day."

Many of Cecil B. Rabbit's special events included elaborate productions of operas, melodramas, and westerns starring the biggest names in

Hollywood. Cecil B., of course, was on a first-name basis with all the stars. He even had a fight with Marlon Brando, who he claimed stole a movie idea from him. Neil Addison chuckles about one particular production of Cecil B.'s that hopped off on the wrong foot.

Neil Addison: "Cecil B. Rabbit was always introduced with a fanfare. It would be up to the audio guy to pick some little thing; I just loved doing that, finding unusual things. So one day I picked the closing bars of "The 1812 Overture," which happens to run over three minutes long. Larry would have to hold the puppet up to dance around this overture. Well, this thing goes on and on and on and on . . . finally he just put the puppet down on the castle parapet and went PLOP! And the thing went on for another thirty seconds. Larry thought that was the funniest thing in the world!"

Jerry Booth: "Cecil B. was the heavy. The extent of his heaviness mostly was his conceit. His subtitle was Cecil B. Rabbit, the World's Greatest Anything (WGA). So he was the best singer, the best actor, the best writer, the best everything . . . He would frequently give me things to do that I would never be able to do so that he could come out on top."

Many of those exploits got Jingles into trouble, as Larry Dlusky recalls.

Larry Dlusky: "I remember one time there was a wrestler on the show and Cecil B. Rabbit was saying to Jingles, 'You could beat up that wrestler!' The wrestler right away turns to Jingles and says, 'You think you can beat me up?' Jingles is going, 'No, no, no . . .' And Cecil B. Rabbit goes, 'He could beat you up with one hand behind his back!' The wrestler again, 'You think you can beat me up?' Jingles, 'No, no, no!' And of course, eventually it turns out that the wrestler picks Jingles up and he has him in the air. Cecil B. Rabbit is going, 'You give it to him, Jingles!' Jingles replies, 'He's giving it to me!'"

Cecil B.'s authoritative demeanor succeeded in pushing some of the audience toward his nemesis.

Marci Wojciechowski: "He was kind of bossy sounding; I didn't like him because he was a know-it-all. Herkimer was a good guy, that's why I liked him."

Which segues us into the reptile antithesis . . .

Neil Addison: "The other puppet character was this lovable buffoon, Herkimer Dragon, who did stupid things all the time."

Jerry Booth: "Herkimer was the dumb guy . . . he was just 'Dum-de-dum-da-dum.' He'd go along with anything. Herkimer usually appeared shortly after I did . . . 'Hi Jing buddy' was usually his first line."

As dumb as he was, he made quite an impression on the kids at home. Does anyone remember Herkimer's subtle hat campaign?

When Herkimer wished he had a hat to wear, the fan response was overwhelming! (Courtesy Jerry Booth.)

Jerry Booth: "One time Herkimer Dragon wanted a hat because somebody else got a new hat and he didn't get one. And because he said he wanted one kids started sending hats for Herkimer to wear. We got tons of them in the mail. Some of them were just made out of paper, and some were just little stocking caps. So Herkimer had hats to wear whenever he wanted to after that."

For anyone who remembers Herkimer's occasional puffs of smoke, here's a little secret: inside the puppet head was a tube that led to a hole in the dragon's mouth. Larry Sands would light up a cigarette and blow the smoke into the tube to simulate the effect of a fire-breathing dragon.

Like Sands through the Hourglass

It's often been said that Larry Sands was the mastermind behind *Jingles in Boofland*. Perhaps that's because his presence could be felt in every aspect of the program.

Jerry Booth: "Larry had to do both puppets plus several other characters. He was Mr. Binki the mailman, he was the King of Boofland, all different voices and characters . . . he was a very talented guy. Mr. Binki we never saw; he just handed mail in and he had kind of an Irish accent. The King of Boofland—he did an 'Ed Wynn' impression on that one. That was a character that wasn't used that often, but he actually appeared on-camera with the crown and beard."

Matt Keelan: "He used to play a grand piano, and we would shoot it in a mirror so you couldn't see who was playing."

Jerry Booth: "He wrote the music for the show, the "Boofland Loyalty Song" and stuff like that."

Marci Wojciechowski: "I still remember the song!

Oh Boofland, my Boofland,
Let us always sing,
And have some fun with Cecil B.,
Herkimer, and Jing.
No matter how big I get,
No matter where I go, go, go,
I'll always watch my TV set
For the *Jingles* show, the *Jingles* show."

Although the "Boofland Loyalty Song" was played religiously at the close of every show; usually sung by Jingles (on the ukulele) and Herkimer, Jerry Booth notes another version.

Jerry Booth: "There was a third- or fourth-grade class, I don't remember what school it was, that also wrote a choral version of it and recorded it. We used that version sometimes for the closing."

Sketches

Jerry Booth: "Most days we would have a premise that would take the whole show to come to some conclusion. Some of the spots would be standard bits that we would do every day . . . like a drawing of some-body's name and they would win something out of the treasure chest."

Neil Addison: "They didn't have line-by-line scripts; they had outlines of what they were gonna do. They used to have a little office up on the second floor of the station, [where] the two of them sat and rehearsed all of these things before they ever came down to the studio. We'd do a bit of a dry run in the studio with them and, boom, away you'd go."

Matt Keelan: "As a director, because we were directing other shows, we were handed [the outline] maybe a half hour before the show and we had to ad-lib along with whatever they did."

Jerry Booth: "Cecil B. Rabbit was usually the impresario that was gonna present these things; like he did an opera one time that he allegedly wrote . . . we'd just sing it in fake Italian. Subtitles would be superim-posed on the screen, and it would be the punch lines to the jokes that we were doing."

Playing the Fool

One of the pleasures of working with Larry Sands and Jerry Booth was sharing in their sense of humor. Whether it was Larry or someone from the crew pulling a gag, the main target of the jokes was Jerry! Was it because he portrayed a jester? Retired CKLW production manager Frank Quinn leads the reminiscences of tittering tales.

Frank Quinn: "Larry would really break Jerry up. Jerry was an affable type of guy, but he was nervous; he wanted everything to go right, and Larry would just screw him up every time. When they would rehearse something, Larry would throw something in that Jerry didn't expect, and it was like he was caught in the headlights of a car. He was always in a state of shock on the show."

Neil Addison: "We had a colorful lighting guy named Leo Johnson. On one show, we had a prop toilet, the bottom half of the toilet. We dragged it out and sat it between the cameras. Leo sat on it with his pants down reading the newspaper. Well, Jerry's got to look at this. Every time he looked at it, he started laughing. He laughed so hard he couldn't finish what he had to do and we had to go to a cartoon."

Jerry Booth: "Art Lang, the weatherman [at CKLW], was a frequent collaborator with us, and his main function was to try to get me to break up. I remember many times I would open the treasure chest to get some-thing out and there would be Art Lang sitting inside holding up nude pic-tures or something like that to get me to break up . . . and I usually did!"

And in the End

Neil Addison: "For a while there, *Jingles in Boofland* was *the* big show. It was a darn good kid's show."

During the golden age of television, there was a philosophy that some shows, regardless of their popularity, could only last so long after they had enjoyed a good run. When that kind of thinking works its way into your show, cancellation is imminent. Larry Sands and Jerry Booth became the recipients of such logic when CKLW management approached them in the early 1960s. They were asked if they could do something other than *Jingles* for an older audience. Believing that their brand of shtick sometimes walked a fine line between children and adults, the dynamic duo invented a new show called *Larry and Jerry*.

A few years into their new program, Larry Sands left Detroit to pursue a career with an advertising agency in Chicago. The ad business eventually led Sands to the coast of Southern California, where he directed television commercials. Tragically, it was while filming aerial shots that Larry Sands was killed along with three other people in a helicopter crash in 1975.

Meanwhile, Booth hosted his third show on CKLW, *Jerry Booth's Funhouse*, and at the same time he was chosen to become Channel 9's first Bozo for a brief period in 1967, when the station took over the series from WWJ-TV. Jerry also saw the summer rise and fall of a Windsor theme park built around the premise of *Jingles* called Boofland.

For a time, *Jingles in Boofland* enjoyed higher ratings than *The Jimmy Dean Show, American Bandstand,* and *The Mickey Mouse Club.* Jerry Booth still has fond memories of the jovial jester he created almost fifty years ago and of the fans who embraced him.

Jerry Booth: "I get a general sense of having a connection with kids. Not only kids, but also when we were doing the show and people from the station would come in and watch and get a kick out of it . . . the mail that would come in . . . just the feeling of being a part of the culture of the kids in that area and connecting with them, contributing something to what they watched every day."

Johnny Ginger

Johnny Ginger was the most physical comic you ever saw . . . and the greatest pantomimist I have ever seen in my life!
    —MASON WEAVER, retired director, WXYZ-TV

Long before the American Movie Classics channel began packaging *Three Stooges* shorts under the guise of *NYUK: New Yuk University of Knuckleheads,* hosted by its Professor of Stoogeology, Leslie Nielsen, WXYZ-TV in Detroit had Johnny Ginger. Posing first as a stagehand, Ginger pulled a curtain every weekday evening to present the Three Stooges on *Curtain Time Theater* from 1957 to 1960. With the dawn of a new decade, the sad but lovable stagehand traded his overalls for a red bellhop's uniform and abandoned the backstage shadows of the theater for the limelight in a ritzy hotel lobby. Renamed *The Johnny Ginger Show,* the bumbling bellboy appeared in a variety of outrageous skits between daily doses of the Three Stooges. Retired WXYZ director Chris Montross defines the program's key to success.

Chris Montross: "It was all Ginger. He did voice-overs, and he would have it all prepared ahead of time. Ginger pretty much did his own show, and he had the whole thing worked out himself. He was very good and funny. He would use all kinds of voices and backgrounds. He was fun to work with. He was a star at the station."

From south of the border in Toledo, Ohio, a young comedian by the name of Jerry Gale had developed quite a reputation on the Motor City nightclub circuit for his brand of squeaky-clean comedy. Johnny Ginger (Jerry Gale) explains his preference for "pure" humor versus filthy one-liners.

Johnny Ginger: "When I was a kid, my dad said, 'If you can fall down and make a face, it'll make the people laugh . . . and that's true comedy. Comedy comes from the heart, not the mouth.' I always remembered that, and to this day I do a strictly clean show."

The Audition

During the spring of 1957, WXYZ-TV had a 13-week vacancy to fill in its summer programming schedule. The station managers hadn't decided what kind of show to produce. Given the popularity of the children's genre, they agreed that the new program should have a kiddie theme.

Stagehand Johnny Ginger in the late 1950s. (Courtesy Johnny Ginger.)

Having acquired the television rights to air the *Three Stooges*, they settled on a wraparound show to highlight the kings of slapstick comedy.

But who would host the program? Pete Strand, the station's program director, launched a search for the hottest names on the local comedy scene. One of those names would be Jerry Gale.

Johnny Ginger: "Pete Strand said, 'Come to WXYZ at the Maccabees Building; we're gonna do a summer television show for 13 weeks.' I flipped out! I called my mother and my dad and my wife and my brother. I said, 'I got a television show.' I went over there that Monday, and I'm playing the part . . . I got the shades on and I'm real cool. I walked up to the desk and said, 'I'm Jerry Gale.' The woman at the desk replied, 'Jerry

Gale . . . you're 28.' 'No,' I said, 'I'm 23.' She said, 'No, no, no . . . you're twenty-eighth in line to go in for the audition.' Here I thought I had it! There were 30 comics trying out for it.

"I went in, and they had a high stool. I had a monologue to do. So I sat down, and this big voice comes booming out of the control room, 'Whatever you have rehearsed forget it, just ad-lib.' So I just [rocked] on the stool, and I just kept going until I fell back and rolled up and went, 'Daaaa . . . .' They said, 'Don't call us, we'll call you,' that old bit. About a week later I get a call, and they said, 'We'd like you to come back.' I thought, 'Whoooo!' They kept eliminating some [comics and] bringing back the rest, and finally it got down to me and I got it. They said, 'We liked the physical thing that you did, the fall, because you reminded us of Buster Keaton.'"

Johnny Bull Ginger Beer

Before Jerry Gale's face would grace the presence of the TV cameras, one "minor" detail needed to be addressed.

Johnny Ginger: "I went into the office of the vice president, John Pival, and he said, 'Come in, Johnny Ginger.' I turned around and looked and said, 'Who?' He said, 'Johnny Ginger.' I said, 'I'm Jerry Gale.' He said, 'Not anymore; you're going to be Johnny Ginger.' I said, 'Where did you get that? That's ridiculous, it's stupid.' He said, 'Well, Jerry Gale just doesn't hit it. All the stories you hear about kids in school are little Johnny walked up to the teacher . . . little Johnny came home . . .' He [then] said, 'Well, actually, I got it off of a bottle.' On the green bottle from Pival's office, embossed at the bottom was Johnny Bull Ginger Beer. And the Johnny and the Ginger were on top of each other. He said, 'I was looking at it . . . Johnny Ginger . . . that's it!' I said, 'I'm glad you weren't drinking a bottle of Budweiser, or I'd be Bud Weiser.' He said, 'You're gonna do real well.'"

From that day on, Jerry Gale would forever be . . . Johnny Ginger! It was another successful name change masterminded by the same man who four years earlier had given Soupy the last name of Sales.

Curtain Time

With the new name in place, the next item on the agenda was to create a character and venue for WXYZ's newest show. All programs stem from the concept of making something out of nothing. But in the case of Johnny Ginger, the young comedian had no forewarning about just how much nothing he'd have to work with.

Johnny Ginger: "We had no budget at all. They didn't have money to build a set, and they used an empty studio. Pete [Strand] got the idea of me being just behind the scenes . . . a stagehand. There was just a rope on a pulley, and they found the coveralls in a locker that somebody had left behind and a sweatshirt. There was an Ivy League cap lying around in props, and they said, 'Put this on, let's see how it looks.' I [also] wore suede desert boots with athletic socks, and that became the costume."

Assuming the role of a stagehand in the summer of 1957, Johnny Ginger hosted *Curtain Time Theater* every weekday evening at 6:00 p.m. Detroit TV fan Larry Dlusky notes how Ginger improvised with what little there was in the way of props to segue into the program's feature presentation.

Larry Dlusky: "There'd be this pulley rope, and it would be the kind you'd expect to pull [to] open a [stage] curtain. He would take the rope and start pulling on it, then they'd go into a short. You'd never see what the rope did, but I guess as a kid you didn't need to . . . you just knew, 'Oh, he's pulling the rope. I'm gonna see the Three Stooges now.'"

Feeling a bit insecure about his ability to carry the program for the full 13 weeks, Johnny played the first show as though it were his last, never imagining that his fear would produce his signature ending.

Johnny Ginger: "On the first show, I thought, they're gonna fire me. That's how my trademark ending, 'Mom, Dad, and Patty and all,' started. My mom and dad and my wife at the time, Patty, were watching, so I wanted to say goodbye to them. The next day the phones lit up at the studio; people saying they thought it was so nice of that young man, acknowledging his mom and dad, but who's Patty? So that became a big thing. [Management] said, 'Don't ever say who Patty is because that could be a mystery. If they find out that you're married, then, all young girls who want to grow up and marry Johnny Ginger, it would ruin it [for them] and they wouldn't want to watch.' That became a big mystery, and that was always at the end of my show . . . Mom, Dad, and Patty."

As audiences continued to watch *Curtain Time Theater* with their favorite stagehand, WXYZ expanded the shorts to include the shtick of Andy Clyde, Edgar Kennedy, Harry Langdon, and Charley Chase. Clutch Cargo and Courageous Cat cartoons were also tossed into the mix. However, despite all the new supplements, the main attraction was still the Stooges . . . but only for a little while.

Voices Carry

In the original format, Ginger appeared between commercial breaks to introduce the movie shorts. It wouldn't be long before boredom crept into the act.

Johnny Ginger: "Being a nightclub comic, [the concept] wasn't creative to me. I said, 'Can I write little bits, maybe, to do in between the things?' They said, 'Yeah, that would be nice . . . it would add something now. You will make this . . . if we provide a writer, and you'll make this . . . if you do it yourself.' I thought, I can write that . . . no problem. So I started writing it, and it was very difficult at first."

But as hard as it was for the young comedian initially, he would come to rely heavily on his voice-over skills to fabricate the existence of other characters.

Johnny Ginger: "Soupy had the dogs. Our budget was nil, and I thought, the kids are gonna get tired of seeing just me. So I thought, I gotta create off-camera voices with just a hand coming in. I created the one who I pretty much copied as a Jerry Lewis voice . . . Killer was a guy who'd say, 'Johnny, are we gonna go see the Three Stooges now? Tell Mr. Rocky that we're gonna go in the back and play.' And Mr. Rocky was almost like a pug; he'd say, 'Ya better get back to work or I'm gonna fire ya.' One stagehand [at WXYZ] was like Robin Williams with the hairy arm; he could have been one of Soupy's dogs, so he was the boss with all of the hair."

The boss, incidentally, was named after Johnny's eldest son, Rocky. So just how did Ginger bring these voices to life on live television? You'd think only a ventriloquist would be capable of pulling off such a feat, but the ever resourceful comic had another method entirely. Retired WXYZ director Mason Weaver, who directed most of Johnny's shows, and retired WXYZ art director Jack Flechsig reveal Ginger's secret.

Mason Weaver: "Every day he came in with a tape with all these voices of these people he'd talk to [that were] off-camera. The thing of it is, he'd have fifteen/twenty minutes of this . . . he knew exactly when to come in, and you'd swear there was somebody standing there talking to him. It was that good."

Jack Flechsig: "He was very innovative in that he was one of the first performers I know of that pretaped bits and then reacted to the taped bits; he would talk to himself on a monitor. He was a master at that. It was very tricky to do in those days, too, because of no electronic editing or anything like that . . . it was kind of all by the seat of your pants."

The ingenuity behind the man who appeared as a stagehand gave way to a whole new production strategy.

Jack Flechsig: "He was sort of an independent producer, much like Soupy, except he came in with his own ideas and we merely implemented them. He would come in and meet with the stagehands, and they'd throw something together for him . . . particularly when he was the stagehand character, because he had no set."

Wearing the hats of producer and writer on top of the checkered cap that viewers saw on the TV screen, Johnny Ginger was now assured by the station that he'd be around much longer than the specified 13 weeks. In fact, his bits were first developed to cover the downtime between the *Three Stooges* shorts. However, as time would tell, a day arrived when Moe, Larry, and Curly were edited down to fit Johnny's time!

The Bellboy

In 1960, Johnny Ginger and his fans would experience a jolt that was as unpredictable as an earthquake. That year Jerry Lewis wrote, directed, and starred in a hit motion picture comedy, *The Bellboy*. One of the people who fell in love with Lewis's character and decided to capitalize on it was Pete Strand. Ginger describes how his growing popularity influenced Strand's decision.

Johnny Ginger: "After a couple of years, the sponsors started standing in line, waiting to get on my show. So the budget got bigger, and that's when Pete Strand said, 'You're going to be a bellhop. We're going to build a hotel lobby for you; there will be an elevator and a lounge where you can do your songs, a switchboard, and blah, blah, blah.'"

Ginger fan and webmaster of detroitkidshow.com Ed Golick, along with Johnny himself, summarize the outcome of the initial character change.

Ed Golick: "The stagehand was kind of a 'sad sack' guy, while the bellboy was brash and he sang; the guy that pulled the curtain didn't do that. Johnny was allowed to do a lot more as the bellboy. He had this whole persona of this guy that pulled the curtain and, okay, all of a sudden you're a bellboy!?"

Johnny Ginger: "I really didn't like it at first because it killed the character of this real sympathetic guy that everything happened to. I mean sandbags would fall on me, lights would fall on me, ladders would fall over . . . With the bellhop thing, I couldn't find anything there. So I finally devised the idea that the bellhop uniform was a cover for me being a spy. I would go into the elevator, down into subterranean things, and I

In 1960, Ginger was unexpectedly promoted from a stagehand to a bellhop. (Courtesy Johnny Ginger.)

became this spy. That worked out pretty good, and that [lasted] for the remainder of the shows . . . the bellhop as a superspy. And none of that came out right; I couldn't do anything right . . . so that character became bumbling, too."

Larry Dlusky also remembers the transition.

Larry Dlusky: "All of a sudden he was working at a hotel, and I think Killer was another bellboy there and Mr. Rocky was still the boss. You never saw any hotel rooms, you never went into the kitchen where they made meals . . . it was always the lobby. There was the front desk and the elevator, and that was pretty much it."

As displeased as Ginger was with the switch at the outset, there would be even more dissatisfaction expressed by mothers, who were appalled by the cut of the red uniform.

Johnny Ginger: "We got a lot of letters at first, saying, 'What happened to this shy guy—everything happens to me type?' They sent me down to a tailor and tailor made [some] outfits for me: one for the studio, one for the summertime, which was more lightweight . . . and it was skin tight! I got a lot of letters from irate mothers who are saying, 'It's disgusting; we can see everything you got. When you turn around we can see the crack in your butt . . .' They were pretty nasty about it. I took all the letters to the producer and said, 'Look what you've done!' 'Don't worry,' he said, 'They'll catch on—they'll adjust.' And they did."

The Genius of Ginger

Things really changed when Johnny Ginger reported for duty at the Rocky Plaza Hotel. With an increased budget, he appeared on the WXYZ schedule twice a day, mornings as well as evenings, under a new title, *The Johnny Ginger Show*. And along with all the thematic alterations came an explosion of ideas that elevated local television to unprecedented heights, beginning with his nontraditional brand of pantomime.

Ed Golick: "He did these crazy bits, and I found out years later that he had an old reel-to-reel tape recorder. He would lip-sync but not to a normal song; he would cut pieces from here, pieces from there, splice it all together and lip-sync to his crazy version of whatever song was popular at the time, with all his sound effects cut in."

Johnny Ginger: "I would take Sammy Davis or Frank Sinatra and just chop the hell out of it. I would either splice in Spike Jones or sound effects or Dean Martin, and it almost sounded like it matched—everything matched. I built a studio in Livonia so I could do all of that for the show. I used the Isley Brothers 'Shout': 'A little bit softer now . . . a little bit softer now . . . jump up and shout now . . .' I used to put that in so many bits, it became [such] a standard thing that people would recognize me for the fact: 'You do "Shout" on your show . . . Yeah, yeah, yeah—wild!'"

As if slicing and dicing lip-syncs weren't enough, the station's move from the Maccabees Building in Detroit to a new facility in Southfield opened the door to an onslaught of radical sketches, all of which were from the mind of a man who a few years earlier had been limited to the confines of nightclubs.

Johnny Ginger: "When we did the bellhop thing, I invented the Anything Machine and it was hooked up with a smoke machine and it was on wheels. I got the idea from the movie with Rod Taylor, *The Time Machine,* where I could go back and forward. I had the Earthmobile, where I would go down into the Earth and visit the mole people. I went back in time to visit my great-great-great-grandfather, Wild Bill Ginger . . . anything far out I could come up with . . . I skydived, I did an army bit . . . one time I portrayed Robin Hood.

"I wrestled a midget one time. Killer got me in trouble, and Mr. Rocky fired me. We're looking through the paper, and it read '100 dollars for anybody who could stay in the ring with Muller McGirk.' With a name like Muller McGirk, I don't stand a chance. Killer said, 'Let's sneak over to his training camp and look.' We go and look over the fence, and here's this dwarf (who was a professional wrestler, Pee Wee James). So I wrestled him."

Having a program that was heavily dependent on live sound effects for gags, mistakes became unavoidable. But, as WXYZ news anchor Erik Smith recalls from his days as an electrical transcription (ET) operator, Ginger the Great could handle any kind of mishap.

Erik Smith: "Doing Johnny's show, for the ET guys, was fairly challenging. His bits often required sound effects. And you had to be on the mark because it's on a record. You had to find the right groove out of 400 groves on this record for, perhaps, a gunshot or a scream. I do remember one morning he was doing a western bit—a fast-draw thing or something silly—but the gun had to go off. So at the moment the gun had to fire I missed the groove on the record and there was no sound. Johnny kept looking at the gun. Finally I got it, and it went BANG at a totally inappropriate time. Not only was he able to respond and quickly improvise in any given situation, I think he enjoyed the challenge of not knowing everything was going to go as rehearsed."

April Fools' Day

Johnny Ginger: "April Fools' Day 1961. I was visiting Bill Kennedy [at CKLW-TV], and Jerry Booth was taping *Jingles in Boofland* in the other studio. So, I went over to see him, and I said, 'I'm your rival.' I thought . . . I wonder if kids ever get confused, if they want to watch my show and they hit Channel 9 instead and think, what is that [*Jingles*]? I started thinking, what if we changed places? Jerry didn't wanna go for it at first.

He said, 'Ahhh, I don't know . . .' I said, 'Well, I think it'll be funny . . . an April Fools' joke! They tune into Channel 7 and there you are, and they turn to your show and there I am.' He finally bought it. The producers and everybody agreed: let's do it . . . it's never been done before."

Larry Dlusky: "I turned on *Johnny Ginger,* and there was Jingles! Jingles was like, 'What is this place? What am I doing here?' He was looking around . . . I'm watching this, and I thought, what's going on? I'm thinking, well, Jingles has his own show on Channel 9, so I switch over to Channel 9, and there was Johnny Ginger! He was like, 'This is a castle, where is this place?' So then I go back to *Johnny Ginger,* and there's Jingles. For the whole half hour, every minute or two you'd switch back to the other station, then back to the previous station again. I remember my grandmother saying, 'He's crazy going back and forth! He's gonna twist the knob right off that set!' And my mom says, 'Right now kids all over Detroit are doing that.' My mother understood what was going on because she knew the characters."

Johnny Ginger: "I played with all the puppets because they'd come up and ask me, 'What are you doing here?' I said, 'I don't know. All of a sudden I walked out here and I'm in the castle.' And of course my guys, who I prerecorded for Jerry Booth to work with . . . Killer was saying, 'You don't look anything like Johnny because you got that funny thing on . . .' It was cute."

Larry Dlusky: "I remember Jingles was lying down; then he got up and stretched, then looked at the camera and said, 'Well, boys and girls, you'll never believe the dream I just had.' By that time, *Johnny Ginger* was over, so I don't know how that show ended."

Johnny Ginger: "It went great and was in *Look* magazine. The only thing the studios got irritated with was the phone lines were jammed; they couldn't make any calls out. Everybody was calling in wondering what was going on with their television sets . . . have the signals gotten crossed or what? They're calling WXYZ, 'I'm getting *Jingles* on Channel 7, what's going on?' They just jammed the phone lines. Afterward, as successful as it was, [management] said, 'never again!' But I thought it was a good idea."

Celebrity Status

By the early 1960s, *The Johnny Ginger Show* was regularly booking celebrity guests into the Rocky Plaza Hotel. Hollywood's A-listers visiting Motown checked in for personalized room service from the city's most notorious bellhop. Everyone from Alfred Hitchcock to the Three

Stooges themselves arrived for a visit. And as part of a television cross-promotion Ginger got to appear in guest roles on *The Real McCoys*, *The Rebel*, and *The Rifleman*. In 1965, the man who hosted a Three Stooges wrap show got his opportunity to costar with Moe, Larry, and Curly-Joe in their final feature film, *The Outlaws Is Coming*, portraying the legendary gunslinger Billy the Kid.

Channel 7 also gave Johnny his own prime-time special with guest star Sammy Davis Jr. As a result of their meetings, both Davis and the Stooges (particularly Moe Howard) developed personal friendships with Ginger that lasted until their deaths.

And, as Detroit's famous bellboy was rising in celebrity, his manager approached him with a profitable proposal that could have cost Johnny his show.

Johnny Ginger: "My manager wanted to come out with a 'Killer doll.' Mattel was going to do it, but I said, 'No because nobody knows what he looks like. Every kid in his head knows what Killer looks like; they got their own idea of Killer. If you bring a doll out, it'll ruin it.'"

Ginger fan Greg Russell relives the day when the local star of WXYZ made him feel like a celebrity, too.

Greg Russell: "My birthday is May the eighth. On May 8, at 7:00 a.m. on Channel 7, he wished me a happy seventh birthday! I remember back then you sent in your postcard and Johnny Ginger said, 'We want to wish a very special happy seventh birthday to little Greg Russell in Detroit.' I was king of the school! Every kid was going, 'Johnny Ginger said your name this morning on TV. You are the man!' And it's like, 'oh yeah!'"

As much as Johnny Ginger loved all the glory that came his way in the name of fame, the star power he possessed was sometimes overwhelming for him . . . especially when it came to his dying fans.

Johnny Ginger: "I went to Children's Hospital all the time and I would take cars, dolls, and toys that Mattel would furnish me. There was one time where there was a kid that was dying, and I couldn't face him. Afterward they told me that they buried the little boy in an Ivy League cap like I had; he wanted to be like Johnny Ginger . . . and that still gets me. His mother and dad buried him with my picture on his chest in his coffin, and that just about destroyed me!"

Johnny Comes of Age

By 1968, after an eleven-year stretch, *The Johnny Ginger Show* was canceled due to the increasing popularity of afternoon talk shows. At 34 years of age, the squeaky-clean nightclub comic found himself without a

TV gig. And of all the things in television that he'd miss it was knowing he wouldn't see his second family anymore that tugged at his heartstrings the most.

Johnny Ginger: "We had a great crew. After eleven years, when I left there I cried like a baby. I was with them more than I was with my family. It was a very traumatic thing. At the end, I wrote a bit where the Rocky Plaza's closing down, and I sang 'The Party's Over.' I couldn't get through it without breaking up. We must've done about 13 takes. I said, 'When I finish this tape, I'm walking out . . . I don't wanna say goodbye to anybody; I'm just gonna go.' So I just sort of walked out into the sunset."

Immediately following the news of his cancellation at Channel 7, WKBD-TV approached Ginger's manager with an offer to become the replacement host of a similar children's show they'd been running since 1965 called *Captain Detroit*. After a summer vacation in Florida, Johnny Ginger faced the television cameras once again for the next year to host cartoons from the captain's deck of the Channel 50 spaceship. Upon his departure, local deejay Tom Ryan assumed control of Captain Detroit's spacecraft as Sergeant Sacto.

Jack Flechsig and Erik Smith share a few thoughts about the man who took Stooge fans on a daily adventure of wackiness for more than a decade.

Jack Flechsig: "He was just a consummate performer. I think he probably understood the media better than anyone of his time. He had a real handle on what it was about."

Erik Smith: "I was sad to see John's show go. Johnny was one of the most creative people I think this industry has produced. He was asked to step into some pretty big shoes. When Soupy left, there was a void, and it was a tough act to follow but he did very, very well—just amazing!"

Wixie's Wonderland

Everybody was shocked that this obscene nightclub performer
would be hired to do a kid show. But nothing ever came of that; he
was very popular with the kids.
—JACK FLECHSIG, retired art director, WXYZ-TV

Within a wondrous land filled with toys and pets, there lived a futuristic
elf named Wixie, who brought music, art, and cartoons to all the little
tots tuned in to the wavelength beaming from the studios of WXYZ-TV,
Channel 7. From 1953 to 1957, youngsters woke up each weekday morning to the sight of toys carried by a train chugging through a terrain of
tiny animals that moved up and down as the theme music played. Anticipation would build while the children at home waited to see their
favorite mystic hero. Retired WXYZ director Mason Weaver sets the
scene for Wixie's grand entrance.

Mason Weaver: "I remember we started with a wide shot of the
set; then Wixie [portrayed by Marv Welch] would squat down so you
couldn't see him. We'd go to the slide with music, and the piano gal
would say:

Taxi your tricycle close to your screen
And take your dolly by the hand.
For there are wonderful things to be seen . . .

And then he [Wixie] would jump up and yell . . . 'On *Wixie's Wonderland!*' "

In the eyes of a preschooler, fantasy mirrored reality for an hour in a
world presented by a boyish creature with the aid of a clown, a piano
player, and a grandfather figure. Laced between cartoons of Bugs Bunny,
Mickey Mouse, Woody Woodpecker, and Silly Symphonies, kids were
entertained with the live performances of Wixie's pantomimes, the piano
lady's sing-alongs, Gramps's lovable critters, and the fastest drawings
you ever saw, leaving many in awe and saying, "gee whiz!"

Blue Comedy to Blue Velvet

As one of the first big children's programs in Detroit, much of the success
of *Wixie's Wonderland* hinged on the talent of its star, Marv Welch, as
pointed out by former WXYZ director Ron David.

Ron David: "Marv Welch is a very colorful story because he was a

Wixie Wonderland (Marv Welch) makes the cover of a 1955
issue of *TV Today*. (Publicity photo.)

nightclub entertainer who looked a lot like Danny Kaye. He lip-synced to
a lot of Danny Kaye records because he looked so much like him. He
could sing, he could dance and do a bunch of stuff, but basically he was
a comedian."

Born on October 14, 1925, Marvin Welch Jr. was the product of a
musical union between a trumpeter father and a pianist mother. As a
young boy, Marv's singing voice began to surface and soon it was incorporated into his mother's piano lounge act during the Great Depression.

Retired WXYZ stage manager Art Runyon looks back at Welch during his teen years.

Art Runyon: "I knew Marv from [Mackenzie] high school, and he was a nice young man. He was a year ahead of me. I got to know him and his family. His sister and his parents . . . they opened a little restaurant in our neighborhood. Marv was just 'Mr. Clean' all the way. I remember he sang in the church choir in one of the big Methodist churches in Detroit. So it blew me away when I found out later he was doing club appearances using what they used to call blue material."

The term *blue material* means obscene comedy, dirty jokes. And blue humor is what made Marv Welch one of the Motor City's top comedians by the early 1950s. Prior to that, after military service in Europe during World War II, Welch came home to Detroit, where he attended Wayne State University to major in music. While going to school, he sang in a nightclub for five dollars a night. It wasn't long before pantomime and comedy were added to his routine. His ability to sing a song with a laugh or two landed him a gig in a new medium called television in 1952. Marv recounts his first appearance on the small screen.

Marv Welch: "My first TV show was on Channel 4. Janie Palmer and I had the first musical program [*Musically Speaking*] ever on local television. She sang, I sang and we had a big band and I'd tell some jokes, naturally. It was only on for fifteen minutes, but back then you'd do it for nothing just to get your face in front of the camera. It was such a novelty."

That novelty for Marv would only last a year. On his return to the nightclub circuit, where he quickly resumed his blue humor, Welch received an unexpected proposition from the WXYZ program director.

Marv Welch: "Pete Strand came to my show one night at the Elmwood. He said, 'Hey Marv, you ever thought of going on TV?' I said, 'Oh, yeah, I was on Channel 4.' He said, 'I mean a big-time, steady show?' I said, 'No.' He said, 'You come and see me.' So I went to see him and it started from there."

What started was an offer that the blue comedian initially refused. It was an offer that many of the folks at WXYZ couldn't fathom, an offer that would make Marv Welch a household name to an audience radically different from the one he had come to know in the clubs.

Marv Welch: "John Pival was the general manager at Channel 7, and he had an idea for a kid show in the morning—a variety show with cartoons and pantomime to kid records. We all met in Pival's office and set the format. We were trying to think of a name for the show, and I said, 'Fred Wolf (who was very big back then) called his radio show *Wixie Wonderland*. Too bad we can't steal that.' Pival said, 'The hell we can't!

That's it, I like it. Your name is Wixie Wonderland.' So I came up with the name; I took it away from Fred Wolf, but Fred was still big and he didn't worry about it."

Wixie the Pixie

Wixie—a play on the WXYZ call letters, became the name of the character that would host the show. Next was the challenge of creating an image of what a Wixie should look like. The end result was an odd little pixie creature presented in velvet and tights. Marv Welch and retired WXYZ art director Jack Flechsig explain the development of the costume.

Marv Welch: "He wasn't a clown. He was a character with a TV antenna on his head and Channel 7 on his chest with lightning bolts [on the chest and sleeves] indicating the 'future.' "

Jack Flechsig: "I was involved in designing his costume, which was ludicrous. There was a costume shop on Woodward Avenue that we used all the time for skits with Soupy. The lady there made it."

Marv Welch: "Mrs. Brusier—she ran the only costume shop in Downtown Detroit. She made costumes, so we gave her the idea of the show, and that's what she came up with. And we really went for it, everybody on the whole staff: Pival and Pete Strand went for it. So that was my uniform."

Jack Flechsig: "The costume was dark blue velvet with points on the tunic like a court jester. It had an antenna, which was another thorn in my side; the damn antenna kept falling over, and I had to keep reinforcing it."

Playing the Parts

Even on the strength of Welch's talent, *Wixie's Wonderland* would not be a one-man show. The plan called for the inclusion of a female performer, another male performer, and a clown. Marv runs down the list of his supporting players.

Marv Welch: "We had Diane Dale, the gal who played the piano and sang kid songs. G-Whiz was the artist; he could draw real fast to kid records—whatever they were playing, he would draw a picture for the kids. And Gramps was an old man, Frank Nastasi. [He] used to sit on a park bench and show different animals. We had a good cast!"

Cartoonist Ken Muse, who portrayed the clown G-Whiz, recalls the day he and the others were assigned their character roles.

Wixie meets a few fans at an appearance. (Courtesy Susan Anastasiou.)

Ken Muse: "I remember when the show first started a woman came and met with all of us in an office: Frank Nastasi, Diane Dale and myself. Of course, we didn't know each other, and she said, 'We're gonna start this show called *Wixie's Wonderland* and [to me] you're gonna be a clown, [to Diane] you're gonna play the piano, and Frank you're gonna talk about animals.'"

With Diane Dale using her own name on the program, where did G-Whiz and Gramps come from? Who thought to name a clown G-Whiz of all things and why? Marv?

Marv Welch: "I thought of that: 'gee-whiz, the fastest artist there is!'

Frank Nastasi already had slightly gray hair, like a gramps, and that was it. I said, 'You're the kids' grandpa.'"

Both Muse and Nastasi stayed with Welch for the duration of the show. Tragically, Diane Dale was recast in 1956 after she suffered an attack of polio, which quickly took her life. Marion Rivers assumed Dale's musical duties until the program's demise the following year.

With the cast firmly in place, *Wixie's Wonderland* premiered in September of 1953. Although its time slot would change over the years, the series never strayed from its main objective: morning entertainment for tots. Marv Welch elaborates.

Marv Welch: "I was on in the morning. I would open the first live show at 7:00 a.m. to get the kiddies up before they went to school . . . all the kindergartners. It was an hour [show] from seven to eight. Everything was aimed at the small generation, where Soupy had the older crowd. He had young ones, too, but we really were for the little ones."

Mother's against Cancellation

Shortly after its debut, *Wixie's Wonderland* fell victim to the ever-changing programming needs of WXYZ.

Marv Welch: "We were on for [a few months], and then they decided to cancel the show—so we got canceled. But, my God, there were so many protest letters . . . thousands of them! They had bags of mail of mothers hollering. John Pival said, 'I'm sorry, I made a mistake. It's obvious you're drawing a hell of a number.' Then we went back on the air."

Ken Muse: "All the viewers volunteered to pay our salaries . . . so they brought us back and we lasted a few more years. That's never happened before on any TV show I know of."

The flood of mail from irate mothers protesting the cancellation validated the popularity of *Wixie*. In the wake of the cancellation fiasco, fan letters gave way to one of the largest mail draws in local television for that era, with 200 letters arriving daily. In fact, much of the fan mail was commonly addressed with nothing more than a drawing of Wixie on the envelope, which never deterred mailmen from delivering them to the studio at the Maccabees Building.

Walkin' in a Television Wonderland

With a major sponsor, Bosco, backing the show, *Wixie's Wonderland* was free to dazzle youngsters in the following manner.

G-Whiz it's Ken Muse, 1956. (Courtesy Dave Muse.)

Marv Welch: "It opened up with me. We put on a kiddie record, and I'd start pantomiming right away. Then I'd talk to the kids and get a cartoon on. When we came back, I'd introduce Diane Dale and she'd sing kid songs. I'd come over and lean on the piano, and we'd sing together sometimes . . . it was cute. Then we'd go to Gramps, and he'd always have a snake or raccoon or something. The pet store owners, they were all there, too, and they'd come on the set with us to sit with Gramps and handle the animals so Gramps wouldn't get bit. He never did get bit. Then G-Whiz would come on to do a drawing of a record. And I'd close it out with some funny song for the kids and say 'bye-bye.'"

Ken Muse: "The *Wixie* set was a little stand where they displayed toys and Marv stood behind there."

Marv Welch: "We'd show toys; we had a Toyland there. There were a lot of toy stores back in those days, and they were glad to bring out their toys. And the toy makers, they'd give us all the toys we wanted. I had two kids of my own, and I'd bring the toys home because the toy makers gave them to us; they didn't want to take them back, so everybody on the staff got whatever toys there were. So it was big time!"

Along with the toy table, there was a miniature model of an amusement park, complete with a Ferris wheel behind a sign that read Wixie Wonderland. The toy park was one of the regular fixtures viewers could see on the set. The piano was placed in front of a black curtain. Mason Weaver describes the backdrop for the Gramps segments.

Mason Weaver: "I remember very well [that] it [had] a little park set that was a threefold with trees where Gramps sat."

And Gramps was seated in the park because . . .

Marv Welch: "We always had animals that the zoo brought us, all the animals we wanted along with the pet shops. Don Hunt [B'wana Don] had a big connection with the zoo, and he was an animal trainer. In fact, he went on a safari to Africa. He had a big pet shop in Ferndale. He had everything—dogs, cats, rabbits, snakes, ducks, you name it . . . all the things kids love—so he'd be on the show a lot of times. We were on five days a week, so we had to have a heck of a lot of animals. Some of the funny shows were when the animals got away. We'd have the cameras follow them. But some days we just wouldn't show animals, [so Gramps] would show artifacts for kids."

So now that only leaves the muted clown, G-Whiz, who stood before an easel with a drawing board flanked by curtains and cutouts of toy clowns. Ken Muse paints a picture of the "fastest artist there is."

Ken Muse: "I'd get all the kid records and I'd draw the covers for the kids on the show while they played the records . . . and I'd jump up and down; they loved that. I had it all timed out. I drew on charcoal paper with a charcoal stick, then I sprayed it so it wouldn't smear and I handed them out to the kids, whoever was there. There were kids, but there weren't many of them . . . just two or three would come down. Marv would invite them or we would invite them, that's all that came down. There were no big grandstands with kids like [some of] the other shows."

The Price of Fame

Ken Muse: "I used to go down to the store on the corner of Garfield and Woodward, and the guy used to say, 'How much do they pay you? What kind of car do you drive?' I never answered him. I was the lowest-paid person on the show. I belonged to AFTRA, which was a union, and because I didn't talk [on the program] they couldn't pay me as much as the people who talked."

While Muse was shortchanged financially, Welch came up short on sleep due to the clash between his day and night jobs.

Ron David: "I remember his show was on extremely early, like 7:00 a.m. I would often sign the station on, and here he'd come in right from the nightclub, and he'd do *Wixie's Wonderland* in his costume and all that."

Marv Welch: "I was working nightclubs then, six nights a week till two in the morning. Everybody was wondering how in the hell I was doing it!"

When Marv wasn't amusing kids on TV during the week, he was busy in the recording studio of Prescott Records.

Marv Welch: "I used to make kid records. I would go down to the studio on Saturday afternoon and knock off some songs, maybe Sunday, too. We only recorded one record at a time. I made a bunch of those, and man I sold those records—old 78s, that's how long ago it was."

One of the truest means of assessing fame can be measured by the attendance at public appearances. In the case of *Wixie's Wonderland,* the crowds spoke volumes.

Marv Welch: "We had a lot of personal appearances at old amusement parks like Jefferson Beach and Edgewater Park. It would be on a platform around the Ferris wheel, and we'd do a whole show for them, just like we did in the morning. I made sure I went through the audience to shake hands with the kids and their moms and dads. Wherever we put on the *Wixie's Wonderland* show, we were sold out. We used to say in our dressing rooms—Diane Dale, Gramps, and I—we can't believe it's this jammed. It was fabulous!"

For those who couldn't go to an appearance, the Wixie gang came to them.

Marv Welch: "We went to Harper Hospital, the center for polio; all of us would go around and talk to the kids. We also went to St. John's . . . once a month we went to different hospitals. I would go around with the records [while] Gramps would bring a little animal in a box and show it to them. And G-Whiz brought along his drawing board."

Ken Muse: "I liked the personal appearances because we could meet the audience. Going to the hospitals and seeing kids, I liked that. That was really the best part of it. I didn't have any records. I'd come in with my paper and my easel, [and] I'd set it up and talk to the kids. I would ask, 'Who likes to draw?' Then I'd ask them to make a couple of marks on the paper and I'd make a picture out of it. They used to love that. I would draw cartoons for them. If they asked me to draw a cat, I'd draw a cat. They were surprised to hear my voice because they really thought I was a mute."

Wixie Signs Off

In 1955, while *Wixie* was going strong, a children's phenomenon was beginning to brew on the national front. It started with the phrase "Good morning, Captain." Ken Muse recollects the impact of this new kids' show craze.

Ken Muse: "What happened was *Captain Kangaroo* killed us when it came out . . . it killed us! Things were changing. All the kid shows were killed after he came out—it was a good show."

After losing its morning battle with the captain, the *Wixie* crew signed off in 1957. The remaining original cast members all went on to enjoy prosperous careers: Welch in the nightclubs, Muse as a cartoonist and college art and photography instructor, and Nastasi as a theatrical performer and Soupy's puppeteer in New York. On June 15, 2004, Frank Nastasi passed away at the age of 81, leaving Marv Welch and Ken Muse as the only survivors of a TV tale once known as *Wixie's Wonderland.*

Sagebrush Shorty

Sagebrush had the first two nickels he ever made still in his pocket.
   —ERROL FORTIN, retired stagehand, WJBK-TV

Blazing the trails of the Motor City in the late 1950s and early 1960s in the tradition of *Howdy Doody* was a fast-talking, glitzy cowboy called Sagebrush Shorty. But unlike Buffalo Bob Smith, whose string-dangling puppet pal stood on a stage, Sagebrush was a ventriloquist with a dummy seated on his lap. Live from the corral at WJBK-TV, Channel 2, then later on WXYZ-TV, Channel 7, *Sagebrush Shorty* served up cartoons, games, prizes, magic tricks, animal acts, and safety tips to all the little cowpokes in Motown seven days a week.

Ted Lloyd, who adopted the name Sagebrush Shorty, was born the son of a vaudevillian magician on December 27, 1916. As a boy, he was introduced to show business while traveling the country with his father. During his childhood, Lloyd studied the art of ventriloquism, and by the early 1950s he was ready to apply his talents to a relatively new medium at the time . . . television. At the Storer Broadcasting station in San Anto-

Sagebrush Shorty (Ted Lloyd) with his premier dummy, Bronco Billy Buttons. (Courtesy Ed Golick.)

nio, Texas, *Sagebrush Shorty*, a name that combined Lloyd's short stance (5′6″) with a western plant, became a very popular children's program featuring Lloyd as a rootin'-tootin' cowboy with a slow-witted dummy named Bronco Billy Buttons.

A Stranger in Town

Meanwhile, back at the ranch, WJBK had just acquired a new studio on Second Avenue in Detroit. Shortly after the move, the station owner,

George B. Storer, began to search for a new general manager, which ultimately led to Sagebrush blowing into the Motor City. Retirees from WJBK, director Dick Dietrich and stagehand Errol Fortin, fill in the details.

Dick Dietrich: "Our general manager was a guy named Bill Michaels. And George Storer, for reasons we don't know, was big on going into Texas to hire general managers. He hired Michaels, who later became chairman of the board of all the Storer stations."

Errol Fortin: "Michaels brought Sagebrush up to Channel 2 in Detroit and put him in business there. He did the commercial breaks on cartoons with children's stuff in the morning every day of the week. Then on the weekends he had a show with audience participation and gags, stuff like that."

In 1957, Sagebrush Shorty saddled up his horse, Snooper, and rode into Motown with Bronco Billy Buttons. It was an era when the television cowboy was all over the dial. The town that was home to the famed Lone Ranger would soon have to make room for its newest and flashiest western hero. Ed Golick, Webmaster of detroitkidshow.com, describes Lloyd's flare for glamour.

Ed Golick: "He insisted on having the best of everything. He had to have the Stetson hat and a hand-tooled leather belt that said Sagebrush Shorty on it and a belt buckle made of silver with his face and his horse Snooper on it . . . first class all the way. Everything had to be the best you could buy."

Those high standards applied to the set design as well. Originally the set consisted of a flat backdrop painted to resemble the interior of a cabin on the western frontier. But as the show grew in popularity and a weekend edition was added to the programming roster, complete with a studio audience, that simple set had to be expanded . . . drastically! And it was up to Errol Fortin to make it happen.

Errol Fortin: "I had to build a lot of stuff for that show on the weekends. It had to be as western as I could make it. I had to build a covered wagon, a corral fence, and a western cabin with a porch."

When *Sagebrush Shorty* debuted on Channel 2, it was meant to be nothing more than a wraparound for cartoons on the weekdays. According to Errol Fortin and Dick Dietrich, the format was a snap.

Errol Fortin: "His weekday show was a walk in the park; there was nothing to it. He just read letters from kids and organizations. He was just there for the commercial breaks—no other reason."

Dick Dietrich: "It was a relatively simple program. Bronco Billy Buttons was his dummy, and he was a ventriloquist. He read birthdays once a week and bridged cartoons in and out, and that was about the substance of Sagebrush Shorty's show."

There may not have been much substance to the program at first, but that would soon change. However, one element that was never altered was the featured cartoons . . . none of which were the latest or the greatest, as remembered by Ed Golick and Dick Dietrich.

Ed Golick: "[They were] Warner Bros. cartoons, old Columbia cartoons, old cartoons from the thirties where they [have] Mickey Mouse with arms that look like rubber hoses, I mean the old, old stuff."

Dick Dietrich: "*Felix the Cat* we played time after time."

Shorty Dummies Up

One thing that overshadowed all of those ancient cartoons was the presence of Bronco Billy Buttons. Lloyd would play the straight man to a dummy whose personality mirrored that of Edgar Bergen's Mortimer Snerd. Bronco Billy took a long time to grasp simple things and eventually the fast-talking Sagebrush would need a dummy that could keep up with him, one that could be a quick-witted smart aleck like Bergen's Charlie McCarthy. This would add a whole new dimension to the show and at the same time change the flavor of its humor. Ted Lloyd didn't have to look very far because he would soon strike gold in Detroit. And that piece of gold's name was Skinny Dugan. Ed Golick explains.

Ed Golick: "Skinny Dugan was carved by the same person who carved Charlie McCarthy for Edgar Bergen. He bought Skinny Dugan from [the wife of] Bill Maher, a big name in the world of ventriloquism, who had the name Skinny Dugan already. Mrs. Maher said, 'I'll sell you Skinny Dugan, [but] you have to promise me not to change his name.' [Lloyd] said, 'Okay, he'll be Skinny Dugan.' But he dressed him up in the western clothes, and he was really superior to Bronco Billy Buttons.

"Skinny Dugan was the most articulated dummy that was ever made. He could wiggle his nose, he could wiggle his ears, he could stick out his tongue, he could spit, he could raise each eyebrow independently [and] he could cross his eyes."

From the day Skinny Dugan was carried into the studio at WJBK till the last day he was carried out of Broadcast House at Channel 7, Lloyd and his little partner were nearly inseparable. News anchor Erik Smith, who worked the electrical transcription for the show during its Channel 7 run, remembers Skinny as an alter ego for Sagebrush.

Erik Smith: "I never really was certain that he separated himself from the dummy. The two seemed to be 'velcroed' together . . . one was never in place without the other. And if the dummy was just sitting there, I was convinced it was going to get up, walk around, and start talking; it was that real. He had a marvelous ability to make that little wooden creation live."

Dick Dietrich: "We had a stagehand [at WJBK] named Jerry. Sagebrush would be at his desk going over his birthdays and his lead-ins and the dummy would be in a box with the door open. The stagehands would be around touching up the lighting and that stuff . . . Jerry would walk by and say, 'You wood-headed turkey, you dumb . . .' to the dummy. And Sagebrush, without moving anything, continuing to work, would answer back in the dummy's voice!"

As much fun as Ted Lloyd had using his dummy for gags, the engineers had their fun with it, too. Retired WXYZ director Chris Montross recalls how it was used to "break in" a new engineer.

Chris Montross: "The [crew] always suckered some new engineer into hanging a mic on the dummy. Sage was a ventriloquist, [so] you didn't need a mic on the dummy. So they'd tell a new engineer, 'Don't forget to put the mic on the dummy.' And he'd hook up a mic and hang it on the dummy."

Lloyd's proficiency in voice throwing eventually went beyond his two main dummies and into a world of puppets and other objects. *Sagebrush Shorty* fans Larry Dlusky and Ed Golick go down the list.

Larry Dlusky: "He had a beer mug on his desk, which he called Toby. He would talk to it and it had a mouth on it that would move."

Ed Golick: "Cecil Rabbit was a rabbit with a speech impediment; [he] kinda sounded like Bugs Bunny a little bit. Ted Lloyd made the Professor himself. He was made from an old Charlie McCarthy dummy. He put him on a little chair and put a little mortarboard and little gown on him. He had a deer on the wall and a buffalo on the wall that moved."

Promotions and Prizes

On the weekend editions of *Sagebrush Shorty*, Ted Lloyd would trade his Stetson for a turban and black robe to perform magic tricks with some of his father's equipment. In addition to the magic segment, there would be animal acts and contests for the kids in the peanut gallery. Some of the competitions included sewing contests for girls and nose egg rolls for boys. But not every child had to be in the gallery to win a prize.

The Pyramid of Prizes, as it was called, became the ultimate reward for any youngster who won the write-in contest of the week. The pyramid consisted of a table full of toys courtesy of Muirhead's in West Dearborn. The contests to win them would involve a cross promotion with a sponsored product. Ed Golick comments on Lloyd's promotional skills.

Ed Golick: "Ted Lloyd was a showman . . . he was a pitchman and a half, [and] he was a good promoter. He had a deal with Schwinn where he gave away a bicycle every week. You'd send in a card and he'd pull the card out of the bike barrel. He had a cop, Sergeant Dusty Rhodes from the Detroit Police Department, who would come on every week [on Tuesdays and Thursdays] to give bike safety tips. Shorty and Dusty Rhodes would pull a card out and give away a bike every week."

Pushing products and prizes wasn't the only thing Ted Lloyd pitched on his show. There was a more important message for all the young buckaroos in TV land.

Ed Golick: "*Sagebrush Shorty* had this thing where you send in an envelope and they sent you a little decal that you put on the back window of a car. It basically said, 'Shut up and do what Mom and Dad say.' He promoted good clean living and say your prayers before you go to bed."

The Spur of the Moment

Beloved by the children of the Metro area, Lloyd's personal life wasn't as fulfilling as his public one. Much of his displeasure came as the result of an unhappy marriage. It was his wife who was directly responsible for his termination at WJBK. Leading this sad chapter of the *Sagebrush Shorty* saga with a bit of background information is retired WXYZ director Mason Weaver.

Mason Weaver: "Sage was a very subdued guy because he had a wife who was a great big woman who was always hollering at him . . . and he was very quiet and polite. So in rehearsal he would have the dummy say all kinds of rotten things that he couldn't say. It was funny, but I really think he was directing it toward that wife of his."

Ed Golick: "His wife's name was Marie, and she was hired by the station as a kid wrangler, to keep the kids in line and keep the guests happy."

Errol Fortin: "To beef up the show, along comes this fellow, Don Hunt [B'wana Don], who had a pet shop in Ferndale. He had a young chimp that he bought [when he was] a little over a year old, and he named him Bongo Bailey. What happened was the station hired him, for about a month, to come on and be one of the features on *Sagebrush Shorty*. He would bring in all kinds of animals every show. And he had the chimp there around the set all the time. Now you just didn't go grab

Bongo Bailey and drag him. I was there when it happed and [Marie] just went up and grabbed him to take him to Sagebrush on the set. She just grabbed him, and he wasn't in the mood to be dragged so he bit her!"

Ed Golick: "Rather than sue the owner of the chimp, she sued the station, and of course the station dropped the show."

And as fate would have it, WJBK replaced *Sagebrush Shorty* with *B'wana Don,* featuring—you guessed it—Bongo Bailey.

Landing another television gig didn't come easy to Mr. Lloyd. He waited for two years before John Pival at WXYZ finally hired him to do the same show he had done at Channel 2 under a new name, *The Circle Seven Ranch.* Getting into Broadcast House took some persuasion.

Ed Golick: "Channel 7 already had all kinds of kid show hosts. The only reason they took Shorty on was because he had the Hires Root Beer account. He had all these accounts lined up. Hires was the main one, so he was on WXYZ for a couple of years and then he left for Los Angeles [in 1965]."

Happy Trails

At the end of every episode, Sagebrush always preached, "Be kind to each other." For his final show in 1965, he scripted a Hollywood ending that was meant to foreshadow his destiny. Larry Dlusky describes the finale that didn't go without a hitch.

Larry Dlusky: "On the last show, he was going to ride off into the sunset. So he went outside the station and they had a horse out there waiting for him . . . and boy did he struggle to get on that horse! Even as a kid looking at him, I was thinking 'It doesn't look like he's ever been on a horse before.' He eventually got on there, and he managed somehow to stay on. It didn't look like he was that secure, but he rode off and they cut away from him . . . that was the end of the *Sagebrush Shorty* show."

In the hope of landing a national audience like Soupy Sales had five years earlier, the ventriloquist packed up his dummies and headed west to live the California dream.

Ed Golick: "He thought he was gonna make it big in Los Angeles, but it just never happened—he never went national. He tried. He appeared as a guest on *The Lawrence Welk Show* [and] he did a lot of industrial shows and kids' parties—enough to make a living—but he never had his own show. He had a Wrigley's Spearmint Gum spot that went national, but he didn't really have the fame that he had here in Detroit."

Ted Lloyd spent the rest of his life in Los Angeles. He died in 1999, four days shy of his eighty-third birthday. Although he did not achieve the stardom he aspired to in Hollywood, in the end the name Sagebrush Shorty was permanently etched in the memory banks of his Motor City fans . . . right, Larry?

Larry Dlusky: "The end of the theme went, 'Sage-brush . . . Sage-brush . . . Shor-ty.' It's still stuck in my head!"

Send in the Clowns

3

Milky

Milky the Clown was a magician; he was performing magic. Kids
would be wide-eyed, and there is where the joy of it was. That
magic stuff was really what endeared him to the kids.
   —BOB ALLISON, Detroit radio and TV host

Well before milk cartons displayed the faces of missing children, the
Twin Pines carton featured the friendly smile of a gap-toothed clown
named Milky. Back in the days when home delivery of milk was a thriv-
ing business, the Twin Pines Dairy Company launched what may have
been the grandest and most expensive ad campaign ever devised in the
history of Detroit TV. A weekly television program was conceived by the
Luckoff-Wayburn advertising agency to market its client's dairy products
to children. The agency convinced Twin Pines that kids often held the key
to their parents' choice in dairy brands. Today such a ploy would be con-
strued as an infomercial, but in the 1950s and 1960s it was one of the
hottest children's shows on the tube. And at the heart of it was the dairy's
own Milky the Clown.

Every Saturday from 1950 to 1967, Motor City youngsters were glued
to the front of their television sets to be dazzled by a clown that was quite
different in both appearance and performance. Detroit TV fan Larry
Dlusky provides a brief introduction to Milky.

Larry Dlusky: "Milky was probably *the* most popular clown in
Detroit—everyone knew him. What was unusual about him was that you
never saw a clown that was all white before; the white suit and the white
facial makeup really made him unique. And there was always magic
involved . . . there were no illusions like a David Copperfield type of performance. Milky didn't make your parents disappear or anything like

that. He would do what was referred to as sleight of hand magic, stuff you'd see in his hands rather than something at a distance."

Making his small-screen debut on December 16, 1950, *Milky's Movie Party* was broadcast from the studios of WJBK-TV, Channel 2. The two-hour format showcased a western feature film wrapped around cartoons, magic tricks, and live commercials.

Larry Dlusky: "They had the Twin Pines milkman for the commercials, and of course, there was a Twin Pines song, which is also embedded in my mind. I can never forget: 'You can have worry-free . . . home delivery . . . call Twin Pines . . . Texas-four-one-one-oh-oh!' "

Every aspect of the show, with the exception of the "features," was a plug for Twin Pines. The company name graced the set's backdrop and the magic table. Even the magic words for the tricks were "Twin Pines," a phrase that was shouted from a live peanut gallery, which was added to the program along with contests in the late fifties. Although the series was a highly successful marketing vehicle for the dairy company, children saw it as a Saturday afternoon full of magical fun, games, and prizes. As WMGC-FM air personality Linda Lanci notes, one prize in particular was coveted by many little boys and girls of the baby boom generation.

Linda Lanci: "I remember that jar full of pennies, and as a kid I always wanted to be the one who could reach in for the pennies. I thought that was really, really cool . . . I liked Milky!"

The Two Faces of Milky

Behind the face of the clown for the first thirteen years was an automobile paint salesman for Du Pont by the name of Clare Cummings. Born on February 4, 1912, in Chicago, Clarence Cummings Jr. was only five when his parents settled in Birmingham, Michigan. During his boyhood years, he developed a genuine passion for magic. After years of practice, in 1929 he staged his first professional magic show at the Baldwin Library in Birmingham. From that moment on, Cummings spent almost all of his spare time perfecting his magical talents, as recalled by retired WJBK stagehand Errol Fortin.

Errol Fortin: "He never considered himself a full-time magician or entertainer. It was strictly a part-time job for him. But he loved it . . . gosh, he loved doing that! He was forever doing research to come up with new tricks. He had a lot of magician friends who helped him."

While performing in 1950 at the Hall Magic Company in Detroit, Clare was approached by a producer from WJBK-TV, who fancied him

Milky's Party Time on WWJ-TV. (Courtesy Peggy Tibbits.)

to host a new children's program they were patterning after *Kukla, Fran and Ollie*. Cummings hosted a 15-minute production called *Peter, Clare and Oscar*, which disappeared after a mere 13 weeks.

That same year, Lou Luckoff and Leon Wayburn's advertising agency pitched and sold to Twin Pines their idea for a television show aimed at selling dairy products to kids. The concept was built around a clown whose name would be a tie-in to their main product—milk—hence Milky. And to give their character a sense of dignity and set him apart from the stereotypical "buffoon," the executives turned to another source of amusement that was known to captivate youngsters—magic.

Born on January 30, 1928, Karrell Fox was only 22 years old in 1950. Known as the King of Korn, he established himself as a top-notch master of illusion on the Detroit magic circuit at a very young age. Detroit TV buff Ed Golick and Fox's widow Marilyn summarize Karrell's showbiz beginnings.

Ed Golick: "Karrell Fox was on one of the first local kid shows called *Junior Jamboree*. This was before WWJ was WWJ, [when it was WWDT]. Fran Harris, an early woman pioneer in Detroit television,

Milky (Clare Cummings) with Creamy in the early 1950s at WJBK-TV. (Courtesy Peggy Tibbits.)

came up with the show *Junior Jamboree* among others. And Karrell Fox was a regular on that as a magician. So his history on Detroit television and Detroit kid shows was way before *Milky the Clown*."

Marilyn Fox: "In his early years, his act was really corny. So [he crowned himself the] King of Korn; he spelled *corn* with a *K* just to make it different. He was topical and funny—whatever he said was funny. He never had a job, never ever had a nine to five job. Entertaining was his job, and he supported us very nicely."

It was the King of Korn whom the executives at Luckoff-Wayburn initially had their eye on to host their new children's show.

Marilyn Fox: "Karrell was offered the job first, and he was going to do it, but then he got drafted into the army for two years."

During the preproduction planning for *Milky*, Fox received his draft notice. In a panic to find a replacement, Karrell was asked by the agency if he knew of any local magicians who could take his place temporarily. He recommended one of his best friends, Clare Cummings. Detroit radio and television personality and Twin Pines milkman number four, Bob Allison, mentions how "green" Clare was compared to Karrell going into the show.

Bob Allison: "Karrell Fox was a professional entertainer. Clare Cummings was a sales rep. Magic was a part-time thing with him, which he enjoyed and loved."

On Fox's advice, Cummings was hired to portray the magical clown Milky until Karrell returned from military service. After receiving his discharge papers in 1952, the King of Korn came back to the Motor City to discover that the TV gig awaiting him had become a smash hit. Although the ad agency guaranteed that he could reclaim the starring role, Fox couldn't bring himself to steal the glory from Cummings.

Marilyn Fox: "When he got out, *Milky* was being done by Clare, who was one of his best friends. And he didn't want to take the job away from him, so he just let Clare do it until he couldn't do it anymore; then Karrell took it over."

In fairness to his friend, Karrell Fox stepped back and offered to be the understudy for Clare when he was on vacation or ill. The two magicians would eventually trade places in 1964 at the onset of the program's "color" years. The transition was opaque to the kids . . . or was it? The makeup and costume were still the same, but there was one sure way to figure out which magician donned the familiar clown suit: check out their dental records.

Bob Allison: "When you see Milky the Clown with the space between his two front teeth, that's Clare Cummings."

Pagliacci

Standing by their decision to package Milky not as a traditional jester but as a dignified clown, the ad agency fell short in its creation of a costume, one that would reflect the spirit of the clown's name. With Karrell Fox out of the picture, Clare Cummings undertook the challenge of producing a costume that would please the agency and Twin Pines. His daughter, Peggy Tibbits, explains the evolution of Milky's unforgettable white suit and makeup.

Peggy Tibbits: "The white clown suit came from my mother [Margaret] thinking of the opera clown Pagliacci. My parents worked on the costume together. My dad always said it was my mother who kind of came up with the design for the suit and her friend, a seamstress, sewed it together. They made white suits to start with on the show, and they were too bright. So for black and white TV they had to be changed to pale blue. On TV, he wore a pale blue clown suit, but on personal appearances he wore white. They were made from a heavy cotton material, and my mother always had to iron them.

"It was all one piece in the beginning, with ruffled cuffs on the sleeves and pant legs. Then it became a two piece so my dad could go to the bathroom more easily without having to take the whole darn thing off. He had white gloves for certain things, but to do magic he wouldn't have the gloves on because he couldn't do sleight of hand with the gloves.

"And on the makeup my dad came up with the idea of just drawing some lines over the white face. He always said that the makeup was one of the things he was glad about when he no longer had to put it on. Getting into makeup and getting out of it for all those shows and the personal appearances was quite exhausting. He spent about an hour to get into the full costume."

An interesting observation regarding the colorless costume was made by local African American television personality Greg Russell of WDWB, Channel 20. Looking back as a fan, Greg comments on how today's politically correct society can easily distort the innocence of the past.

Greg Russell: "Milky was cool. He was all white, and it's kinda funny now because you look at him and say, 'Wow, Milky's wearing a Klan outfit.'"

Peggy Tibbits: "That image of the pointed hat, the all-white suit, and the white, made-up face, I can see how that's a very strong KKK [Ku Klux Klan] image . . . and yet I don't think that ever entered my dad's mind. It was much more about the milk theme and patterning it after the classic opera clown, Pagliacci."

As a testimonial to the acceptance of Milky by the African American community, Peggy Tibbits shares a personal story from her father's funeral service.

Peggy Tibbits: "After my dad died, many people came to his funeral. It was a surprise because it was so huge. We opened it up for people to come up and talk. This one man came up to the front, a very well dressed, distinguished-looking black man, and he said, 'I just have to say that I got my start on the *Milky* show.' There used to be a talent contest on the show ["Stars of the Future"]. He went on to say, 'At that time, there weren't opportunities like that for blacks on television, but that show gave me a chance to compete and win.' He went on to become some kind of producer in entertainment; he spoke very eloquently about that."

Milky's Movie Party

Live from the WJBK studios at the Masonic Temple, *Milky's Movie Party* aired Saturday afternoons from 4:00 to 6:00 p.m. compliments of the Twin Pines Dairy. The lengthy format showcased a one-hour western movie sliced up between cartoons and wrap segments of Milky. Retired WJBK stagehand Errol Fortin reviews the quality of the *Movie Party* features.

Errol Fortin: "They were really old black and white cartoons, ancient stuff from the thirties. And of course the western was a C or D movie that was really very bad. Movies were rated way back then by their quality. Usually a B movie was the second film on a double bill—all the movies were double billed at the theaters. The C and D movies were usually for children on a Saturday morning . . . they'd see a Gene Autrey, Bob Steele, or Tex Ritter picture. Usually that's all *Milky* got . . . the C and D movies . . . very cheaply made little cowboy one reelers they'd stretch into an hour."

In 1952, a marionette segment, "Willy Dooit," joined the party to add a little more variety to the movie show. Years later Willy Dooit's creator, Ed Johnson, broke away from *Milky* to expand the adventures of his characters into a series of his own. But whether it was the cartoons, the cowboy flicks, or the marionettes that kids appreciated most, they all took a backseat to the mystifying magic of Milky. Peggy Tibbits and retired WJBK director Dick Dietrich elaborate on the style and practice of Cummings's trickery.

Peggy Tibbits: "He did things that could be put on a table that he would stand behind, stuff that was big enough to show up on TV. He didn't do many card tricks or coins or that kind of close-up magic."

Dick Dietrich: "He never wanted the cameras to be too tight on him. In those days, we had cameras that you flipped the turrets on, and the 10-inch lens was the close-up lens. After a while, he could look at the monitor and see that we would betray his magic tricks with a close-up. If the trick was at a table and it had a little box of something, while he turned it around or flipped it we'd take a fast shot of it and he'd kind of cheat it, but he wasn't hip enough to cheat it toward the camera. And sometimes we'd see him do something wrong in the back that would reveal the trick. It was live, and there was nothing we could do about it . . . so we all learned not to take close-ups. We just widened the shots."

Peggy Tibbits: "My dad would come home from the show and always ask my mom and me, 'How did that trick look?' My mother always watched the show, and she would give her honest feedback to him. My dad would practice all of his tricks before he would leave, and he would want me to watch. It would be, 'Let me show you this . . .' Then he would go through the whole thing and say, 'Oh, wait, wait . . . I messed up. Hold on, let me start again.' And I got to the point to where I knew how all the tricks worked because I saw the mess up.

"He kept an elaborate card file listing every trick he had done for every TV show so he wouldn't repeat anything for about two years. Then he would start to repeat the tricks. He was given a budget to buy magic tricks, so he had to buy quite a bit because he might do four tricks per show and they all had to be different."

A specially chosen child would help for the week. In the beginning, it was the Sunshine Smile winner. Children would send in their names and their pictures, and one would be chosen by the producers to appear on the show and help with the magic tricks.

In addition to assistance with magic, Milky employed the service of another little helper when it came to safety tips. A small hand puppet of a white rabbit named Creamy could always be counted on to advise the children on how to act and play safely. Though Creamy never uttered a peep, Milky was there for the translation.

Peggy Tibbits: "He would say, 'That's right, Creamy, it's important to tell the boys and girls when they're out riding their bikes to . . .' whatever. Every week it was always some safety tip."

As meticulous as Clare was in preparation for his lead-ins, whether it be a magic trick, a commercial tag, or a "word" from Creamy, his timing was subject to an occasional rattle when it came to production mishaps or practical jokes. And when it came to the latter he took it like a clown.

Dick Dietrich: "There was a guy who worked on the floor named Gene Johnson who was a very clever innovative guy, but when he would direct he would have no idea where he was with time. I remember a few incidents when the western was run at the end of *Milky*. At the climax, when the villain who was being chased by the posse would fly off a cliff and was in midair, Johnson, because there were only two minutes till the end of the show, would just 'cut out' of the western at that climactic moment and suddenly, here's Milky! And Milky would always look surprised!"

Errol Fortin: "He didn't take himself too seriously. Clare was the most easygoing guy you could imagine. Sometimes as a gag the crew would hide his puppet Creamy just before he went on the air so that he would panic before going on live. But you could tease Clare like that and get away with it—he didn't have a vindictive bone in his body."

Because *Milky's Movie Party* was owned by Twin Pines, which purchased the airtime, the show aired on whatever station the sponsor chose.

Milky joins the peanut gallery for a group photo on a birthday show. (Courtesy Peggy Tibbits.)

In 1955, WXYZ presented Twin Pines with a better deal, and consequently, Milky packed up his bag of tricks at the Masonic Temple and headed for the Maccabees Building, where he repeated the same format until 1958.

The Milkman

Playing second fiddle to Milky was the ever-present Twin Pines Milkman. A salesman himself, Cummings figured that the most effective way to pitch the products in the commercials would be to use a gimmick that was both representative of the sponsor and familiar to the children at home. The innovation called for the emcee to host the commercials dressed as your friendly neighborhood milkman—Twin Pines, of course. Larry Dlusky recalls that the concept worked like a charm.

Larry Dlusky: "The milkman would come out in the Twin Pines uniform, and he carried one of those baskets with the six bottles of milk in it. He'd talk about why Twin Pines milk was the best milk and about other Twin Pines products—how good they were."

Unlike Milky, for whom the men behind the makeup could trade places anonymously, the face of the milkman was quite noticeable when it changed over the years. The original milkman was the Channel 2 news director, Earl Hayes, who passed away just a few years into the show. In 1953, WJBK staff photographer Dale Young suited up for a brief stint. But it was Bob Leslie, a former radio announcer and the Santa Claus in the Hudson's Thanksgiving Day Parade, who became the third and longest-running milkman from the mid-1950s until his untimely death in the early 1960s. Dick Dietrich describes how Leslie handled the commercials.

Dick Dietrich: "Bob Leslie was a radio announcer going back to the thirties, and he was also an actor. When he appeared in his Twin Pines suit to do the commercials with Milky, they normally stood at a table, one on each side, with a product on the tabletop. I don't remember if they used cue cards, but regardless Bob Leslie would memorize the entire script. They would do maybe three commercials. There were no time limits in those days, so it would be two or three minutes at a crack, which was a lot for him to memorize."

After many years on the *Milky* show, Leslie's life came to an unexpected halt on a cold day in 1963, as recounted by his replacement, Bob Allison.

Bob Allison: "His furnace went out one night and he went down to relight it and it blew up. It was a very tragic accident. Bob was a super guy! After Bob died, suddenly, I was asked to be the milkman."

While hosting the popular *Ask Your Neighbor* program on WWJ radio, Allison was approached by his director, Vic Hurwitz, who also directed the renamed *Milky's Party Time* and had a connection with Luckoff-Wayburn. On his acceptance, Allison would wear the uniform until the show's demise in 1967.

Milky's Party Time

The move to WWJ in 1958 created an entirely new way for Milky to interact with his fans. The most noticeable difference in the format was the introduction of a live peanut gallery. Renamed *Milky's Party Time,* the program still featured cartoons, but the westerns rode off into the sunset to make room for a serial, *The Adventures of Sir Lancelot,* and a live talent segment, "Stars of the Future," hosted by a young girl called Mary Lou. Milky still performed his magic, but with the assistance of a Frenchman named Pierre who also coordinated games for the kids in the studio audience. Larry Dlusky and Bob Allison critique the mannerisms of the children in the peanut gallery.

Larry Dlusky: "Milky had a lot of interaction with the audience. The kids would say their names, give their ages, and say what school they attended. [There was] a line [of children] that would come by, and Milky had a handheld microphone."

Bob Allison: "There were about 40 kids in the audience every week. They were very well behaved . . . they were easily controlled . . . if I said do this, they did it, if I said don't do this, they didn't do that. Everybody on the show, whether it was Milky, Mary Lou, Pierre, or myself, we were their friends; we weren't authoritarian figures. So when we told them to do something it wasn't like having Mom or Dad tell them. This was something that was done very gently, and I don't ever remember a problem . . . the kids were very nice."

Every Saturday children from all over the Metro area flocked to Channel 4's Studio A on Lafayette Boulevard to see Milky, Mary Lou, Pierre, and the milkman hop out of the Twin Pines milk truck parked on the set at the beginning of the show. The demand to get on *Milky's Party Time* was so enormous that the thousands of letters and postcards requesting tickets created a backlog that took months to answer. Nonetheless, audiences both at home and in the studio cheered as youngsters typically competed in some sort of timed race.

Larry Dlusky: "The contests were what stood out most about the show. But the prize was really, really cheap. There was this big jar full of pennies, and you got to stick your hand into this jar and grab as many as you could fit in your hand. If you had 200 pennies in your hands, that would be two dollars. Now I dare you to try and get 200 pennies in your hands and hold onto them. So I was thinking, what do these kids get, 83 cents!? But that was such a big thing at the time—to get your hand in that jar of pennies and pull out as many as you could."

As the production budget grew, so did the quality of the prizes. The famous penny jar was tossed away in favor of actual toys courtesy of the "Twin Pines Toy House." However, the games weren't the only form of competition highlighted on *Milky's Party Time*. Bob Allison outlines another contest segment so popular with the viewers at home that the producers attempted to turn it into a spin-off.

Bob Allison: " 'Stars of the Future' was a half-hour segment of *Milky's Party Time*. In that segment, they usually had three or four musical performers—singers, dancers, and musicians—[that] would come on to perform. I was the emcee for that. The gal that was in charge, Mary Lou, was one of the judges, and we always had a couple of guest judges. They went through a period where they had quarterly winners, and at the end of the year they had a grand 'Stars' competition. The yearly prize was either money or a scholarship of some sort. They took this show and tried to turn it into a regular prime-time weekly program after *Milky* went off the air, and I got to be the host. It ran for 13 weeks and died. They just couldn't find sponsors for it."

Worry-Free Home Delivery

As "worry-free" as Twin Pines home delivery may have been, its commercials were not. Although the content of the show was completely ad-libbed, a lot of time and thought went into staging the commercials. Retired WWJ director Jim Breault recalls the rehearsals.

Jim Breault: "We'd rehearse everything backward. We'd set up the last commercial first, and we'd rehearse them right [up to] the first commercial, so the first one was already set up to go by the time we started live. We very rarely rehearsed anything of Clare Cummings's; we just ran with it, and it just seemed to work out quite well. We'd rehearse the commercials, but that's all."

In *Milky's* later years, when videotape was available, Karrell Fox's son Karlin was at the high end of the single-digit age group when his father arranged for him to appear regularly in the "heated" ice cream commercials.

Karlin Fox: "I sat there and ate ice cream and smiled while the milkman did the voice-over. The lights are what I remember the most because they were so hot and the ice cream would melt in like two minutes. And we'd do take after take after take because the ice cream had to look fresh. They used to have a dozen of them set up, and they'd bring a new one for each take."

The pressure of executing the commercials smoothly was intense, especially when they were live! If a spot was about to go sour, it was crucial that the performers have their thinking caps on or else the entire pitch was certain to flop. Bob Allison ought to know because it happened to him.

Bob Allison: "This one particular day, we were pushing a prepared pancake mix that was in a quart milk bottle. We had a griddle that was heated up, and the idea was I'm pitching how easy it is to make pancakes for your family. I've got a spatula in one hand and this mix of pancake batter in the other. I poured out six pancakes and I'm talking, going over the whole pitch . . . and when I took the spatula to turn over the first pancake, it was much too soon. So when I scooped it up, it scrunched into this bubbly ball mess that looked awful; it resembled a piece of dog manure on top of that spatula.

"So I knocked it down, and I said, 'Oh, I know what's wrong.' Then I took my Twin Pines milkman's hat and threw it down and yelled, 'Pierre . . .' He came in, and I said, 'Bring me your chef's hat.' He had a chef's hat because he'd been in a commercial earlier that day. I said, 'I need the hat.' He brought me the hat, and I put it on. By this time, the rest of the pancakes had cooked. So then I flipped the pancakes and said, 'See how easy that is . . . you can make them at home!' After that, Alan Luckoff [Lou's son], the advertising agent who represented Twin Pines and produced the show, said, 'I don't know whether to get mad or laugh or hug you, but that was the most beautiful thing I've ever seen.'"

For as many guidelines as there were in the production of the commercials set forth by the sponsor, when it came time to wrap up the show for the day the crew had an even bigger rule to follow . . . never let anything (in the way of props) go to waste!

Jim Breault: "It was interesting because we would have all the products that Twin Pines sold in the studio. As soon as the commercial was over, the stagehands took all the products. The items would end up in their cars."

Bob Allison: "My kids used to love it when I came home because I'd bring ice cream or whatever Twin Pines products we were pitching that day. We would split them up among the crew, and I would always bring something home to the kids, so they thought I was a big deal."

Another big deal revolved around the print promotion of Milky. It wasn't enough that his picture appeared on the product containers or even the side of the milk trucks. The Twin Pines magical clown had to be bigger than life! According to Peggy Tibbits, he was.

Peggy Tibbits: "There were billboards that had my dad's picture on them. In fact, one of them was all black except for my father's face, and all it said was, 'What are the magic words?' It won some big billboard award because it never mentioned the product. I remember it was real classy looking. You'd see several of them driving through Detroit."

Sometimes Clare Cummings himself dabbled in a little self-promotion while he was on the road for Du Pont. During his visits to the collision and body shops in the tricounty area, he freely distributed small autographed photos that the employees could give to their kids. They read, "Best wishes, keep smiling—Milky!"

Milky's Public

Like many of the local children's TV stars, Milky made appearances at schools, churches, hospitals, parties, and any other event that was asked of him. Cummings spent nearly all of his waking moments appearing in public as Milky. The popularity of the Twin Pines clown had escalated over the years to such heights that on the tenth anniversary of his television debut, December 16, 1960, Detroit mayor Louis C. Miriani presented Cummings with a key to the city on what was officially declared Milky the Clown Day!

Maintaining the illusion that Milky was real presented a few challenges. It was important to Cummings that his true identity never be revealed so that no child's impression of the clown would be shattered. Peggy Tibbits recounts some of the precautions her father employed to secure his privacy.

Peggy Tibbits: "He was very careful that when he was in costume [he stayed] in character. He knew to be attentive to children and families that were there. He would never talk down to a child. He never wanted to embarrass children or make them feel badly in any sort of way. He wanted them to feel comfortable. He would certainly never swear, although my father was not a person who swore. He wouldn't come out with something off-color . . . that was very important to him, to keep that image.

"Sometimes he was given less than secure places to change, and that became written up in his contract. He had to have his own private room; he couldn't have the boys' bathroom to get ready in and risk having the bathroom be used by anybody else . . . it had to be off limits so no one would see him.

"Only one time do I remember him coming home still in his clown suit. He came home from a personal appearance and he just drove in costume—he must've been close to the house somewhere and decided not to change until he got home. My mother and I were sitting in the living room, and he came up to the window and just stood there. Suddenly, there was this 'face' at the window we didn't expect and he just scared the pants off of us!"

Despite the pains Cummings took to conceal his identity, he wasn't entirely incognito out of costume, particularly when he opened his mouth.

Peggy Tibbits: "He never used a character voice for Milky; he always used his normal speaking voice. Someone once recognized him. He was standing in line at a Wendy's ready to order and a lady there said, 'You're Milky the Clown.' He said, 'How did you know?' She said, 'I can tell by your voice.' That was amazing [because] it was so much later in his life, like when he was already in his seventies. Of course, when he smiled the lady recognized that big gap between his two front teeth."

A Cub Scout assists Milky (Karrell Fox) with a magic trick.
(Courtesy Karlin Fox.)

The Old Switcheroo

Ed Golick: "If you remember *Milky the Clown* in black and white, it was
Clare Cummings. If you saw *Milky the Clown* in color, then you saw
Karrell Fox."

The year was 1964. Much of society was changing at that time, and
along with this came a major reincarnation for Milky. The magician originally chosen to mystify the kids as the magical clown was ready to
reemerge. Bob Allison revisits the changing of the guard.

Bob Allison: "A year after I started on the show, Clare decided he wanted to retire. So what they did was a flip-flop. Karrell became Milky, and Clare became the backup. That's how the switch happened. It wasn't anybody replacing anybody . . . they just changed places. There was no animosity whatsoever; everybody got along very well. I don't think maybe but once, for either one of them, that they missed a show. They were really good performers and very steady people."

During Clare's long tenure as Milky, Karrell Fox was busy taking his magic act on the road, where he prospered and became a world-renowned magician. Karlin Fox affords us a personalized glimpse into the incredible career of the King of Korn.

Karlin Fox: "*The Wonderful World of Ford* was dad's big break. It was a traveling show. He invented a big robot made entirely of car parts, and it had lights in the top with a speaker and a microphone. Somebody offstage would talk through it, and that created a lot of attention. He drew it all up and sold it to Ford. He went to Ford's world headquarters in Dearborn and did a card trick for William Clay Ford. The trick was where he forces a card, you know, pick a card, any card. Then he would say what the card was, but it would be wrong. So when William Clay Ford said 'That's not my card,' Dad says, 'Oh, no! This is my big break. You're real important. I was trying to make a good impression here, and I blew it.' Then he got Mr. Ford to go over to the window. Dad had hired a skywriter to write the "Ten of Clubs" in the sky, which was the correct card! And that's how he got the job. He did auto shows from then on all over the country until his death.

"His specialty was just being a great entertainer. He was on *The Ed Sullivan Show* along with *The Tonight Show*—Johnny Carson was interested in magic all the time. When he did magic, he told jokes along with the magic, so he was a comical magician. He was really, really good at magic. He was the president of the International Brotherhood of Magicians, so he traveled all over the world. I remember I asked him once why he was going to Australia and he told me because he'd never been there; he'd been just about everywhere else. He was highly respected in the world of magic. He never stooped to working in Vegas . . . he was offered to go to Vegas and work the clubs, but he didn't drink and he didn't like to be around drunks. The bottom line for him was always magic.

"Every time I walked through the kitchen or something, he would stop me and say, 'Let me do a trick for you . . . let me do a trick for you.' It was constant; he always wanted to show me a new trick. He was a perfectionist, so it took him a long time to put the makeup on to become Milky the Clown. I used to go with him when he'd get there early at

WWJ and go back in the makeup room with the big mirrors and a table that wrapped all the way around. I was just a little kid. I'd sit there and watch him put on his makeup, and it took him a long time. He'd sweat a lot, so he never used the cheap makeup that's water soluble . . . he used grease that had to be taken off with makeup remover. He was a true showman."

Crying over Spilled Milky

By 1967, supermarkets had waged a full-scale war on dairy home delivery by instituting a massive price cut on milk. In fact, the price cut was so severe that it literally killed the business entirely by the early to mid-1970s. By the end of the city's turbulent summer of 1967, *Milky's Party Time* had become an astronomical expense for Twin Pines. With their "worry-free" enterprise on the decline, the company's management was forced to pull the plug on the golden goose that had made them number one in home delivery.

The cancellation of *Milky's Party Time* may have closed the curtain on the magical clown in TV land, but off-camera the show was far from over.

Peggy Tibbits: "The baby boomers as they became adults sort of drew my dad out of retirement, and he got back into his clown suit to start doing appearances."

Karlin Fox: "My dad did appearances as Milky for quite a while after the cancellation of the show . . . so did Clare, but Dad did a lot more of them than Clare did. I think it was probably around 1978 when Milky faded out."

Sadly, both Milkys have since passed on. Clare Cummings was 82 when he died of congestive heart failure on October 31, 1994. His daughter Peggy remembers how the magic stayed with him to the very end.

Peggy Tibbits: "He was a magician from the time he was a kid up to the day he died. I mean he did a magic trick on the day he died; it's quite amazing. He did this trick for his hospice nurse. His nurse came out and told me, 'Your dad just showed me a magic trick.'"

Three and a half years later, on March 12, 1998, Karrell Fox passed away at 70 years of age in Palm Desert, California, where he and his wife had retired to in 1985. Vanished from the airwaves Milky may be, but the memory of the magical clown survives in the hearts of a generation that grew up with him.

Peggy Tibbits: "I think there's a real nostalgia in the boomers remembrance of him as being someone who was really important in their childhood life."

Ricky

Clowns, at times, can be frightening to kids and sometimes even frightening to adults . . . there's a phobia about clowns. Ricky was not threatening at all; he was a very soft-spoken, quiet clown and had a calming effect—more than the wild antics. He was my personal favorite of the clowns.

—LARRY DLUSKY, Detroit TV fan

Ladies and gentlemen . . . boys and girls . . . . Under the tent of WXYZ-TV is a clown like no other. This clown wasn't dreamed up for television, he was born from the trunk of the circus. Yes indeed, the circus! He enters your living rooms five days a week with a show full of music and dancing . . . acrobats and animals . . . but most important of all he comes to entertain you with plenty of laughs. So, without further delay, here he is . . . Ricky the Clown!

For 12 long years, Channel 7 was home to the only genuine clown on local television. Having spent his whole life performing with circuses, including the Shrine and Ringling Bros., Irv Romig was more than ready to amuse children all over southeastern Michigan with an endless number of gimmicks and gags that only live audiences that bought tickets could see. Sandwiched between Laurel and Hardy and Little Rascals shorts and cartoons, Ricky brought the circus home for every little girl and boy to enjoy.

Irvin Romig was born in Detroit on February 1, 1920. His dad was a cowboy, and his mother performed a high-wire act. Growing up under the big top, little Irv fell in love with the laughing, clapping, and cheering of live audiences. The shy youngster discovered his confidence behind the mask of a clown. After studying the routines of professional clowns, Romig wasted no time in developing fresh new material of his own under the name Irvie the Circus Buffoon.

The Greatest Show on Earth

As the years passed, Irv expanded his talents to include animal training, bareback riding, and complex gags that often required the construction of special props, which he built himself. So, with all of these talents to his credit, what kind of a clown was Irvie supposed to be? To answer that question, here is the clown himself, Irv Romig.

Irv Romig: "What portrayal would I be? Emmet Kelly. In fact, I took

Ricky the Clown (Irv Romig). (Courtesy Ed Golick.)

his place in the Ringling Bros. Circus when he left to make his first movie
[*The Fat Man,* 1951]. I was a tramp clown but a high-class tramp because
I wore a plaid suit. The hobo clown was more like Emmet Kelly, all
rags."

Although he replaced Kelly in "The Greatest Show on Earth," Irv
would get the chance to appear with the famed clown in the celluloid version, *The Greatest Show on Earth.* The 1952 release directed by Cecil B.
DeMille and starring Michigan natives Betty Hutton and Charlton Heston, featured Irv, his wife, and his sister, billed as "The Romigs," in bit
parts.

Irvie Becomes Ricky

During an appearance in New York City in 1953, Romig was approached by a man who appreciated his brand of shtick and thought he should have a career in television. While considering the idea, Irv returned home to Detroit, where he immediately began to write letters to all the TV stations, pitching a concept for a new children's show: a small-screen circus hosted by a genuine clown with a live donkey in front of a studio audience. Channel 7 program director Pete Strand responded favorably. Romig recalls how the news went from good to bad to good again.

Irv Romig: "I really got a surprise when my mother said, 'A man [Strand] from WXYZ called and wants you to come down and have an audition.' So I gave him a call, and he said, 'Bring that little donkey that you got and I'll bring a peanut gallery.' I was never much into auditioning because in our line of work they see you somewhere else and if they want you, they'll get you . . . so I didn't have to audition. I went down there, and we went all through it. Wards Baking Company [makers of Tip-Top bread] was kind of interested. Later Pete Strand says, 'Well, it didn't work out.' So I said, 'The heck with this, I'll go back to the Shrine.'

"While I'm with the Shrine Circus, my mother called, saying, 'That man [Strand] wants you to come back again.' So I went through the whole thing with the donkey again up on the fifteenth floor of the Maccabees Building. Anyhow, when we got through it I said, 'Well, how was it?' Strand said, 'You start this coming Sunday at 4:30 p.m.' It was a half-hour show with Laurel and Hardy [shorts] in front of a peanut gallery with the donkey."

In the days before the premier, the station management was experiencing a bit of discomfort with the name Irvie. Fearing that kids wouldn't remember it, the program director suggested an alternative.

Irv Romig: "Pete Strand said, 'Hey can we come up with another name? How about Ricky?' And I said, 'Gee . . . that sounds great.'"

In October 1953, one month after Soupy Sales took to the airwaves at WXYZ, Ricky the Clown made his debut on *Tip-Top Fun*. Just like Sales, Romig became his own producer and writer; responsible for all of the skits wrapped around the Laurel and Hardy films. The demand for fresh material thrust Ricky into a whole new arena, one that was foreign to seasoned circus clowns. Performing clowns traveled from town to town which afforded them the luxury of using the same bits over and over again. Television wouldn't be so kind.

Irv Romig: "I had to change my gags a lot because when you're on television you've got the same crowd tuning in."

Channel 7 retirees, director Mason Weaver, and art director Jack Flechsig, cite a few distinguishing characteristics that separated Ricky from the other TV clowns.

Mason Weaver: "He knew all the circus tricks—physical stuff . . . Milky didn't do physical stuff; he was a magician and more of a manufactured clown."

Jack Flechsig: "Ricky had pupils painted on his eyelids, so when his eyes were closed, he appeared to be staring! It was hilarious. And I think he painted them off kilter, so when he talked to you he'd close his eyes and it would look funny."

With Tip-Top bread backing the program, the Federal Communications Commission (FCC) soon forced WXYZ to change the name of the show due to a regulation that prohibited the sponsor's name from appearing in the title. As disruptive as the ruling may have been at the time, the intervention turned into a blessing. The new title, *The Ricky the Clown Show,* reflected the name of its star.

Sideshow Ricky

With the program increasing in popularity, the station extended Ricky's airtime from Sundays to Monday through Friday. But as Ricky fan Ed Golick points out, the new schedule evolved into a juggling act.

Ed Golick: "He wasn't on from this year to that year continuously. Sometimes he would have just a 10-minute show for a while. Other times it was 15 minutes, other times it'd be a half hour. I think the reason for that was he would leave to be in circuses, then he'd come back. He didn't have a half hour for five years or whatever; they'd kind of have him on sometimes in the morning, the afternoon, and on the weekends in different lengths."

Utilizing his numerous contacts in the circus, Ricky showcased a number of acrobats and animal trainers, who were more than happy to perform on the small screen when they came to Detroit, including members of his own family. Kids all over Motown were in awe of the variety of live tricks broadcast into their homes. It put a whole new spin on the phrase, "The circus is coming to town." *Ricky the Clown* was the circus you could visit without leaving your house. And as spectacular as the performers were it was always the comical tramp clown who took the spotlight in the center ring. Fans Larry Dlusky and Ed Golick remember one of Ricky's most famous routines.

Larry Dlusky: "One of his bits was pantomiming old records. He

Where to, ma'am? (Courtesy Irv Romig.)

wouldn't pantomime something that was a contemporary hit. Like he wouldn't do Eddie Fisher or Frank Sinatra—he'd be doing Al Jolson. So he'd be doing all of Jolson's movements, like getting down on one knee, spreading his arms, and singing something like 'You find your castles in Spain . . . through your window pane . . . back, back in your own back-yard . . .' They were these old songs from the twenties and thirties."

Ed Golick: "I was like six or seven years old. I didn't know Al Jolson from anybody. He would have the calliope and he would play *Is It True about Dixie* and he would sing along. A few years later I was watching

Bill Kennedy and I saw an Al Jolson film. Here's this strange man with Ricky the Clown's voice coming out of him. I thought, 'This man ripped off Ricky the Clown.' Irv did Al Jolson impressions for years and years."

Reproduced with permission from his unpublished autobiography, *The Show Goes On,* Irv Romig describes another bit that satirized one of his circus comrades.

Irv Romig: "I went onstage like a Russian dancing guy. I would do the dance where they would kick one leg up in the air at a time. But once in a while I would stick both feet up in the air and I wouldn't fall down. Each time I would put my feet up in the air I would yell, 'Hey,' then some hay would fall down on me. When the number was over, I would turn around to walk off and they would all see a stool tied to the back of me. The stool is what kept me from falling down when I would lift both feet up."

Although his comedy sketches were well choreographed, Ricky believed he could captivate an audience just as easily by going back to the drawing board.

Irv Romig: "I was pretty good in school doing artwork. So I got into these trick drawings where you draw something then turn it upside down and it becomes something else. I'd draw a wigwam in front of the kids with some trees on each side and a track going across that I'd say was a railroad track. Then I'd draw a little more and say, 'You never saw the Indian in the wigwam; would you like to see him? Well, I'll do a little more then turn it upside down and see if you can tell me where he is.' Then the drawing becomes his face."

Studio Tents

Ed Golick: "He had on the set a log cabin . . . it was just the front, but he would sit on a chair in front of the log cabin and do some stuff. He also had a backdrop that looked like the inside of a circus tent."

Irv Romig: "When I first started, it was one little curtain, but then it went to flats. Jack Flechsig was very nice to me because anytime I came in to ask him about something I hated to do it because he had enough work of his own. But I'd say, 'If there was any chance of getting this or that . . .' He'd say, 'Oh, yeah . . . we'll get it for you.'"

Jack Flechsig: "We did a set especially for him, and it was a very simple set . . . three flats in a book shape with circus tent stripes. He had some sort of table in front that was used for a lot of props [and] he had a set once with faces painted on it, too."

Donkeys and Llamas

To help maintain the circus motif, *Ricky the Clown* had a couple of costars: Bambino the Donkey and Fonda the Llama. Though Bambino accompanied the clown on his auditions at WXYZ and subsequently appeared on the show, it was the llama he purchased from the zoo that was more impressive to the kids.

Ed Golick: "That live llama just got to me. On other kid shows you'd expect to see somebody in a llama suit, but Ricky had real animals."

And, having real animals, in many instances one must expect a certain amount of unpredictability. Retired WXYZ stage manager Art Runyon recounts a couple of mishaps with Fonda.

Art Runyon: "Sometimes the llama would be in this little house that he had. I can remember one time when he was doing the show one of the kids in the audience started saying, 'Ricky, Ricky, the house is leaking!' And so it was . . . so was the llama. One of our best cameramen at that time was a fella named Sheldon Broadly. For some reason, he and the llama didn't take to each other. One time the llama got very unhappy with him and spit all over Sheldon's face."

In addition to Bambino and Fonda, Romig maintained an extensive collection of live and taxidermic animals. His diverse collection led to the opening of a small theme park on his private estate called Rickyland. The park included two rides: a small fleet of five electrically powered airplanes, which accommodated two kids per plane; and a little train of wagon cars pulled by Irv's lawnmower. Animals and rides weren't the only attractions at Rickyland; there was also a fun house and circus performances for the children to enjoy. At the end of the day, Ricky supplied each kid with a balloon, a bag of popcorn, and a picture of himself before he or she exited the premises. Sadly, in the following year Rickyland was forced to close due to a lack of funding.

Lu Lus

Larry Dlusky: "Just like Soupy referred to his fans as Birdbaths, Ricky referred to his viewers as Lu Lus. He'd say, 'All you Lu Lus out there . . .' and you'd hear a chorus of 'Lu-lu-lu-lu-lu . . .' from off-camera. That's what he called us, we were the Lu Lus. Just like the Birdbaths, we didn't know what that meant."

Sharing in the mystery about the meaning of *Lu Lu*, Channel 7 news anchor Erik Smith attempts a hypothesis as to its definition.

Erik Smith: "I watched television and saw *Ricky the Clown* like everybody else. Then I came to Channel 7, and Ricky was in his final years here at that point. I never quite understood his 'lu-lu-lu-lu,' but it became somewhat of a password. Whenever things went wrong, you'd hear 'lu-lu-lu-lu,' and that became Ricky's codeword for all hell's breaking loose and the show is going down the chute."

So for all of the Lu Lus out there who've pondered the question for the last 40 or 50 years, here's the chief Lu Lu himself with the final answer.

Irv Romig: "There was this French clown that I started clowning with named Marcus Hunkler. When they used to put tables on top of each other, way up high, with a chair at the top . . . he'd climb up there without it tipping over. This guy was very clever; while he did it, he never talked . . . he'd go, 'Lu-de-do-de-do . . . lu-de-do-de-do . . .' So I got to doing that, and then when I was on TV I'd use that every once in a while. One of the stagehands or cameramen said to me, 'I know when you're doing that what you're thinking.' I said, 'What? Can you guess?' He said, 'Yeah, you're thinking what you're going to do next.' I said, 'You're right!' So it started taking effect. Then I would say to the stagehands and cameramen, 'How are my Lu Lus today?' They'd kid back by going, 'Lu-de-do-de-do . . .' So then I started using that. I even brought in a wagon that read, 'The Lu Lu Wagon.' It got to be a running joke."

Ricky's Rules

One of the things that wasn't a joke on the program was Ricky's Ten Rules, a children's guide to clean and healthy living.

1. Get up with a smile.
2. Brush your teeth after every meal.
3. Wash your hands before every meal.
4. Take a bath every day.
5. Eat your breakfast, lunch, and dinner.
6. Drink four glasses of milk and eat six to eight slices of Tip-Top bread every day.
7. Straighten up your room.
8. Help your mother all you can.
9. Be careful crossing streets.
10. Go to bed on time.

Everybody Loves a Clown

During Ricky's heyday in the mid-1950s, he was approached by the station to cohost another program, an odd sort of spin-off from his circus show. Ed Golick describes the sponsor-driven premise.

Ed Golick: "They had an idea; it was called *The Robin and Ricky Show*. This woman that they named Robin, it wasn't her real name; her real name was Lally Deene. They tried this for about a year, *The Robin and Ricky Show*. It took place inside of a diner. Robin was the cook, and Ricky was the busboy. For some reason, in this diner they had a donkey also. It was just a bizarre premise, I recall . . . It worked really well because, 'Oh, what's on the menu today?' 'Well, we have Hostess fruit pies.' And then she'd pull out from behind the counter Hostess fruit pies, which happened to be the sponsor. That worked really well, but that didn't last long. After that, they went back to the previous format [for Ricky]. Robin bit the dust, and nobody knows what became of her."

By 1965, after 12 years, Ricky played his last gag at WXYZ. During his tenure at the station, he often filled in for stars such as Soupy Sales and Johnny Ginger when they vacationed or called in sick. Because he was asked by the station to substitute for the other talent so frequently, Irv Romig bought a house on Ten Mile Road, just a few blocks from Broadcast House, so he could be there on a moment's notice.

Another milestone that Ricky accomplished was obtaining a sponsorship from Hanley Dawson Chevrolet. His was the only children's show in the United States to be sponsored by an auto dealership, a crowning achievement he wears with pride to this day. On October 16, 2001, Irvin Romig was officially inducted into the International Clown Hall of Fame in Milwaukee—on the very same day as Charlie Chaplin. Although Ricky spent a lifetime traveling the country with the circus, Detroit's baby boomers will forever hail those 12 years on the TV screen as *his* "Greatest Show on Earth!"

Bozo

I remember being on the *Bozo* show, it was around 1971 when I
was eight years old. All of us kids were crammed in this little grandstand, and we were looking out at Bozo. It didn't matter what he
did; we were all so excited we'd scream and yell. Everybody was so
enamored that we were all just like little puppy dogs.
  —JOE HUMENIUK, Detroit TV fan

"Wowie kazowee!" and "Whoa Nelly!" are just a couple catchphrases
from the world's most famous clown—Bozo! Chiefly recognized by his
fluffy red-winged hair, this franchised circus buffoon was a fixture in the
lives of millions of children worldwide from the mid-1940s on. And in
Detroit Bozo was the only clown to entertain not one but two genera-
tions of Motor City kids. From 1959 to 1979, Motown's version of the
manufactured clown evolved from a wraparound host of cartoons on
WWJ, Channel 4, to a singing ringmaster of live games and magic shows
on CKLW, Channel 9, and the first nationally syndicated Bozo on WJBK,
Channel 2.

Regardless of when you tuned in to Bozo during his 20-year reign, just
about every youngster that grew up in the Metro area carries a fond
memory of their old pal . . . just as *Access Hollywood* correspondent/
anchor Shaun Robinson and Detroit TV fan John Hilt do.

Shaun Robinson: "I was real little when I watched Bozo. He was kind
of like the babysitter for us because my grandmother would say, 'Okay,
sit down there, watch *Bozo,* and be quiet' so she could get her work done
and not have to worry about us. I just remember being glued to the TV
for however long he was on, and I remember just wanting so badly to be
able to be in the audience on *Bozo.*"

John Hilt: "I was in awe of watching this man on TV; this guy who
was a clown had his own show with music. He would march around and
have the kids come in and he'd talk to them—Bozo actually incorporated
himself with children. But I was more in awe of the man himself than the
show . . . just how clean and crisp his costume was. Everything I noticed
about Bozo was perfect. He was a clown that everybody saw at one point
in their lives when they were younger."

Bozo the Clown (Art Cervi) at CKLW-TV. (Courtesy
Art Cervi.)

The Capitol Clown

Because Bozo is not a Detroit original like Milky, Ricky, or Oopsy, we
have to travel to the Capitol Records Building in Los Angeles to learn of
his origin. In 1946, writer/producer Alan W. Livingston was hired by the
(then) small record company to create an illustrated "read-along" book
that would accompany a record designed to crash the children's market.
Livingston developed the distinctive crowned red hair and blue suit for
the central character in his story; a lovable clown whose name hailed
from circus slang identified with hobo clowns. Thus, Bozo the Clown
was packaged and marketed to children on what became the first ever
book-record combo, entitled *Bozo at the Circus.*

The multitalented Vance "Pinto" Colvig, a former circus clown, cartoonist, and actor, had been voicing animated features and shorts for
Walt Disney and Max Fleischer when Livingston contacted him for an
assignment. Some of Colvig's most notable voices include Disney's
Goofy, Grumpy, and Sleepy, along with Popeye's nemesis, Bluto. When
asked to characterize Bozo, Colvig simply elevated one of his recognizable voices. Playing Bozo for a brief period in 1967 on CKLW, Jerry

Booth (who also played Jingles) explains the formulation of the clown's voice.

Jerry Booth: "As I recall, the way the voice is created is you think of Goofy, but then you constrict your throat a little bit more and 'Wowie kazowee, boys and girls . . . this is your old pal Bozo!' "

Having sold over a million copies, the success of *Bozo at the Circus* led to a series of more illustrated records based on Capitol's new mascot. As the popularity of Bozo increased, so did the demand for merchandise and ultimately a live television program. In 1949, Pinto Colvig became the first Bozo on TV in a broadcast from the studios of KTTV in Los Angeles.

The Harmon Factor

To help with the promotion of Bozo, Alan Livingston hired a man by the name of Larry Harmon. From the day Harmon was employed, he recognized the marketing potential of Bozo, which subsequently launched his relentless pursuit of ownership of the clown, as described by local CKLW and WJBK Bozo, Art Cervi.

Art Cervi: "Somewhere along the line, and it gets very, very vague, Larry Harmon started acquiring all of the rights to different products— Bozo bread, Bozo forks and spoons, etc.—and began marketing them. Bit by bit he was buying up all of the rights to these products, but the last thing he could ever get his hands on, as much as he tried, was the actual rights to Bozo, which were owned by Capitol Records."

After years of persistence and a sizable sum of money, Harmon was able to purchase the licensing rights to the Bozo character in the late 1950s. Around that same time, when Jayark Films sought to animate and release a series of Bozo cartoons, Harmon seized the opportunity to syndicate them to local television stations. And along with the cartoons came the franchising of Bozo himself. In other words, any station opting for the cartoons was allowed to develop its own Bozo and have a *Bozo the Clown* show . . . for an annual fee, of course. Retired CKLW director Matt Keelan and Art Cervi detail the Larry Harmon rule book for *Bozo*.

Matt Keelan: "Larry Harmon came in with a great big fat book that said how the makeup should look, what the costume would look like, and the format of the show."

Art Cervi: "He broadened the show out with a book that had the 'dos and don'ts' and so forth in them. He would use the various characters in that if you did something, say, in the Chicago show, it became *his* property. If you did a bit and that bit was successful and it became a running gag, then he would tell the other Bozos about it. He had each of them interweaving while he was sitting back taking all the credit for it."

And taking credit for sketches wasn't the only bold move on Harmon's part. The shrewd businessman who charged the franchisees for anything and everything Bozo, right down to the makeup, proclaimed himself the originator of the character.

Art Cervi: "Larry Harmon never played the part of Bozo on television or ever interfaced with children as such. He took the character and embellished him a lot. But as the years went by a lot of untruths came out. Through the years he convinced himself that he created this character, and he didn't! So when I would be interviewed in the past, I would try to explain to everyone that he was indeed a smart businessman who was able to embellish this character but he did not create him. The Clown Hall of Fame gave Larry, several years ago, a plaque recognizing his efforts in creating Bozo the Clown. Fortunately what happened, just a short while ago, is that they took the plaque back because they realized after checking with people, like myself, and in doing their homework that he was not the creator. So they stripped him of the honor."

Bob McNea: Bozo, 1959-67

While Larry Harmon was out selling Bozos across the country, he made a stop in the Motor City in 1959. His *Bozo the Clown* package was licensed to WWJ, Channel 4. With Schafer's Bread waiting in the wings to sponsor the program, the station needed an actor to portray the fluffy red-haired buffoon.

Robert J. McNea was born in St. Thomas, Ontario, on June 12, 1929. Beginning at the age of 11, "Bob" spent much of his youth performing as a clown with various circuses and the theater. He first appeared on Detroit television in 1950 as part of a promotion for the Michigan State Fair's grandstand show, which was broadcast on WXYZ. Working as a carpenter at Channel 9 in 1954, McNea was afforded the chance to fill a summer vacancy with a clown show of his own, *Moppets*. As short-lived as the program was, McNea's clown was not forgotten. Five years later Moppets the Clown resurfaced in live bread commercials aired during *The Mickey Mouse Club* on Channel 7.

Prior to the bread commercials, McNea appeared as a character actor for WWJ in its early courtroom dramas. It was his connection at Channel 4 that steered him into auditioning for Larry Harmon's clown. He remembers how the director's advance notice gave him an edge over his competitors.

Detroit's original Bozo (Bob McNea) at WWJ-TV in 1961.
(Courtesy Walter P. Reuther Library, Wayne State University.)

Bob McNea: "I heard through the grapevine that Channel 4 was look-ing for a person to portray a clown called Bozo. I never heard of Bozo prior to that. So I shopped around and found out it was a Capitol Records clown. I got my name in for the audition through a guy by the name of Bert Wright who was a director at WWJ. I came across him because I was doing acting parts on all those old court shows—*Night Court* and *Juvenile Court*.

"Bert came to me first and said, 'Bob, nobody here knows what the hell's going on; how this Bozo's supposed to be. Will you do it?' I said, 'Yeah, but with this one proviso: I can come over there and look at a couple of the *Bozo* cartoons to get a feel for him?' 'Sure.' Then I said, 'But don't tell anybody.' He says, 'I won't.' So, I went over one morning and looked at some of the cartoons and thought, well, that's enough. Then when I went to the audition I put three or four little juggling balls in my pocket and a clown's rubber nose. There were nine guys altogether auditioning for the part of Bozo the Clown. I was asked to go first, but I said, 'No, I'm not gonna go first, I'll go in the middle.' I knew I had this thing sewn up because I could tell that none of the other guys there were clowns. And, sure enough, the first three or four of them they interrupted them right in the middle of what they were doing and said, 'Thanks for coming.' That's the kiss of death when you go for an audition and they say that.

"So I get up to the camera, turn my back, put the nose on, reach into my pocket, and start to turn around saying, 'Hi boys and girls . . . it's me, Bozo the Clown. I'll show you a juggling act.' I juggled, and the other guys left to do the audition got up and walked out. It wasn't until years afterward that both Bert and I admitted that he allowed me to see the cartoons."

According to the Harmon bible, all Bozos were supposed to mirror each other; however, that wasn't always the case, at least not in Detroit. Matt Keelan points out how McNea's background called for an interpretation of the character that differed from what Art Cervi would portray eight years later.

Matt Keelan: "Bob had clown experience, and his [*Bozo*] show was different because he would do clown acts. He was extremely talented, and he leaned toward entertaining kids himself, where Art Cervi was a people person. I had difficulty getting Art to do anything clownwise. He bounced off the kids more, so they were totally different."

Bozo's Motor City Debut

In the final year of the Fabulous Fifties, Detroit's baby boomers received their first dose of a clown craze that was captivating the nation. Bob McNea paints a picture of the *Bozo* show he introduced to Motown.

Bob McNea: "There was just a curtain background with some circus animals hanging down that we cut out from circus posters. There was a big trunk that said 'Bozo,' and I would stand behind the trunk. That was the counter, and I would do the shtick standing behind it. For a half hour, I led in and out of the cartoons. We used to look at all the cartoons before we used them that day. I used to go and sit for like an hour watching these cartoons and make notes. I juggled, and I did magic tricks; I always had a different trick or two for each show. I also had guests on the show . . . firemen, policemen, the Shrine Circus clowns . . . I worked the Shrine Circus for 15 years, so I always had the guys on as guests."

Although the curtained set would be replaced with animated flats depicting a circus atmosphere, as the years went by the format routines that wrapped around endless reruns of the staling *Bozo* cartoons remained the same. Nonetheless, they were a hit with the kids. In fact, they were such a hit that at one point in time WWJ altered its program schedule to include an afternoon edition.

Bob McNea: "At one time, I was on the air, believe it or not, for nine hours a week! We did an additional one-hour show every day from 4:00 to 5:00 p.m.; we used to lead in to *George Pierrot Presents*."

While other local clown shows gyrated "on-air" excitement with lively studio audiences, *Bozo* did not. Despite Harmon's demand for a peanut gallery, WWJ's lack of one came at the behest of its star.

Bob McNea: "There was no live audience because I said that it's unfair to expect parents to bring their kids to Downtown Detroit and sit for two hours while we do a kid's television show. So we never used kids on the show."

As the technology in television advanced into living color in the mid-1960s, Channel 4's *Bozo the Clown* would become the first local children's program to be broadcast in color. Meanwhile, tension between WWJ and Larry Harmon was steadily mounting. The more popular Bozo became in the Motor City the more Harmon raised the franchise fee. This continuous game between the powers that be lasted until early 1967, when the station decided it was time to end its eight-year association with Mr. Larry Harmon. *Bozo the Clown* on WWJ was abruptly canceled. But, not to worry, the beloved red, white, and blue clown was about to make a dash for the border.

Jerry Booth: Bozo, 1967

When Canada's CKLW-TV bought the *Bozo* package from Harmon to continue the Motown franchise, Jerry Booth was already one of the station's biggest stars. As the jester in the highly successful *Jingles in Boofland*, he was the hands down choice by the management to don the costume of their newest clown. But, unlike Booth's previous programs—*Jingles in Boofland*, *Larry and Jerry*, and *Jerry Booth's Funhouse*, which were creations of his own, *Bozo* was a "cookie-cutter" production from A to Z. The restrictions placed on creativity coupled with the intense facial makeup proved to be overwhelming for Booth.

Jerry Booth: "They picked me to do *Bozo*, and I agreed, although I had never done anything with that kind of makeup and all that stuff. So in order to learn that bit I went to 'Bozo School' in Boston for a week with Larry Harmon, and of course I studied the Bozo [of Frank Avruch] that had been running in there for years and years. I went to *Bozo* and watched him do his show. I sat down in a hotel room with Larry Harmon, and he told me how to create the Bozo voice, the Bozo walk, the 'wowie kazowee,' and the expressions that were taken from the cartoon. He also taught me how to put the makeup on.

"When I came back, we would do a live show every morning and then keep the same peanut gallery there to tape one that ran the same day in the afternoon . . . so that was a job! There was a lot of interaction with the kids. We would do games and stunts with the kids. I had that Bozo makeup on for a lot of hours every day, and I did that for about four months. I just never got into it like apparently Bob McNea did and other Bozos. As it turned out, I had started a part-time business that all of a sudden became more profitable. I just decided that I was gonna spend more time doing that, so I suggested they find another Bozo.

"It was a fun thing to do, but when you're doing a show like that with kids in the audience you're actually doing two shows. You have to do one for the camera, and while the cartoons are on you have to keep the kids entertained in the studio. So it was a lot more work than the *Jingles* show and a lot more stress."

Art Cervi: Bozo, 1967–79

After Jerry Booth's departure, CKLW executives began a search for a new Bozo. Little did they know that the man best suited for the job was already in their midst working behind the scenes on their hot dance-party show, *Swingin' Time.*

Art Cervi was born on September 4, 1934, in Mt. Pleasant, New York. During his youth in the 1940s, the Cervis moved to Michigan. Wishing to continue his schooling in New York, he traveled back east to live with his grandmother. Upon completing his education, he rejoined his parents in Michigan in the early 1950s. By the time he reached his twenties, he had embarked on a career in radio at WEXL and then WOMC. By 1960, he switched stations again when he became the music director at WKMH-AM 1310, which later turned into WKNR, Keener 13. It was there that he struck up a friendship with the station's top morning deejay, Robin Seymour.

In 1963, Cervi cocreated with Seymour a teen dance-party show for CKLW-TV called *Teen Town,* which ultimately became *Swingin' Time.* During his tenure as Channel 9's talent coordinator and head of guest relations, Cervi's personable nature convinced many in his social circle that he should audition for *Bozo's Big Top* in 1967.

Art Cervi: "They had open auditions . . . and anybody that you can think of at that time tried out for the *Bozo* show. My friends and even people within the station kept saying to me, 'Oh, why don't you try it? You work well with kids, and you're nice to people.' And I'm thinking, 'That's the last thing I wanna do—no!' So they finally coaxed me into going in and putting the makeup on. That was the audition. They had a small set, and they would bring in a dozen or so kids and have you put on the face and suit. They taped each one of these to see the interaction between the character and the audience.

"At least two months went by, and one day I came in and the switchboard operator says, 'Mr. Metcalf [the general manager] wants to see you.' And of course, because we're sooo secure in this business, what's my first thought: 'Oh god, I'm canned! I haven't been doing something right . . . I'm out of a job.' So I go down there and say to the secretary, 'Mr. Metcalf wants to see me?' She says, 'Yeeaahh . . .' I walked in there and he had three-quarter-inch tapes all stacked up and he said, 'Sit down. I don't know what to do with you.' And of course my mind was going in every direction imaginable. He said, 'You remember when you did that audition for the *Bozo* show? We've looked at all these tapes, and we're really in a quandary. We have all these so-called television-experienced people. Your [talent] background is more in radio, but we keep looking at these tapes, weeding them down, and you keep popping back up! Everybody likes the way you interact with the audience better than anybody else on these tapes. But you have the least amount of on-air time. So we're going to give you a 30-day audition, but it's going to be live. We'll put the show on the air, and you got 30 days to show us that you can do this thing.' That audition lasted until today."

Matt Keelan reaffirms the station's decision to go with Cervi.

Matt Keelan: "Art was a natural. What I liked about Art Cervi was when he put the makeup on he became another person . . . he became Bozo. Even as a director, when I talked to Art [out of costume], I talked to Art, but once he had the makeup on I only saw Bozo. He had a perfect personality for being with kids. No matter what was going on, he never got upset—he accepted everything as a challenge. There was one kid who swore at him from the stands, and he just made light of it. Another one of the things the kids wanted to do all the time was stamp on his feet, but he had the personality that could handle all that kind of stuff."

That special quality of being able to relate to children on their level not only felt right to Cervi but it became the standard by which he would portray the character . . . regardless of what Harmon's playbook said.

Art Cervi: "I was probably one of the biggest thorns in Larry Harmon's side because I did it unlike any book or manual that he had. The way you talk to kids, the way you shake hands . . . he had a way of when you're shaking hands with a child you're not really shaking their hand. And I thought, 'C'mon!' If you did it his way, it wasn't genuine, it was false . . . and that was one of the biggest things. I would also go right into the peanut gallery to sit with the kids and talk to them. Right away that was not in the manual; you don't do that because someone could grab you from behind. Well, yeah, they could, but if everybody's enjoying themselves I'm not gonna get them in that frame of mind to want to do something like that. Harmon would say, 'No, I want you to do it this way.' It finally got to the point where they ousted him from the station, saying, 'We'll send you your check each year and you just stay away.'

"I can't speak for the other [Bozos] because a lot of them did Larry Harmon's manual, which was a rigid 'this and this and this . . .' So what I was doing was going out there and having fun! And letting the kids enjoy themselves. Laughter is infectious. I would never ever ever use a child to benefit me by making that child the brunt of a joke. If the joke is going to be on anybody, the joke is going to be on me. I think that's why our particular show was successful. I tried to make other people and the kids the stars of the show as opposed to having all the emphasis on me."

Bozo's Big Top

The debut of *Bozo's Big Top* on CKLW sparked a revolutionary new way of showcasing the famed clown. It was 1967, and the next generation of TV viewers was on the rise. The baby boomers that grew up with Bozo on WWJ were entering their adolescence, and consequently the production staff at Channel 9 sought to revamp the series in an effort to appeal to the up and coming Generation Xers. Aside from Cervi's interpretation of the character, the most noticeable deviation from Channel 4's presentation was the inclusion of a live audience.

Within a vibrantly colored circus atmosphere of reds, yellows, and blues, local kids were invited to sit in a framed "circus wagon" grandstand encased by flats with animal cages painted on them. At home, children routinely watched Bozo running through the streets on film as he made his way into the "big top." Once inside, the fluffy-haired clown would break into a hand-clapping rendition of "Bozo Is Back."

Hello world, every boy and every gal, I'm Bozo the Clown.
Yes, this is your old pal.
I brought you a bag of rootin'-tootin' tricks,
One, two, three, four, five or six.

The funniest man in the whole human race
Is gonna put a smile on your face.
Just keep laughin'.
Get rid of that frown.
Bozo is back,
The one and only Bozo the Clown!

As the years progressed, *Bozo* director Matt Keelan eventually scrapped the "canned" opening for the sake of production value.

Matt Keelan: "I got away from that because I didn't like the idea of the "film" going into the live show. I was never that impressed with it, so we ended up doing a live opening after a while."

Once the opening number got under way, *Bozo's Big Top* quickly spun into a fun house of guests and games in between those same old Bozo cartoons. Like his predecessor at WWJ, the new Bozo featured policemen and firemen to teach safety, but CKLW opened the door much wider to attract dance troupes from Disney, skaters from the Ice Capades, singers, musicians, and even race car drivers. Live circus animals were brought in regularly along with exotic pets courtesy of B'wana Don Hunt. A couple of sidekicks were also added to the roster to perform music and magic. Thus, the entertainment on *Bozo* was significantly improved from that of Channel 4.

And along with all of this revitalization came an increase in production. The format originally conceived by Harmon called for a half-hour program. Though WWJ briefly produced additional hour-long shows, CKLW pushed the envelope even further by producing two one-hour episodes. Larry Thompson (who played Bozo's sidekick Mr. Whoodini) and Matt Keelan review the production.

Larry Thompson: "For many years, we were doing two one-hour programs a day. The first one was in the morning, and then there was another one in the afternoon. The morning one we did live, then we'd take a break for a half hour or 45 minutes. We had the next group of kids come in, and we did a taped version for the second program."

Matt Keelan: "I prided myself on the fact that when we did stuff on videotape, it was still live . . . we did not edit the thing. We never edited one thing out of a *Bozo* show."

Outlines for the shows were primarily developed by Keelan and Thompson while Cervi rehearsed his musical numbers with pianist Wally Townsend (known on the show as Mr. Calliope). The program was never scripted with lines of dialogue; every outlined segment was filled with ad-libbed performances. The talents of Cervi and company, combined with his audience magnetism, paved the way for CKLW to secede from the

Larry Harmon school of thought and shift the premise of the show in an entirely new direction . . . one that was undeniably different from those of the other franchises.

Matt Keelan: "Harmon was the one responsible for laying out the whole show—the idea. We just simply took that and built on it, mainly with the kid audience. I think that was the main difference between what we did compared to other Bozos . . . there were times we thought Bozo was just an emcee. But Art connected with the children, and they loved him. Originally they had cartoons and kids related Bozo to the cartoons, so we dumped the cartoons and did the show so that Bozo could be Bozo and not a cartoon character."

Sidekickin' Out the Cartoons

In an effort to help expand the show, Bozo was given a couple of sidekicks, who were instrumental in filling the time originally allotted for the cartoons. The first one to come along was Mr. Calliope. Wally Townsend was a veteran studio musician at CKLW by the time *Bozo* went into production. Already on the payroll but not assigned to any program, station management decided to make use of Townsend's musical abilities and wasted time.

Art Cervi: "They came up with this brilliant idea of putting a striped jacket on him and a straw hat. Mr. Calliope [pronounced cal-lee-oh-pee] was just a play on ca-ly-o-pee. But, Bozo being as dumb as he is, couldn't get it right, so it became Mr. Cal-lee-oh-pee instead of Mr. Ca-ly-o-pee. We had this upright piano painted green, and all of a sudden I became the singer. We would sing kids' songs where kids could clap along. But, for as much fun as Mr. Calliope appeared to be having on the set while the cameras were rolling, his persona off-camera and out of sight was a complete reverse."

Matt Keelan: "Mr. Calliope was an accomplished musician, and he had a hard time dealing with Bozo. He tried to rehearse with Bozo in a backroom somewhere and people would be going by all the time and Art would acknowledge them. And Mr. Calliope would be really upset with Art because he wasn't concentrating on what he was doing. Mr. Calliope was temperamental. One day we put all kinds of balloons inside his piano, you know, things we thought were funny—and were funny—but he didn't think so. He was an interesting character."

Approximately three years into *Bozo's Big Top,* as the cartoons were being slowly phased out, Larry Thompson was hosting his own program at CKLW called *Magic Shop.* Dazzling youngsters as the red-suited, tur-

Top to bottom: Mr. Whoodini (Larry Thompson), Mr. Calliope (Wally Townsend), and Bozo (Art Cervi) in the late 1970s. (Courtesy Larry Thompson.)

baned Mr. Whoodini, Thompson was asked to appear in crossover segments to incorporate magic into the *Bozo* format.

Larry Thompson: "It helped the ratings, and then from there they said, 'You guys make a good team, let's make this thing happen.'"

From that moment on, the Detroit Bozo show possessed a character ensemble that was unmatched in any other television market. Bozo fans

John Hilt and Joe Humeniuk cite a few of their memories of the magical man with the pointed goatee.

John Hilt: "I remember Mr. Whoodini a lot because he came on as a sidekick doing magic. He was clean and precise in his magic, and Bozo would become the butt of some of his jokes."

Joe Humeniuk: "Mr. Whoodini's daughter went to my school [Clay Elementary in Livonia], and he would come to do shows. We had this little theater in the school; it was just a cool little constructive room that we called the 'Theater.' Mr. Whoodini would show up every year to do magic acts for us. Everybody loved that!"

Born in 1942, Larry Thompson reminisces about how his childhood love of magic led him to the studios of CKLW and the evolution of his alter ego, Mr. Whoodini.

Larry Thompson: "Most kids when they're growing up do magic tricks—both male and female. I just never got rid of them; I kept doing them. So when it came to my college days I was doing shows and actually supplemented a great deal of my college [tuition] by doing magic shows. When I got my bachelor's degree from Central [Michigan University], there was an opening at Channel 9 for *Magic Shop*. I was very good friends with Jerry Booth, and he said, 'You got to come in and take a shot at it.' And I said, 'You've got to be kidding!? I don't have a shot at it.' He says, 'Well, you do.' They were originally going to call it *Tinker Tom's Workshop*. I said, 'Jerry, I don't have a clue what *Tinker Tom's Workshop* is.' So I called a magician friend in Lansing, and he says, 'Larry, why don't you call it *Magic Shop?*' BANG—the lights went on—and I thought anything can happen in a magic shop. So when I went in for the audition there were like 50 people. I said to the director, 'I'm sorry, I have another concept I'd like to present.' He said, 'Well, we're here, let's tape the thing.' Low and behold, I got the job.

"When it came to a name, my name is Larry Thompson. They said, 'Larry Thompson is not very magical, let's call you some magic name.' So they came up with different names, and either the director or somebody else came up with Houdini. I said, 'That's good, but that's the father of magic.' Then they said, 'Let's call you Mr. Houdini.' I said, 'Okay, but let's spell it W-H-O-D-I-N-I.' And they said, 'No, let's make it W-H-O-O-D-I-N-I.' I said, 'Go for it!' About six months into the program, they said, 'You look nice, you're a kid, you look really good, but you need to look more magical.' So at that time I was wearing a red suit, and we kept the red suit, but we needed to add a turban, so I got a turban and a false beard and mustache, which looked very cool. But it was clear to me that I would have to grow a beard and mustache because in those days I was doing it seven days a week. And spirit gum seven days a week did not help my face, so I grew the beard and mustache."

Art Cervi: "When they decided to add Larry to the show as the second banana, we started dropping the cartoons in favor of the magic bits. It gave us another reason to use more children. If Larry was doing a trick, he could use a child instead of Bozo all the time. So there were fewer and fewer cartoons. We jam-packed the shows as much as we could."

Winners and Almost Winners

Matt Keelan: "On the *Bozo* show, you never had a loser . . . there were 'almost winners.' "

Perhaps the single most important element of the program in both fun and philosophy were the games. Art Cervi explains.

Art Cervi: "First of all, the objective was, in our minds, you don't have to have academics to teach life's lessons. By your own actions, the 'please' and the 'thank-yous' and so forth, you're teaching. And when you play a game there's a winner and an almost winner. You don't win everything in life, so if you don't win you can still accept it gracefully with good sportsmanship. And we stressed that. Just because you didn't win, you're not a loser. We always kept that in the back of our minds.

"We played more games with children than any other *Bozo* show that was going on in the country at that particular time. We had the foot in the bucket, sit on the balloon, a banana-eating contest, a cracker-eating contest, the spoon and the egg, and on and on . . . there was a virtual endless supply of games that the kids could play."

John Hilt: "I remember the bucket game. You have a ball, and you stand behind a line; then you toss the ball into a bucket. You won a prize for every time you got it in. And then you got another ball that you'd have to toss into the next bucket, and the farther you went up the better the prizes were."

Joe Humeniuk: "I remember being overwhelmed with excitement because at that time, being a kid, Bozo was the big thing in the early seventies. I remember being picked for a ring-toss game, and I won a prize. I got some sort of [Mattel] Hot Wheels set, and I just loved that thing."

Art Cervi: "Nobody ever went home empty-handed; everybody got a goody bag when they left the *Bozo* show."

Larry Thompson: "We had a lot of sponsors that would send us gifts for free. We had a guy who was in charge of our prizes, and we had cribs loaded with stuff. In those days, we used to have a running gag about

The foot in the bucket game at CKLW-TV. (Courtesy Frank Quinn.)

Orange Crush because every kid got a six pack of Orange Crush when they came on, and every kid used to get a big giant Tootsie Roll too. It was a running piece of business because we used to get thousands of them."

One of the reasons why the Motown *Bozo* played so many games per episode was its commitment to making every kid on the show a star. Children in the peanut gallery were selected at random to participate in the competitions. If a child wasn't chosen for a game, he or she was asked to assist Mr. Whoodini with a magic trick or Bozo with a bit. Every effort was made by the staff to include as many youngsters as possible in some kind of event that would put them in the spotlight.

Only one contest was ever left up to a lottery: the highly anticipated Treasure Chest game. Each kid had a number on his or her name tag (along with an animated picture of Bozo). When it came time to play the "World Series" of games on *Bozo*, a hat was brought out filled with all of the corresponding numbers. A number was drawn, and that lucky child got a crack at winning an awesome prize of their choice from the chest. Joe Humeniuk relives the moment.

Joe Humeniuk: "What I thought was really cool was when they rolled out that chest with the siren on the top of it. That was when all the kids got really excited. And I remember every kid in that audience was waiting for that chest to come rolling out. That was the big thing. Where's the chest? When's it coming out? Everybody was just waiting to see what toys were in there."

Unknown to audiences in the studio and at home, the treasure chest became an ongoing gag between the stagehands and Bozo. And, as Art Cervi recounts, his attempt to turn the tables on his pranksters resulted in the program's most embarrassing moment.

Art Cervi: "When the treasure chest was rolled out, Bozo would stop it with his foot. So it became a game of how fast we could send it in to the clown! It was always done coming out of commercials. The siren would go off—the sound effect of a siren—it [the chest] was sent out, and Bozo would stop it. Then he'd open it and talk about what was inside. Well, one day I decided I'm really gonna fix these characters. While we were into spots, they're getting this thing ready to send in. The siren goes off, we go on live, and they push it in. Because I'm gonna fix these guys, I sidestepped, which I had never done before, and I did the matador bit— olé! The chest goes past me, and I start talking. All of a sudden people start laughing; the crew is virtually on the floor. I don't know what the heck's going on, so I turn around to look . . . and we could not have planned this any better. The chest just caught the corner of the set in such a way that it started to slowly fall over, like an implosion in slow motion that was almost surreal . . . first one flat fell, then another flat fell, then another one . . . it was like dominos, and we were LIVE!"

Bozo on the Road

Larry Thompson: "Personal appearances were huge! You would swear we were the biggest celebrities in Hollywood. It was very gratifying to see these turnouts. We did a show live for many years at many of the Detroit area theaters on Saturdays. We might do two a day, and they were always sold out. And these were big theaters, not your little 300 seaters you have today; we're talking your 1,500- to 1,800-seat auditoriums."

Art Cervi: "The reception was fantastic—unbelievable! It would be raining, and they would be standing out in the rain a block long waiting for my appearance. All of the shopping malls would have me for an hour on a Saturday, and the lines were so long that I would end up staying for two to three hours . . . especially in the summer and around the holidays."

Matt Keelan: "I can recall people hiring Art for personal appearances. I remember one time when the people that hired him said, 'We're gonna have you here, and we're going to charge admission to see you.' He said, 'No way. I'll sit on the other side of the gate then. There's no way you're charging admission. That wasn't the deal.' So that's the kind of ethics he had."

Art Cervi: "One of the things that I insisted on, even if they [the sponsor] had a camera there to take pictures so that people could buy the picture—everybody looks at a way to make a buck—no Bozo stuff was to be sold where I was. Nobody was going to be forced or embarrassed or goaded into buying a Bozo product for their child while they were waiting in line. I always looked at it from the standpoint of what people can and can't afford."

Larry Thompson: "We did the State Fair a couple of years in the big amphitheater, and we would fill that audience. There were probably 8,500 seats there. I'd bring out some illusions at that time because it was such a big audience. The show was basically built around more magic in those days, and we would do a couple of games. We had one game that had a father and son come up and we'd dress the father in a baby cap and bib and give him a baby bottle filled with water. The contest was the kid had to feed the dad and the winner was the one who drank the most water. It was a nothing thing, but the response was stupendous! People loved that."

Art Cervi: "The communication between the character and the people, even today, boggles my mind! I say this in all modesty, I am overwhelmed by not having one person ever come up to me and say, 'I couldn't stand you.' I mean, it's like they almost have tears in their eyes; they're just overwhelmed. And it's like, oh my God, you never think of how you're touching people."

Larry Thompson: "We used to do a lot of charity work. We did the Leukemia Foundation, and we would go out onstage with hundreds and hundreds of families where two-thirds of the kids were bald. And we would do our program; we're onstage in character—we don't break [character]. After the show, these kids come up and they hug you and you're still having to be in character . . . so afterward we'd go in the backroom and both of us would cry!"

Art Cervi: "I was a fanatic about not breaking character. When I was Bozo, I was Bozo. I wouldn't so much as take a glove off in front of a child. If I had to go to wash my hands or do whatever else I had to do, I made sure there was no one anywhere near that room. Even going to an appearance—or better yet coming back from an appearance—while I was in that suit, no matter how tired I was, until I walked in the door that headpiece or glove never came off. I believed in that character, and I was not about to destroy any child's image of him."

Syndication

The mid-1970s was a pivotal period for both CKLW and *Bozo*. In 1974, the CBC (Canadian Broadcasting Corporation) acquired Channel 9's broadcast license. The following year the network took possession of the station and changed the call letters to CBET. An attempt was made to syndicate *Bozo's Big Top* throughout Canada from the studios on Riverside Drive, but unfortunately the bid failed. By 1977, the Canadian border protection rules, in conjunction with the station's finances, forced the cancellation of *Bozo* and brought about the end of an era. Larry Thompson elaborates.

Larry Thompson: "When CBET-TV took over CKLW, they basically let all of their American talent go. So that was probably the end of the TV generation for Channel 9 as we think of it. CBC in Toronto was huge! They had *The Friendly Giant* and *Mr. Dressup* and all of these great programs for kids out of Toronto. Since they were franchising Windsor, they didn't need the local stuff anymore. They could just pipe this stuff out of Toronto and save a lot of dough. Obviously, it was crushing to us because we thought we were doing a pretty good job . . . and we were."

After their release from Channel 9, Art Cervi was determined to continue the *Bozo* show with Thompson in Detroit. He purchased the franchise from Harmon and negotiated a deal with WJBK, Channel 2, to duplicate the winning format he and Thompson had crafted at CKLW. However, Cervi's vision for the show wasn't limited to the Motor City market; he had his sights set on national syndication.

Larry Thompson: "For two and a half years, we tried to syndicate the program nationally. The first year was dismal. The following year we picked up a couple more sponsors, but it just didn't work out, and basically that was the end of the [Detroit] *Bozo* show. However, at one point we were in some pretty serious markets [in addition to Detroit] as I recall: Los Angeles, New York, Vegas, Wichita . . ."

Packing Up the Tent

Like so many other local programs, especially the kids' shows, which were fading at the end of the seventies, *Bozo* packed up its television tent once more. This time it would be for good. In 1979, the *Bozo* franchise in

Motown was officially canceled. After 20 years of fun and laughs, both Bob McNea and Art Cervi joined the ranks of the many men (such as national weatherman Willard Scott), who earned the distinction of playing Bozo the Clown, each doing it in his own unique way!

Art Cervi: "I can tell you in all honesty it was a labor of love!"

Oopsy

The fact that he was appearing at the Christmas Carnival, I was tugging at the hem of my mother's skirt for quite a while. It was like, 'Mom, we gotta go!' Oopsy took precedence over Santa Claus any day of the week.
—MARK NOWOTARSKI, Detroit TV fan

When WWJ-TV made the decision to cancel its eight-year run of *Bozo the Clown* in 1967, the program's star, Bob McNea, had no idea that the station's termination of the famous clown would propel him into a whole new arena of creativity. McNea recalls the day he received the bad news that turned out to be a blessing in disguise.

Bob McNea: "They called me into the studio one day, and the program director, Ian Harrower, said, 'Bob, we're gonna cancel the *Bozo* show but not you.' He says, 'We want you to replace yourself.'"

Originally, Harrower wanted McNea to revive Moppets the Clown from his *Mickey Mouse Club* days in the 1950s. However, due to copyright and other legal technicalities, Moppets would have to stay locked in the trunk permanently. As disappointing as that may have been for Harrower, McNea presented him with an alternative.

Bob McNea: "I said, 'I do have a character in mind; let me work on it. How long do we have?' He said, 'Two weeks.' So I hurried up, had a costume made, and then made a 10- or 15-minute tape of the character . . . I came out and said, 'Hi, it's me . . . Oopsy the Clown. I got a new suit and a haircut, do you like it?' Well, they laughed like hell at the station. The program people thought that was hilarious! So they decided, 'Okay, we like it, let's go with Oopsy.'"

The death of Bozo at WWJ-TV gave birth to Oopsy at the old studio on Lafayette Boulevard in Downtown Detroit. But how would the sta-

Oopsy the Clown (Bob McNea). (Courtesy Bob McNea.)

tion make the transition? Why is Bozo leaving and who's this new clown anyway? Why is he here? What happened to Bozo? The Channel 4 staff knew they'd have a lot to explain to their loyal Bozo audience, so, with McNea's input, here's how it all went down.

Bob McNea: "This was the gag . . . Bozo decides to call his cousin Oopsy to come look after the boys and girls while he [Bozo] takes off with the circus. We did a split screen; this was when tape first came in. First we taped the part with Bozo calling his cousin Oopsy on the phone, just a one-sided conversation, then the next morning we taped the half of Oopsy for the split screen, and it worked like a charm. Then we had Bozo leave, saying, 'Well, I gotta go. I can't wait anymore.' He goes out the door . . . then there's a knock and the door opens a crack, 'Bozo? It's me, Oopsy. Where are you? I guess I must've missed him.' And Oopsy comes in . . . it was beautiful.

"People would call up the station and say, 'We know that's the same guy who played Bozo.' And the instructions were to say, 'Yes, he got a new suit and a haircut, do you like it?' We never denied it . . . didn't you used to play Bozo? Play who? And they'd laugh. Our slogan was 'Now it's Oopsy for those who think young!'"

For the next 12 years, *Oopsy Daisy* captured the attention of youngsters all over the Metro area who awoke when the sun came up on Saturday and Sunday mornings.

Miracle Grow

With the restraints of a manufactured and franchised clown washed away for good, Bob McNea was free to develop his new clown any way he desired. Looking back to his own childhood in the 1930s, McNea's grandmother would be the inspiration for the clown's name and signature line.

Bob McNea: "My grandmother was German, and she used to say to us when we were kids, she'd pick us up and say, 'Oopsy-daisy.' Upsy-daisy is what she said, but to me it always sounded like oopsy-daisy. So 'upsy' didn't look right but o-o-p-s-y . . . hey, that looks pretty good."

As appealing as the name was for McNea, the stem that rooted from the 1930s needed more growth in order to move through the airwaves and blossom in the hearts of Motor City children. It was 1967, the Summer of Love, with "flower power" everywhere . . . hence the seed of a brilliant idea was planted in McNea's brain for a striking costume pattern that would reflect the sign of the times in the spirit of his grandmother's phrase.

Bob McNea: "At that time, kids were sticking daisies on their Volkswagens and garbage pails and everything else. So, I thought the guy's gotta wear a flowerpot hat with daisies coming out of the top. So I designed the hat and the costume. Those are daisy petals around the sleeves and collar, daisy buttons, and a daisy patch on the back."

Avid *Oopsy* fan, John Hilt, otherwise known as Gonzo the Clown, recalls the uniqueness of the costume.

John Hilt: "I remember the green and yellow costume; it was always bright, [so] Oopsy was the one that stood out more than anything—the set and the characters. He stood out more because of his green and yellow suit and his checkered shoes. His shoes were large, and when he would walk you could hear a clomp, clomp in his step. You could hear him, and it made a difference."

The Greenhouse

Like the brightness of his costume, McNea designed a set that matched the colors of Oopsy's wardrobe . . . lots of greens and yellows.

Bob McNea: "The idea was there would be a counter with shelves at the back and it was supposedly an empty store. Oopsy, who had retired from the circus, decided to come and live in Daisyville. So he lives in this old store—he doesn't sell anything, but that's where he lives. There are a table and chairs [by the window and] a counter with a cash register that doesn't really work, though it has a crank on the side of it."

Additionally, there was an old-fashioned wall phone with a daisy-petal mouthpiece, for telephone bits, mounted to the right of the counter. Next to the phone was a storeroom closet door jamb draped with a green and yellow checkered curtain. The closet was key when Oopsy needed to fish out a prop for an upcoming skit. And there were balloons painted on the walls. The set was constructed as a storefront, but the decor had to be daisy fresh.

Bits and Pieces

Maximizing his showbiz expertise to its fullest, Bob McNea planned a clown show that would have it all . . . a little something for every child's enjoyment.

Bob McNea: "We had bits of business, puppets, marionettes, a magic segment, a song segment, and a craft segment."

Wrapped around Felix the Cat cartoons, Oopsy's main shtick, like that of most clowns, was good clean comedy for the kids. Retired WWJ director Jim Breault, along with McNea, outline some of the typical Oopsy gags.

Jim Breault: "He would pantomime a record, like, for example, 'Puff the Magic Dragon.' When the word *sea* came in, 'lives by the sea,' you'd hear a roar of seawater and we'd hit him with water."

Bob McNea: "Every time I played the calliope, it would explode at the end and all these worms would shoot out of the tubes."

But not everything about the happy-go-lucky clown was intended to be humorous. Some kids, particularly those who were accustomed to the liveliness of Bozo, viewed Oopsy as reserved. Fans John Hilt and Joe Humeniuk explain.

John Hilt: "Where Bozo was more of a circus clown, I found Oopsy to be practical . . . he ran a business kind of deal; he was in a store. Oopsy really didn't have a sidekick, [unlike] Bozo, who relied on sidekicks mostly. Oopsy was more of a straight clown."

Joe Humeniuk: "I remember Oopsy was just kind of an odd clown; I didn't quite understand or get what Oopsy was really all about. It just seemed like an odd show. It seemed more like he'd show kids how to make things. I'd see arts and crafts; making little houses with Popsicle sticks and it was kind of like an educational thing."

Passive, funny, instructional, whatever . . . Oopsy was a gentle soul, whose soft nasally voice and kind demeanor were soothing to children who were often intimidated by clowns . . . most of the time, that is . . .

John Hilt: "I remember what always scared me was he would walk out from the stage into the camera and go, 'We'll be right back after these messages' or something like that. And I was always scared because I thought he was coming to get me, so I jumped behind the couch. 'He's coming to get me . . . he's coming to get me' For some reason, I could never figure out why, I got scared, but when the show would come back on, my eyes were glued to the TV again: 'Oh, he's back.' "

Pouches and Puppets

Joining Oopsy on-camera was a goofy-looking mailman reminiscent of the Keystone Kops. With a saggy oversized mailbag slung over the shoulder of a uniform that didn't fit, Mr. Pouch was an eccentric man who sprouted a walrus mustache underneath a twisted cap. Usually when Mr. Pouch arrived at the store's doorstep it was to deliver mail, but his visits always evolved into a quirky skit at the expense of Oopsy. Much of the success for the Mr. Pouch bits was attributed to the man behind the sack. Jim Breault remembers Daisyville's comedic postal carrier.

Jim Breault: "Jerry Snyder was Mr. Pouch. He was the station's booth announcer upstairs, and he was funny. He and Bob worked well together—they played off each other."

Along with Mr. Pouch, *Oopsy Daisy* had a trio of regulars in the way of puppets who inhabited the store, as Bob McNea and John Hilt describe.

Bob McNea: "There's a mouse that lives in the cash register—that's Miser Mouse. And the chicken sleeps in a box up behind the counter on a shelf. They were all cute and funny: Miser Mouse, Squiggly Wiggly Worm, and Henrietta Peck."

Mr. Pouch instructs Oopsy on the finer points of bicycling.
(Courtesy Bob McNea.)

John Hilt: "Squiggly Wiggly Worm, from what I do remember . . . was a worm that lived in a flowerpot. He was always trying to be smarter than Oopsy was in conversation, but Oopsy would always come out winning."

Bob McNea: "[The plan] was to come up with ideas that nobody else had. We watched other kids' shows, thinking who has a chicken on the show called Henrietta Peck? Nobody!"

John Hilt: "They were all done by Frances Kay, Bob's wife. His wife designed all the puppets, and that's where she became involved in the show."

Near the end of the Detroit run, Frances Kay McNea also appeared on-camera as the milk lady, Dairy Dora. Outfitted in a pink uniform, Dora would always drop off a quart of Oopsy's favorite grade of milk— skim.

Daisyville

John Hilt: "They showed a cityscape [on the program intro] that was supposed to be Daisyville. Then they showed him, and he would walk past this big picture window and there were flowers in the window. He would walk in through the door and greet the kids."

Bringing Daisyville to life on-screen was the job of retired WWJ director Jerry Burke, who remembers the day it happened.

Jerry Burke: "Bob hired the station crew to do an opening. We spent one whole day in the big studio down there with a big setup of going through a little village that's built up. We just dollied a camera and did a truck shot along the edge of this city model that was probably 12 x 8 feet. It was the same thing Mr. Rogers did. Bob used the opening we taped that day for years."

Burke and his crew not only pleased McNea with their depiction of the fictitious community, but they even fooled some of the kids at home into believing it was real. Case in point . . .

John Hilt: "When I would think about it, I thought, 'Gee, this was so neat as a child; if this place exists, I wanna go there . . . I wanna go to Daisyville.' After the show was done, I used to get ready to go to church with my family on Sunday mornings. When I would come back [home], I'd still be thinking about the Oopsy show. I'm like about six or seven years old, and I always used to tell my dad that I wanted to go to Daisyville. 'Dad, can we go to Daisyville for summer vacation?' And my dad didn't know what I was talking about."

Rolling Tape

Unlike many of the local shows from the 1960s and earlier, *Oopsy Daisy* had the benefit of being taped. Much of it had to do with the program's weekend time slot. The production staff, with the exception of the news department, didn't work on the weekends. This meant that *Oopsy* would have to be taped in advance for the Saturday and Sunday broadcasts. Jerry Burke and retired WWJ stage manager Bob Stackpoole roll us through a normal day of production.

Jerry Burke: "There really wasn't much planning on it. I'd go down to Oopsy's dressing room downstairs in the basement of the building where they had some old dressing rooms. While he was putting his makeup on [which took 20 minutes], we'd chat about what sequence he was going to tape with his friends, like Henrietta Peck. We'd spend about a half hour going through it like that, and that was the amount of preprogram planning that we did. We never rehearsed anything."

Bob Stackpoole: "Production facilities and time allowed to use them were pretty limited at the station. If you had a one-hour show to tape, you were lucky to get two hours from start to finish with the crew allocated to you. They'd have something before and after, so Bob was pretty well expected to have things ready to go when he came in there. It was squeezed in between [the evening] newscasts."

Jerry Burke: "Each show went the same. He saw the same characters, went to the same places on the set . . . so we knew where the movements were going to be just from what particular character he was visiting. There wasn't much to it; it wasn't complicated at all. We never did any editing. I don't remember any full-out disasters on that show."

The Daisyville Art Gallery

One of the biggest highlights of the show was Oopsy's routine visits to the Daisyville Art Gallery. At the midpoint of each episode, he would always take a walk over to see what was happening at the gallery.

John Hilt: "He would walk out the front door of the store—off set. Then they would show a picture of the gallery/museum, and then they would show the artwork with the children's names and ages."

Bob McNea: "I was sitting on a stool with two boards and two cameras and a monitor. I was very close to the monitor. I never paid any attention to the cameras, just the monitor. As the pictures came up, I'd spend a second or two on them. I told the director to start out on the kid's name in a close-up, then zoom back and fill the screen with that picture so I could say, 'Here's a drawing from Billy so-and-so who lives in so-and-so, and it's a pretty picture.' We knew how many it would take to do a four-minute segment."

Much of the popularity of this segment rested on its interaction with the audience. Kids had the opportunity to send in a drawing of anything they could think of and it would appear on the program. Well, most of them anyway . . . right Bob?

Bob McNea: "The stacks of boxes and bags of mail . . . it was physically impossible to go through them all; we just couldn't."

And, while the cameras panned across the boards from left to right, row by row, as Oopsy read the names, classical music could be heard playing in the background. Why classical pieces instead of children's tunes or pop music? Was it because art and the symphony tend to go hand in hand? Let's ask the man who made the call.

Bob McNea: "I said let's get away from the orangutan stuff and do something nice."

Oopsy in Public

Watching Oopsy on TV was one thing, but when the chance to see him in person came along the fans just had to be there! Oopsy followers Mark Nowotarski and John Hilt recount their off-screen impressions of the flowered clown.

Mark Nowotarski: "Where Oopsy was there had to literally be several hundred children ranging in age from still in diapers to kids in their pre-teens. The place just went wild! Everybody was with their moms . . . just a tremendous following. Oopsy was very kind, very courteous, and everything was as orderly as possible. Oopsy could control a crowd."

John Hilt: "Bob is a tall man [6'1"] for most clowns. When you finally see the man in public and you're a stone's throw away, you look at him and go, 'Whoa, he is tall!' That surprised a lot of people about him. I was about 10 years old when I first saw him in a [street] parade, and he came out with the Daisyville Marching Band; he had a baton and was conducting. I looked and went, 'Wow, he's taller than everybody in the band.' He commanded a presence, and everybody took note of him because he was so tall."

Years later John had another opportunity to see Oopsy at a shopping mall, and this time it would be a lot more personal.

John Hilt: "I finally got to meet this man, and he was dressed all clean and crisp. I was in awe of this man. I said, 'Hi, I'm John, and I became a clown because of you.' So basically I met my other idol. I became a clown because of Oopsy and Bozo."

Oopsy Leaves Detroit

John Hilt: "I remember Oopsy at the end [of the show]; he would leave the store and walk past the window and wave."

In 1979, Oopsy waved through the window for the last time in Detroit. After 12 years in a store that sold nothing, the management at the new

WDIV-TV decided it was time for Oopsy to close up shop in Motown. In the year prior to *Oopsy*'s cancellation at Channel 4, McNea clinched a deal with CKCO-TV in Kitchener, Ontario, to repot his lovable clown in a new home, one that would last for the next 15 years. Jim Breault and Bob McNea have some final thoughts about *Oopsy Daisy*.

Jim Breault: "My memories of Bob McNea are of how hard he worked on the job. He worked all the time on that character, and he was doing what he loved to do. He was always professional, always a gentleman, and very easy to work with at all times."

Bob McNea: "I always had fun doing it, and that's the thing . . . if you can't have any fun doing something, then don't do it because you can't fool the kids. They know whether you're being sincere and whether you're having fun . . . if they can feel you're having fun, then they'll have fun, too!"

Let's Dance!

4

Swingin' Time

Swingin' Time came on at four o'clock in the afternoon. That's when
I learned how fast I could run. After the school bell rang, I ran home
and would be there just in time to catch the start of *Swingin' Time.*
They showed all the Motown artists, which was so cool because at
the time, of course, they all lived here. It had all the latest dance
moves, and it was truly our version of *American Bandstand.*
—GREG RUSSELL, air personality, WDWB-TV

If you can recall the day Mary Wilson, Florence Ballard, and Diana Ross
received keys to the city, then odds are you saw it on the hottest hour-
long dance-party show in Motown: *Swingin' Time.* From the day it aired
in 1963 as *Teen Town* until it faded out in 1971 as *The Lively Spot,* the
studios of CKLW-TV were packed every afternoon with local teens from
both sides of the river. On a black and white "chessboard" floor, they
swiveled their hips and tapped their toes to the beat of the latest records
and live performances by the music industry's top-selling artists.

Hosted by "Detroit's oldest teenager," veteran disc jockey Robin Seymour, *Swingin' Time* epitomized the Motor City's youth culture during
the most turbulent decade of the twentieth century. When television's
first generation, the baby boomers, were entering adolescence in the
1960s, it was imperative that local programming grow up with them. And
Swingin' Time did just that. It had a party format that catered specifically
to the fickle interests of teenagers, as Detroit TV fan Marci Wojciechowski remembers.

Marci Wojciechowski: "We'd watch it to see the newest dances and to
hear the latest songs . . . catch the latest styles and hairdos—the bee-
hive—and to see cute guys! When you were a teenager, you watched it

Host Robin Seymour greets some of the *Swingin' Time* dancers backstage. (Courtesy Frank Quinn.)

for all the teenage reasons. Robin Seymour was a nice, friendly guy, and even though he wasn't a teenager we accepted him as one."

Although it wasn't the first dance show produced on Detroit television, it was the first to showcase a homegrown phenomenon that was about to take the world by storm in 1963—MOTOWN! Well before *American Bandstand, Shindig,* and *Hullabaloo* ever heard the Motown Sound, *Swingin' Time* had the honor of being the premier venue for some of the label's supergroups. *Swingin' Time* fan Larry Dlusky recalls a couple of them.

Larry Dlusky: "There were so many times that the Supremes appeared on the show, the Temptations . . . The first time I saw a performance of "My Girl" was when they did it on *Swingin' Time*."

Bobbin' with Robin

When Freddie Cannon sang "The Dedication Song" on *Swingin' Time* in 1966, he shouted a few rounds of, "Oh yeah!" at the end. As he encouraged the kids to raise their arms and shout on every "Oh yeah," an older

Robin Seymour in the 1950s. (Courtesy Robin Seymour.)

man wearing a sport coat and vest stood on a riser with his arms in the air to cheer along with the crowd. Dancing his way in and out of the acts, Robin Seymour often portrayed himself as one of the gang. His connection with teenagers was unlike that of any other local television personality of his era. In many ways, it was much better than that of his network counterpart, Dick Clark.

Even though Clark was a radio disc jockey prior to hosting *American Bandstand,* he was unfamiliar with the escalating teen scene. Much of his initial success hinged on the fact that he befriended teenagers by asking them what they thought would be the next hit record, the next cool dance, or the next fashion statement. But, unlike Clark, who was pretty green at the outset of his *Bandstand* debut, Seymour was a seasoned pro at gauging the whimsical trends of adolescent pop culture by the time he landed his TV gig. To elaborate, here's the man himself, Robin Seymour.

Robin Seymour: "I was a disc jockey, that's all I was. I dug music. I was young when I started and I wasn't far from high school kids and I dug everything that was there. I prided myself in having an ear. For the most part, when I heard something, I would think, 'Man, this is gonna be a big record!' I was always excited about what I did!"

Seymour's radio career began on June 1, 1947, at a tiny AM station, WKMH, located in the attic of the Gagnon Furniture Company in Dearborn, Michigan.

Robin Seymour: "I started at 90 cents an hour, and my folks thought I was crazy. In those days, I lived on Taylor and Linwood by Clairmount on the West Side of Detroit. To get to Dearborn, I'd have to take the streetcar to make a connection to a bus that would go down to Michigan Avenue so I could open up the station at six o'clock in the morning. It took me about two hours, so I'd get on the streetcar around 3:30 or 4:00 in the morning. I did that six days a week until February 1948."

That year Seymour got his lucky break when the station owner, Fred Knorr, assigned him the two to six afternoon air shift. It was then that he adopted a gimmick that still remains fresh in the minds of his loyal listeners.

Robin Seymour: "When I came on the air, a buddy of mine—one of the [record] distributors—said, 'You gotta have a gimmick . . . like Ed McKenzie is Jack the Bellboy.' He said, 'Robin . . . what goes with Robin? Bobbin'! Bobbin' with Robin!' Then George Weiss and Bennie Benjamin wrote a song in 1956, 'Bobbin' with the Robin,' and it was recorded by the Four Lads with the Percy Faith Orchestra. And that became my theme song."

With the passing of the big band era, a new sound unfamiliar to white audiences captured Seymour's attention—rhythm and blues. By the mid-1950s, Bobbin' Robin was one of the first deejays in town to regularly play "black" records on a predominately "white" radio station, thus becoming a leader in the Motor City's introduction to rock and roll!

Having the right instinct to foresee the success of rock and roll, some might say he missed the boat when it came to predicting the future of the music's king, Elvis Presley. In 1956, Seymour stirred up a bit of controversy when he blasted the former truck driver from Tupelo, Mississippi, on the air; proclaiming him a surefire flop.

Robin Seymour: "I got headlines on that; it was a gimmick. In 1956, here's this guy, Elvis Presley, who appeared on *Ed Sullivan* shaking his hips. I got on the air the next day and said, 'I think that's absolutely terrible! It's sacrilegious that they allow anybody to do that on TV . . . this guy will never make it . . . he's a fad!' I had 200 hundred kids in front of my house that night on their bikes with signs: 'Don't listen to Bobbin' with Robin! Robin stinks! Robin doesn't like Elvis!' It was a gimmick

. . . it got headlines in the *Detroit Times*. So there you go, it's absolutely true . . . but really I thought [Elvis] was absolutely terrific!"

After more than a decade of spinning records on the radio, Bobbin' Robin was growing tired of the medium and dreamed of graduating into the more glamorous world of television. His dream would come true in 1963 at a hip stopover he helped to create called *Teen Town*.

From *Teen Town* to *Swingin' Summertime*

In the late 1950s and early 1960s, many local television stations across the country began to duplicate the dance-party format made popular by *American Bandstand*. Given that Detroit was the fourth-largest television market in the country in the late 1950s, the timing was right for Motor City deejays to launch their own dance shows. Among the earliest were *Ed McKenzie's Saturday Party* and *Dance Party,* hosted by Bud Davies. By 1963, WXYZ introduced *Club 1270* to a new generation of teenagers who were still in grammar school when the genre was born.

At WKMH radio in Dearborn that same year, Robin Seymour was ready to pursue a career in television. He and his friend, Art Cervi, the station's music director, hoped to hop on the teeny-bopper bandwagon with a program of their own, *Teen Town*. And, just like *American Bandstand* or the *Hollywood-a-Go-Go* out of Los Angeles, or, for that matter, Channel 7's *Club 1270*, *Teen Town* highlighted the latest records, dances, and fashions along with live performances by recording artists. But there was one thematic difference: every show would feature a salute to a different local high school. Kids from the high school of the week were invited to dance and be interviewed on the show, thus allowing for an easy transition in audience.

To produce the program, Seymour and Cervi teamed up with an advertising agent, Jerry Kurtis and a representative from the Electronics Institute of Detroit, Sam Gardiner. The four of them formed Teen Town Productions, Inc., and immediately began strolling their new "baby" around to the local TV stations. Their goal was to find a facility that would produce and air their independent project. As Robin Seymour recalls, a new general manager at CKLW gave them the break they needed.

Robin Seymour: "We went to Channel 9 and met Ed Metcalf, the general manager. He was from RKO General in New York, and he was looking to take the TV station in another direction, [one that] would mean something in the market other than just Captain Jolly, Poopdeck Paul, and Jingles. I went with Art and met him up at his office and said, 'This is who I am . . . I've been on the air for years, and I want to put together a show for the kids . . . there's nothing like it on now except for *Club 1270* on Channel 7 . . . once a week we'll salute different high schools, and I've got 7-Up, Federal's Department Stores, The Electronics Institute of Detroit, and the Patricia Stevens Modeling School . . . so I have commercials I can put on.' The show was already coming in with several thousand dollars worth of advertising, and Metcalf said, 'Let's do it!'

"*Teen Town* went on for a while. It was very successful, and a [year and a half] later Metcalf came to me and said, 'In the summer, we'd like to put you on and have you do *Swingin' Summertime,* but it can't be an independent deal. It's got to be for Channel 9, and we'll pay you to do the show every day.'"

In the summer of 1965, Teen Town Productions was dissolved upon Seymour and Cervi's acceptance of employment at CKLW. While Robin hosted *Swingin' Summertime,* Art became the station's talent coordinator and head of guest relations, which basically meant that he was in charge of recruiting people, whether they were talent or audience participants, for all of CKLW's programs.

Swingin' Summertime continued the dance-party format of *Teen Town* with the exception of the high school salutes. The new show opened with a shot of a girl seated on a lawn swing, hence *Swingin' Summertime.*

Robin Seymour: "We'd have to draw straws when kids would come to the show because the girls would fight; they all wanted to sit on that swing."

The shows became a combo of both indoor and outdoor performances. The indoor set had a patio theme, with lawn furniture and a sunshine "smile" painted on the backdrop. Whenever possible, weather permitting, the show went on the road to scenic locations such as Bob-Lo Island for fun in the sun with the stars.

Flashing back to late October 1963, WKMH-AM 1310, which stood for Knorr, McCoy, and Hanson, was about to undergo a change in ownership. Fred Knorr had bought out his partners and changed the call letters to reflect his name . . . WKNR. "Keener 13," as it was officially nicknamed, was still Seymour's home base during his *Teen Town* days. The dual exposure boosted his radio ratings to the top of the chart in the nine to noon time slot. By the summer of 1965, tension was brewing between Keener's general manager, Walter Patterson, and Seymour over his "cross-promotions." After 18 years of loyal service going back to the infancy of the station, Bobbin' Robin was confronted with an ultimatum.

Robin Seymour: "Ed Metcalf had foresight. He said, 'Look Robin, what you can do on your program [is] every time you finish your morning [radio] show say, 'Don't forget to watch us on Channel 9 this afternoon at four o'clock.' And when you finish your TV show [say] don't forget to tune me in every morning on Keener radio, nine to noon.' Great plug! You're reaching your audience. Well, Patterson called me in, and he says, 'You're paying more attention to TV than radio, so you gotta make up your mind . . . you're either going to do TV or you're going to do this.' In those days, you didn't cross-plug. He said, 'You can't do that. I don't want you to do it.' So I said, 'Okay then, I'll leave.' He said, 'You can't just quit. You're number one in the market from nine to noon.' I said, 'Well, what do you want?' He says, 'You gotta give us six weeks.' 'Okay.'

"So I left and it was one week before the [*Swingin' Summertime*] show was supposed to go off the air and Metcalf tried to open up something. At that time, CKLW was in the process of making changes. He said, 'We'll have a deal for you.' We had lunch at the [London] Chop House, and he said, 'We'll put you on five days a week and on Saturday you'll have a special production-type show and we'll call it *Swingin' Time*. For the first three to six months, I want to put you on [CKLW radio] from four to six. Your [TV] show will go from three to four, and then you'll go on radio from four to six because we want to build up your name.' I said, 'Great!' Well that only lasted a few months and they pulled me off the radio thing."

Dance, Dance, Dance

In the fall of 1965, *Swingin' Time* was off and running—strong! Reclaiming its original four o'clock airtime, Seymour continued his tradition of inviting teenagers from all the local high schools to join the party. Just like the earlier *Teen Town,* kids were asked to bring pennants from their schools for permanent display behind Robin's podium. Any teen that showed up not only had a chance to "bust their moves" on the floor; they were also interviewed and asked to rate the latest records in a "Make It or Break It" segment.

Unlike many of the other dance programs, both in and out of town, which auditioned dancers, *Swingin' Time* was a lot less stringent. It was the one show that gave every kid a fair shake. Art Cervi and Robin Seymour explain.

Art Cervi: "There was no audition to get on the show. A lot of the really good dancers we kept inviting back, but most of them would just show up. We'd get singles, brothers and sisters, and couples. We had a nice cross section. If we knew we could put 50 kids in there, then we would take 50. We tried not to send anybody home, so we'd put them in the bleachers, where they could see the show but they weren't on the actual dance floor."

Robin Seymour: "The only barrier was that the kid had to be 15 to get on the show. But it's amazing how many 12 and 13 year olds sneaked in and many of their mothers would be sitting in the lobby. And they would say, 'Robin, you gotta shoot my daughter a little more.'"

Of all the kids that strutted across the floor over the years, were there any that stood out? Seymour acknowledges the top three.

Robin Seymour: "The Tiptons—Lester and Leslie—they were probably the most famous. They were a black couple and great dancers; they were on the show every single day and the Saturday show. Lester and Leslie would do things, and the other kids would try to copy them. They entered this national contest that Dick Clark had and won . . . they won two Pontiac automobiles, so they were well known on the program. There was also Lana Drouillard, a sweetheart from Windsor. She would get a couple hundred letters a month, and her sister was also on every day. There were some others, but the most popular were Lester, Leslie, and Lana."

Saturday editions of *Swingin' Time* had an entirely different format from what was aired during the week.

Robin Seymour: "We had no dancing on the Saturday show; it was like an *Ed Sullivan* type thing. We would maybe take the best of what we had during the week, and it was all artists performing. We'd tape it Saturday morning, and it would go on the air Saturday evening. *Swingin' Time* was live on the weekdays."

For all the adolescents either too young or too shy to cross the river to the Windsor studios, *Swingin' Time* Fan Club memberships were available to the many viewers at home, complete with a card that entitled the bearer to a few perks, as noted by Larry Dlusky.

Larry Dlusky: "Being local gave them the ability to issue a card that would give you discounts at different places. And there was a *Swingin' Time* card that you could get, and it got you discounts at different restaurants or clubs, like maybe 20 percent off at the Walled Lake Casino or something."

Seeing the Stars

Be it the dancers or the music that caught your attention, nothing was more spectacular than to see the biggest names in the music biz on stage on Riverside Drive. Anybody who was somebody made an appearance on *Swingin' Time*. Whether an artist was coming to town to promote a

new record or as part of a concert tour, he or she took the time to perform a number or two on the program.

Art Cervi: "This was almost like a 'must do' show when you came to
Detroit because Detroit was a 'happening city.'"

Larry Dlusky: "The artists would come all dressed up like they would
normally be if they were appearing on *The Ed Sullivan Show,* and they
were performing 'here.' You got out-of-state talent that was coming
through to do a concert . . . I can recall Frankie Valli being on when
'Can't Take My Eyes Off You' was first breaking around May of 1967."

Who can forget the back-to-back performances of Johnny Rivers
doing "Under Your Spell Again" and "Secret Agent Man" engulfed in a
sea of vibrant dancers? Or the tenderness of Dee Dee Sharp in her ballad
of "I Really Love You"? How about the excitement generated by the
Everly Brothers when they stood above the crowd on a high platform to
sing a medley of "Wake Up Little Susie," "All I Have to Do Is Dream,"
and "Bird Dog" before breaking into a rendition of "Cathy's Clown"?

There was just no telling who would show up. It could be Bobby
Goldsboro one day, then the New Christy Minstrels the next . . . or one-
hit wonders like Norma Tanega or Jackie Lee singing their forgotten
songs, "Walkin' My Cat Named Dog" and "The Duck." Even comedians
stopped by for a chance to entertain the hometown television audience.
Tony Micale, lead vocalist of Detroit's own quintet, the Reflections,
recalls when his group was on the program with a certain impressionist
who was on the cusp of stardom.

Tony Micale: "We were on *Swingin' Time,* believe it or not, with Rich
Little. He was in the dressing room with us and we were talking to him
and he was doing all his different voices. We didn't know who he was
because he was fairly new at the time. He came from Canada and was a
big star there, or at least he was on his way to becoming a star, so they
put him on the show with us. But that's what it was like; it was always
casual. You never knew who you were gonna meet there. We were on
with Paul Anka once, too."

With all of the major talent that entered and exited the studios of
CKLW, one might wonder about the ego trips of the stars. Were these
entertainers, many of whom appeared on *American Bandstand, Shindig,
Hullabaloo,* and other national programs, difficult to work with? Was
appearing on a local Detroit show beneath them? Were they as demanding as the stars you read about in the tabloids today? As the program's
talent coordinator and head of guest relations, Art Cervi ought to know.

Art Cervi: "What was really amazing was the bigger the name the eas-
ier they were to deal with, believe it or not. I mean people like Pat Boone,
Patti Page, and Frankie Laine knew the value of promotion and what you

Pat Boone sings one of his hits. (Courtesy Marilyn Bond.)

have to do to maintain your popularity. Like I said, in most cases the bigger they were the nicer they were. The ones who would hit sudden stardom were some of the most difficult people you ever had to deal with . . . and you never heard from them again. It was really interesting; it was a study in personalities."

And from the talent's viewpoint, Tony Micale describes the advantages *Swingin' Time* had over those national shows.

Tony Micale: "*Swingin' Time* was more of a party to go to. When we went there, we never felt that we were just an act because we knew everybody . . . we knew the dancers; many of them were the same kids that would come to see us. Art and Robin were always great to us, so we would enjoy going there. Some of the other shows we were really apprehensive about doing, like *American Bandstand* and *Shindig*. Those were national shows, and we were all intimidated by those shows because we didn't know anybody."

The Motown Song

Robin Seymour: "Berry Gordy and I go back to 1957, when I first met him. There was a company that wanted him to start a record label, and I introduced them. Berry thanked me for it, and he said, 'I'm going to start my own record company.' So when I did my TV show it was at the start of Motown in 1963. I am proud to say that every Motown artist ever recorded [in the 1960s] was on my show first! The Supremes, the Temptations, Smokey Robinson and the Miracles, Stevie Wonder, Martha and the Vandellas, the Marvelettes, Marvin Gaye . . . every act back then was on [and] they made the show! They were the hottest up and coming recording company in the country . . . the kids just took to them like crazy . . . it was the first big 'Detroit's own.'"

Back in the 1950s and into the 1960s, disc jockeys used to host record hops on Friday, Saturday, and Sunday nights at the local high schools and dance halls. This lucrative business not only benefited the deejays assigned to them, but they proved to be a valuable outlet for talent exposure as well as an opportunity for kids to see the stars up close. One of the people who understood the power of the record hops was Berry Gordy. As Art Cervi and Motown superstar Mary Wilson of the Supremes fame remember, Robin Seymour became a tremendous resource in the promotion of Gordy's new ensemble.

Art Cervi: "Berry Gordy would come to us and say, 'I've got a new group, and I really need some exposure for them. Is there anything you can do?' And his new groups were the Supremes, the Temps, the Four Tops . . . doing record hops! You tell that to people today and they think you're nuts. Yes, they went on to become megastars, but we had them when they were kids."

Mary Wilson: "Robin Seymour used to always have us on his record hops. He was a really fun kind of guy, and he always requested to have us. I think we were still the Primettes when we first met him because we were doing all the local shows and didn't have a hit record out. He was always good about calling us to come and perform."

Once the Supremes had a record, the hits just kept coming until they became the label's number-one act. Retired CKLW director Neil Addison, who directed many of the *Swingin' Time* shows, looks back with particular fondness at how the legendary trio touched him personally.

Neil Addison: "The Supremes were great ladies to work with, and it was a real thrill! I really enjoyed that. As a matter of fact, one of my favorite memories of all time was Diana Ross coming into the control room after a show and planting a big smacker on me. I think I turned four shades of red, but that's my claim to fame—Diana Ross kissed me!"

Already an international sensation by 1966, Mary, Flo, and Diana returned to the studio of CKLW once more for a very "unusual" appearance.

Mary Wilson: "Robin Seymour had us on *Swingin' Time* doing a *This Is Your Life* kind of show once where Berry Gordy came on."

Robin Seymour: "We did a salute to the Supremes, and Berry was on the show; this was on a Saturday. About a week or two before we were to go on, Berry's office called and said, 'The girls cannot sing on the show. We have a contractual deal [of some sort] that they cannot be on anybody's show to sing but they can be there for the interviews.' So what we did is we had a couple of three-gal groups; one was a white group and one was a black group, and they lip-synced to all of the Supremes' stuff. And it was the cutest thing in the world. The Supremes were sitting there, and every time the [camera] flashed back to them, they were swaying and lip-syncing to it, too, but they couldn't get up and perform. So it worked out real good."

Hailed as "Supremes' Day," the girls sat in swivel chairs alongside the dance floor dressed to the hilt with bouquets of flowers on their laps. In addition to the two "pretend" Supremes, Mary, Flo, and Diana enjoyed performances from Johnny Tillotson, singing his latest single, "Our World," and fellow Motown trio the Marvelettes, who warned everyone "Don't Mess with Bill." And of course the mayor, Jerome P. Cavanagh, was there to present each of the Supremes with her own key to the city.

Performances

Swingin' Time was a low-budget, local show, but you would never know it by the look of the performances. The stagehands at Channel 9 exercised an enormous amount of care when it came to showcasing the stars. The sets had to be every bit as rich as the million-dollar artist appearing on them. A series of backdrops, lighting effects, and props were in constant demand to reflect both the mood of the song and the personality of the performer.

A great example is when Frankie Avalon covered the popular love ballad "Moon River." To create a romantic night in the park, the perfect atmosphere for such a song, Avalon was seated on a wooden bench in front of a nighttime riverfront cityscape. The studio lights were dimmed, and a lamppost was placed next to the bench to simulate the only source of luminance, other than the moon, on a peaceful summer night. Another example is when Motown diva Kim Weston sang her hit "Take Me in Your Arms." As she was appearing in a glittering gown, a "cosmic" backdrop was brilliantly chosen to compliment the many "starlike" sparkles on her dress and suggest that her dynamic voice was out of this world.

With all of the controversy surrounding lip-synced performances these days, the pressure for artists to sing live is overwhelming. Even the public access cable channels run the risk of being blasted for allowing singers to mouth the words. High budget, low budget, no budget . . . audiences today are unforgiving when it comes to lip-syncing. Turning back the hands of time, 35 or 40 years ago it was commonplace.

Mary Wilson: "The majority of those performances were lip-syncing. The show couldn't afford to have a band there, and we couldn't afford to hire one either. That's why most of those [dance] shows were lip-synced."

For the most part the guests on *Swingin' Time* either lip-synced or sang live to a band track . . . but not always.

Art Cervi: "I can remember going outside with Paul Revere and the Raiders. When you come out of the lobby doors of CKLW, you're under a concrete canopy with brick posts every so often. The canopy comes out and makes a 90-degree turn into the parking lot. We actually did the show outside. We brought all the cameras and everything else outside. We had Paul Revere and the Raiders up on this concrete canopy, and they performed live!"

The Summer of 1967

Art Cervi: "We used to do a Swingin' Time Review at the Fox Theater with a lot of mixed [professional and amateur] acts. In fact, we were there doing a review in 1967—smack in the middle of the riots!"

As unpleasant of a memory as the 1967 riots were for the city, the morning of July 23 started out the same as any other Sunday for Robin Seymour. Heading down to the Fox Theater on Woodward Avenue, he looked forward to the review that day; Martha Reeves and the Vandellas were scheduled to appear. Little did he, or anybody else going to the theater that afternoon, realize what a historic performance it would be.

Robin Seymour: "We got down there early on Sunday; we heard there were some problems Saturday night on Twelfth Street—a shooting or something of that nature—and didn't pay that much attention to it. The first show I think was at 1:00 p.m., and then the second one was at 3:00. Well, the first show is usually only half filled. By 3:00, which is always full, that day it was still only half full with the same kids from 1:00. We heard some reports that there were riots, and sure enough a couple of policemen came walking up to the stage in the middle of the show. Martha was onstage doing a song, and they stopped the show. They asked the kids to exit quietly to the lobby and their parents would soon be there; they had to close the show. And Martha got up and gave a nice long talk to the kids, 'I'm sure it's temporary . . . don't worry kids, your moms and dads are gonna be here . . . everything is fine, just be comfortable.' We went outside on Woodward Avenue to look, and all we could see were puffs of smoke. The rest, of course, is history.

"The next day we went on the air, and we ran tape. I mentioned on the show something to the effect of, 'Something really terrible has happened to our city and I'm sure everything is gonna be fine.' The next day we went live, but we only had about 15 or 16 kids from Windsor on it. Then slowly kids started coming back."

The Music Must Change

As sad as the summer of 1967 was for Detroit, to the rest of the country it was the Summer of Love! Music was changing drastically. The release of the Beatles' *Sgt. Pepper's Lonely Hearts Club Band* in June of that year altered the direction of rock and roll from snappy little ditties to elaborate studio productions designed more for listening than dancing. Dark groups with deep lyrics such as the Doors and the Grateful Dead from the West Coast were emerging on the American teen scene, leaving the toe-tapping teeny-bopper artists to blow in the wind. Times were indeed changing, and so were the tastes of *Swingin' Time* fans such as Marci Wojciechowski.

Marci Wojciechowski: "I thought the psychedelic music out of San Francisco was cool, so if *Swingin' Time* had anything that came out of California or something else that we didn't usually see that was a big deal to me."

Along with the change in music came an entirely new breed of musicians from our own backyard, ambitiously waiting their turn to shine on the program that had been so instrumental in launching the careers of the Motown artists. Robin Seymour revisits a couple of struggling performers whose television debut just happened to be on *Swingin' Time*.

Robin Seymour: "You may have heard of Ted Nugent and the Amboy Dukes. You may have heard of Bob Seger and the Last Heard . . . With the advent of the bands, practically every band in Detroit was on my show first. It was a stepping stone—a localized national-type show."

The year 1970 brought a close to one of the most turbulent decades in the history of the United States—and for that matter the world. The new year was not only a fresh start for society but for CKLW as well . . . or so it thought.

Robin Seymour: "By 1970, Ed Metcalf had left and they got a new program director and so on. That's when they called me in and said, 'We're giving you 30 days notice . . . we're looking for a more youthful image.' I said, 'I beg your pardon?' And that was it. They gave the show to [CKLW disc jockey] Tom Shannon. The daily show lasted six months and they lost all the commercials for the show, so they canceled it. They kept the Saturday show, and they got George Young."

After Seymour's demise and Tom Shannon's failure to carry the show, Channel 9 turned to a familiar face that appealed to the Detroit youth. George Young had been a repeat guest on *Swingin' Time* for many years. His musical career dates back to the late 1950s, when he made appearances on *Ed McKenzie's Saturday Party:* playing his guitar behind his head and on his shoulders . . . a gimmick Jimi Hendrix employed over a decade later! George's name epitomized his image: young. Although he was balding by the 1960s, he was still very witty, energetic, and full of life, as Neil Addison attests.

Neil Addison: "I remember George as being easily excitable and physically dancing around all over the place all the time."

When Channel 9 began its search for a new host, Young's photo just happened to be in the right place at the right time. He relives the day he got the call.

George Young: "It was a Saturday morning; I was sitting in my condo in Trenton watching television when the phone rang. It was about twelve o'clock in the afternoon. The girl [on the line] says, 'This is CKLW calling. Mr. So-and-so, the station manager, would like to talk to you.' Now, I'm thinking, 'Sure. What the hell does he wanna talk to me for; it's a Saturday?' So, I'm like, 'Mmm-hmm, okay.' He says, 'I was walking to the office, and I noticed your picture on this girl's desk. And I asked her about you; who is this guy?' And she said, 'Oh, this guy comes in and does *Swingin' Time*.' 'Well, what does he do?' 'He's got a band, and he's pretty funny; he's got a great personality, and he tells jokes. Every time he comes on he does something different; it might be a comedy routine or a song.' So she told him.

"He said, 'Well, I'll tell you, as you've probably noticed, we haven't been using Robin because his ratings have been pretty low. So we've been using deejays from CKLW as hosts every week, and we've kind of run out of hosts . . . we'd like to use you until we find somebody. So would you like to have the show next Saturday? You might have to get up early.' I said, 'How about if I slept in the parking lot?' That's how bad I wanted that job!"

Originally hired as a substitute host, Young convinced the management that he could be of greater value to them by acting as the producer also. After Cervi resigned in 1967 to become Bozo the Clown, Seymour's radio trafficker, Olga Chocreff, assumed the duties of booking the guests. By the time Young arrived, Chocreff was ready to call it quits; the program had dramatically strayed from its dance-party theme, and Young felt it needed to get back on track.

George Young: "The show was more of an outlet for hard rock; psychedelic rock groups out of Ann Arbor . . . groups from the Eastwood Gardens type of acts, basically white groups. That wasn't really my bag. I was more into the black music and not really into hard rock. This was a dance-party show, so I didn't think it always had to be in the Top 10. I mean, let's face it, everything in the Top 10 on CKLW radio [at that time] wasn't danceable, especially some of the psychedelic music."

So what if the record's an oldie? Young's theory was that as long as the tune got people movin' and groovin' everything else was irrelevant. Having secured his position as both host and producer, George began booking such performers as George Clinton; Isaac Hayes; and an up and coming Detroiter named Vincent Furnier, better known to the world as Alice Cooper; and a blast from Motown's past, David Ruffin. Young recalls the day he persuaded the former Temptations' vocalist to sing an all-time favorite.

George Young: "I remember when I had David Ruffin after he left the Temptations. I had in my script that he was going to open up with "My Girl." When he walked in and we were having coffee, I said, 'I have you opening with "My Girl."' He said, 'I'm not doing "My Girl." I don't sing it anymore.' I said, 'You don't sing "My Girl"? What do you mean, you don't sing "My Girl" anymore?' He said, 'That's when I was with the Temps; I don't sing it anymore.' He says, 'I'm not gonna sing it; I'm only gonna do songs on my new album.' I said, 'Well, wonderful.' Now, I'm saying to myself, 'You better do "My Girl" . . . I'm worried about the show, not your new album.'

"I said, 'David, I'm a musician, too.' I told him who I was and what I did. I said, 'As far as the people out there watching are concerned, there's only gonna be one guy in the world—forever—that can sing "My Girl" and guess who it is . . . David Ruffin . . . not anybody else. It's your song and nobody else's, and no one can sing it like you! And if you don't sing it like it says on that script . . . do you know how many people are gonna be disappointed, because it's your song. When you die, they're gonna say that's the man of "My Girl."' And he says, 'Really? You really think so? I didn't know that . . . Well then, sure, no problem.'"

In 1971, CKLW retired the name *Swingin' Time* in favor of a title they perceived to have more pizzazz, *The Lively Spot*. Later that year George Young's personal life took an unexpected turn, which forced him to give up the show. Robin Seymour was asked to resume his throne. Unfortunately, the second time around for Seymour would be a very short reign. The days of record hops and TV dance parties, except for *American*

Bandstand, had run its gamut. The once prestigious show was failing to attract the caliber of talent it had become so famous for. The personal touch was gone, and by the end of the year so was *The Lively Spot,* formerly known as *Swingin' Time.*

Robin Seymour: "Guys watched the show because of the girls; it was the beginning of the miniskirt. Girls would watch because these kids would get dressed to the teeth in their outfits. But I would have to say it was a combination of seeing the artists—the stars—watching the dances, seeing the girls, and finding out which records were hot. We played the records, and the kids danced. I loved what I was doing, I loved the kids, and I loved being there every day because it was a lot of fun."

Club 1270

They were the dirtiest bunch of guys I think I'd ever seen. This was at Broadcast House. They were coming out; there was this crummy old-time convertible, and they all piled in it and left . . . that was the Rolling Stones.
   —JIM BURGAN, retired engineer, WXYZ-TV

Ahh . . . springtime . . . the season of change. After a long, harsh winter, the grass grows, flowers bloom, and birds sing as life regenerates itself. And in the spring of 1963, the weekend dances that disappeared on WXYZ-TV with the departure of *Ed McKenzie's Saturday Party* were reborn with the opening of a hot new cabaret called *Club 1270* (pronounced "twelve-seven-oh"). One of the many viewers tuning in to the small-screen discotheque was Detroit TV fan Larry Dlusky, who remembers some of the club's distinct features.

Larry Dlusky: "It was a teenage dance format, but what was different about it was the name—*Club 1270.* Twelve-seven-oh was the frequency of WXYZ radio, and *Club* would be like going to a nightclub. When you go to a nightclub, you don't sit in bleachers, nor do you sit in chairs lined up like in a theater; you sit at tables, and you're served food while the performers are on. This was set up like a club. Kids would have Coke to drink, and they'd sit in groups. When they played a record, the kids would get up from their tables to dance. Then afterward they'd go back

Leslie Gore takes center stage on *Club 1270* in 1963.
(Publicity photo.)

to their tables. When guests came on, they performed their songs just like they would on *Swingin' Time*, but then they would sit at a table with the kids and talk to them."

Every Saturday afternoon, *Club 1270* opened its doors to the beat of Les Elgart's "Varsity Drag," and for the next half hour Motown teens tore up the dance floor in their Sunday best to the rhythms of the hippest records slid between performances by the day's coolest artists.

Rockin' New Year's Eve

Flipping back the calendar to the fall of 1962, *Club 1270* producer John Dew explains how the show was carved out of a promotion for the coming New Year's Eve bash.

John Dew: "One of the sales guys, Bill Hendricks, came in with an opportunity—he had advertisers that wanted to sponsor a local New Year's Eve television program. It was specifically Coca-Cola and Better Maid Potato Chips . . . so he had money to put down on the table for a local show. John Pival came up with the idea of doing something with the radio station [AM 1270] to cross promote the two; so he lined up [WXYZ disc jockeys] Joel Sebastian and Lee Alan to cohost a New Year's Eve program. They started by pretaping appearances as artists would come through [Detroit].

"So basically as recording artists arrived to make appearances at record hops [the station] pulled them into the TV studio and taped them. They would tape them with kind of a nondescript, dark, draped background so it would blend in with whatever they were going to do on New Year's Eve. They built up a pretty good little repertoire over a couple months. Then on New Year's Eve they brought in a bunch of kids from the Walled Lake Casino. As I recall, we picked out some kids that were pretty good dancers and invited them to be on the show. We had maybe a hundred or so in the studio in a cabaret-style setting with tables and pretended to have these artists come on and entertain. It was a big hit! It got a huge rating share. From that, John Pival decided he would do a regular weekly television dance-party show . . . so the idea was born for *Club 1270*."

Sebastian and Alan

Choices for the hosts of the New Year's Eve show boiled down to two of "Wixie Radio's" top jocks, Joel Sebastian and Lee Alan. Hailing from the streets of Chicago, Joel Sebastian possessed a mellow voice that resonated eloquently every afternoon through the tinny speakers of the transistor radios while kids headed home from school. Sporting blond hair, a light complexion, and boyish features, Sebastian became one of the city's first deejays to introduce teenagers to the exciting new Motown Sound. Detroit's own Tony Micale of the Reflections shares a warm thought about Joel Sebastian.

Tony Micale: "Joel was a real good guy—a very sincere person. What he told you is what he did. He was very nice to all of the acts. If he asked you to do something, he 'asked' you . . . he wasn't telling you that you had to do it in order to get the record played like many others. He wouldn't take advantage of you . . . I've always liked Joel."

On the flip side was the boastful chattiness of evening personality Lee Alan. In contrast to the record-spinning Sebastian, Alan's air shift concentrated less on music and more on banter, much of which centered around what he called a finely tuned Pakistani horn. Hailed as the most perfectly tuned musical instrument in the world, in actuality, it made the worst-sounding noise imaginable! The gimmick became known as "Lee Alan on the horn."

As individual as they were in radio, when it came to television Sebastian and Alan succeeded in igniting a spark that resonated with the dance-party crowd by presenting themselves as a comedy team instead of radio rivals. John Dew elaborates.

John Dew: "Rather than just having two hosts going back and forth, taking turns doing stuff, and to make it kind of stand out a little bit, Lee played the wild man—the fool—and Joel played the straight guy. That seemed to work quite well. It was the first dance show in Detroit to have two hosts."

From the spring of 1963 to the end of 1964, Sebastian and Alan would kick off every episode of *Club 1270* with a light comedy sketch to break the ice with the audience before moving into the first toe-tapping segment. For the next half hour, the duo would announce the dance records and introduce and interview the guest performers.

The Cabaret

Although it was the "first" music hop show in Motown to score with two hosts, *Club 1270* wasn't the first to present that type of format on local TV. Having to follow in the footsteps of the highly successful *Saturday Party*, *Club 1270* was pressured into creating a fresh venue in which to showcase its live talent. So, without revamping Ed McKenzie's old set or copying the concept of WJBK's failed *Detroit Bandstand*, that New Year's Eve cross promotion between the commercial sponsors and radio proved to be the winning combination for the establishment of a TV nightclub. John Dew describes the atmosphere that set the mood.

John Dew: "It was cabaret style, just as if you were in a nightclub. On your left was a raised platform with the *Club 1270* logo and a small bar. Behind that bar on the raised platform would be Joel and Lee. The logo was also on the front of the bar, so when the camera was on them you could either tilt up and see the logo of the show or you could dial on either one of them in a close-up and see the bar logo.

"You had the same kind of small round tables with chairs typical of a cabaret, and there was a dance floor out in the middle. Kids would get up from the tables to dance. Now what you would occasionally see, but we didn't do a lot of it, was along the side or in the back there was a little bleacher section where additional kids could sit. But the ones that were on the floor were pretty much the regulars and they would be at the tables. I think there were between eight and ten tables, which were set up for two to three kids at each of them."

Now Appearing

Because Detroit was such an important market in the world of entertainment during the 1960s, recording artists from all over the globe flocked to the city in an effort to promote their latest records or concerts. And in doing so they would often book an appearance at the *Club*. Retired WXYZ stage manager Art Runyon recalls some of the famous headliners.

Art Runyon: "Mr. 'Goodboy'—Pat Boone—was there, Leslie Gore, Aretha Franklin, Dionne Warwick, Martha and the Vandellas . . . there was a big tie-in with Motown, which was new and sensational at that time."

Indeed it was . . . Not only did Berry Gordy create an international music empire out of the basement of his home on West Grand Boulevard, but he had the foresight to use the local dance programs as an outlet to prep his ensemble for national television appearances. In conjunction with *Swingin' Time*, *Club* 1270 had the honor of hosting the world premier of many of Motown's biggest names.

John Dew: "The Supremes were on multiple times, Stevie Wonder . . . every Motown act at one time or another appeared there. They were easy to work with, they were pleasant, they were humble, and they'd do whatever you wanted. All of the Motown acts were totally classy!"

Another Motor City act making multiple appearances on the program was the Reflections. Lead vocalist Tony Micale revisits a couple of them while describing the experience of lip-syncing . . . under good and bad circumstances.

Tony Micale: "Our group at the time wore sweaters, and we always looked like college kids or the kids next door. So when we sang on *1270* for the first time we wore them. It was the kind of show you walk on to pantomime. They didn't have a mic system that picked up anybody's voice, nor the technicians that could mix you properly. I always sang with it live while I'm there because they had these speakers really blaring with the music. And if you turned them off you could hear me sing with it and the guys; we would all sing with it because nobody knew how to pantomime. So we always sang with it, but we weren't really miked. All the shows were that way back then—even *American Bandstand*.

"One time we came out in a new Mustang convertible and nearly killed a cameraman. We're all sitting up in the back of it singing as the stage door opens and the car comes in. It was a stick shift, and the driver popped the clutch so the car lunged forward toward the cameraman. All of us fell into the car while we're on-camera, and we still had to sing because the record was still going!"

So, with this wealth of talent lined up at the stage door of Broadcast House, what was the criteria for booking guests? Could any lesser-known local group gain exposure on the show?

John Dew: "The artists pretty much had to have a record to be on the show, with the exception of some of the local bands—we would spotlight a few of the local bands. We had a group called Sonny and the Sunliners on a number of times—very, very good local band. They were later signed by Motown and came out under the name Rare Earth! And another group that appeared a couple times on the show was Billy Lee and the Rivieras . . . well, Billy Lee became Mitch Ryder and the Detroit Wheels. So both of those bands really started with us."

The Greatest Satisfaction

In 1964, Columbia Records released a single called "I'm the Greatest" backed with a cover version of the Ben E. King classic "Stand by Me." The artist on that 45 was a rising athlete who professed to "Float like a butterfly and sting like a bee." And two of the guys he knocked out the day he popped in were the former electrical transcription operator and Channel 7 news anchor Erik Smith and retired director Mason Weaver.

Erik Smith: "Muhammad Ali, when he was Cassius Clay, came in when he was on his ascendancy in boxing. He came to *Club 1270* and was all over the building; just an incredible presence. He came up with me [to the control room] and sat there; I was spinning records for the show, and I remember him being a loud man in the room while we were attempting to do the show. It was great fun! That was the first time I met him . . . [and] he so impressed me as being this absolutely free spirit."

Mason Weaver: "Chuck Snead was the regular director. I filled in a few times when he was on vacation, one of which was when Muhammad Ali was on the show. My gosh, in the control room walks Muhammad Ali! He sat right next to me and was quite intrigued with what we were doing. Then they came up and got him; down he went and into his routine of 'I'm the greatest . . .'"

That same year, while America was being besieged by the "British Invasion," a virtually unknown rock group from London finagled its way into the studios of WXYZ. Larry Dlusky, John Dew, and Erik Smith present a unique account of this particular band's Motown debut from both sides of the TV screen. It would be an afternoon they'd always remember.

Larry Dlusky: "They came on, and I think their song was "It's All Over Now," which they lip-synced. And then, when they were done, they sat around at the tables with the kids. Here was Keith Richards [and] Mick Jagger drinking pop from a bottle with the teenagers sitting at this table."

John Dew: "The Rolling Stones were really weird! The way they were dressed was like they couldn't have cared less . . . They would spit gum on the floor and use foul language . . . and at that time they hadn't had a hit yet."

Erik Smith: "We were in the middle of a taping. I don't remember if a camera went down or what, but we had a technical glitch. It stopped the program for a considerable length of time—it might have been an hour. So here we are: we got kids in the studio, we got the Rolling Stones, Lee and Joel, the production crew . . . [and] we're all sitting around waiting for something to happen.

"In those days, the studio doors opened onto what was a green belt area alongside the driveway. And somebody came up with a football. So here we go, all of us. Lee and Joel, myself, Mick Jagger and the Stones go out on the lawn and play a touch football game! At the time, they were not the huge success that they ultimately turned out to be, yet it was just one of those impressions and indelible memories: 'Yeah, I played touch football with the Rolling Stones back in 1964.' It was great fun—great fun!"

The Last Call

At the end of 1964, *Club 1270* began to suffer a series of talent changes that contributed to the demise of the program. The first to go was Lee Alan. In a dispute with radio management regarding an outside venture that involved the Walled Lake Casino, Alan was dismissed from WXYZ, leaving Joel Sebastian as the sole host for a short period of time. Early in the following year, another popular deejay from AM 1270, Dave Prince, was picked to replace Alan. Unfortunately, the pairing of Sebastian and Prince didn't produce the magic that existed with Alan.

John Dew: "Ratings had declined, and it lost its spark. I think Joel and Lee, the two of them together, were not on this kind of level but like Martin and Lewis, each had talent, but together they were better than either one was individually."

In the summer of 1965, Lee Alan managed to patch up his differences with WXYZ. With the support of John Pival, Alan spearheaded an ambitious production he hoped to syndicate on ABC. *The Swingin' Kind* was a collection of elaborate outdoor performances pretaped at picturesque locations such as Metropolitan Beach and Edgewater Park and edited into a single show. The special aired on August 11, 1965, featuring performances by Stevie Wonder, Marvin Gaye, Leslie Gore, the Coasters, the Shangri-las, and others. Discouragingly for Alan, the network passed on the project; shattering his dream of becoming a household name across America. In the subsequent years, he purchased a broadcast school that had fallen on hard times. The Lee Alan School of Broadcasting operated until 1970, when he sold the institution to a struggling deejay named Specs Howard.

Back in 1966, Joel Sebastian accepted a radio position in his hometown of Chicago. After his departure from the Motor City, Dave Prince hosted *Club 1270* until its cancellation at the end of the year. Twenty years later the fair-haired boy with the soothing voice contracted pneumonia. Joel Sebastian died at the young age of 53 in Evanston, Illinois.

Despite *Club 1270*'s brief life span, it entered Detroit living rooms at a time when pop music was undergoing a revolutionary change. In those three years alone, 1963–66, America saw the end of doo-wop, the rise of Motown, the assassination of a president, an "attack" by the British, and the cries for peace in protest of the war in Vietnam. Music is a reflection of society, and *Club 1270* helped to teach the kids to sing by serving it note for note to their tabletops every Saturday afternoon with a fresh bottle of Coca-Cola.

The Scene

This was something everybody watched after school every single day. The people on *The Scene* were stars! And when we saw them at Northland shopping mall, just walking around, we would go crazy. They were celebrities for us.
—SHAUN ROBINSON, correspondent/anchor, *Access Hollywood*

When Don Cornelius laid the tracks for *Soul Train* to cross the country, he didn't bank on a 12-year derailment through one of the nation's biggest stops—Motown. From 1975 to 1987, *Soul Train* had to make a detour due to a local dance program beamed into Motor City living rooms. It was called *The Scene*. The new kid on the block, WGPR-TV, Channel 62, was victorious in broadcasting the spirit of Detroit's inner city teen culture to the Metro area five days a week.

Regardless of who you were or where you lived, teenagers from all over the Metro area gathered around their TV sets at 6:00 p.m. for an hour-long trip to "Geektown" to catch all the latest trends in music, dance, and fashion. Along with the styles came the recording artists and a shot at fame for any local who could sing or bust a move in front of the cameras at the small studio on Jefferson Avenue. And for those less daring individuals who simply wanted a chance to work in television career opportunities were available "behind" *The Scene*. In many ways, this was much more than a dance show; it was a rare phenomenon that turned dreams into reality, especially for African Americans seeking an outlet for their talents.

At the nerve center of this pulsating vibe was a relatively unknown disc jockey by the name of Nat Morris. In 1972, with the help of a good friend, Ray Henderson, Morris arrived in Detroit from Flint to fill an air shift at WGPR radio. The station was in the process of obtaining an FCC license to launch a new television channel on the UHF dial. Shortly after WGPR-TV, Channel 62, signed on the air in late September 1975, *The Scene* made its debut. Nat Morris explains how the show came to be.

Nat Morris: "The program director, George White, already had ideas on how they were gonna do this local station. They had intended to produce quite a bit of their own programming, and they thought a dance show was a natural for the channel since the channel originated from the radio station. They had experienced the show *Swingin' Time;* [so] basically, they put the deejays up there and let them host the show while the kids danced. Ray Henderson had already been designated as the host of the show, but I think my ratings with the radio station kinda helped the program director decide to also put me up there with Ray. I was very apprehensive about going on television, but they thought I could handle it."

On October 13, 1975, Ray and Nat began to host *The Scene,* but, unlike the successful pairing of Joel Sebastian and Lee Alan on *Club 1270,* the necessary on-camera chemistry was sorely lacking in these first-time cohosts.

Nat Morris: "It was a basic total disaster because they just put us up there. No scripts, [it was a] 'you guys just play off each other' type of situation. About six months later Ray Henderson decided that he would change careers, so I wound up as the sole host of the show."

Nat Morris (*left of center*) with *The Scene* dancers in 1977. (Courtesy Nat Morris.)

Henderson's departure would be the first in a series of changes that were waiting on the horizon. The next major overhaul came in 1979. Believing the show was in serious danger of failing, Morris concluded that he needed to do something about it.

Nat Morris: "I approached the president/general manger about taking over the production of the show because it had gotten very stagnant and the station hadn't seen fit to make any more investments in it. In March, they allowed me to basically become the producer of the show in that I would buy the props and pay the staff to try and take the show a step up or to another level."

So that year, under Nat Morris Productions, *The Scene* went from being a live show five days a week to a taped program Monday through Thursday with a live edition every Friday. In fact, Friday nights became much livelier than anyone could have imagined. To help offset the cost of producing a complete show each day, Morris opted to tape two programs on Fridays in addition to the live broadcast. These would be shown on Mondays and Wednesdays as fresh episodes. He inserted repeats on Tuesdays and Thursdays. Thus, a week's worth of live shows was now covered on a much reduced budget.

It's Six O'clock

Another peeve of the new executive producer was the absence of a structured format. Originally the program featured whatever records were popular, with an occasional artist popping in once in a while. It was plain and simple, a little too simple for Nat.

Nat Morris: "I did begin to develop a different format. I wrote it, really, after not being able to watch the show. I thought it was kind of boring just sitting there watching kids dance. It was like the same 20 or 30 kids for an hour, especially when you had no guest. This [new] format opened up with a scenario that included some kids 'taking the dance floor.'"

One of the show's most popular dancers, LaWanda (Gray) Anner, further elaborates.

LaWanda Anner: "It was called the Scene Circle. Everybody's closed up, you know, you're dancing, and then they blow the whistle and you've already picked who's gonna stay out there. When the crowd opens, there's either a couple or one person dancing, and when the whistle blows you close back up again."

With the new opening going full throttle, there needed to be a standard track that would capture the essence of *The Scene*. The old theme song composed and released by Johnny Griffith and Ernest Kelly, which went "Hey, hey, I wanna be . . . be on *The Scene*," had to go. Morris wanted something that would stick in the minds of viewers, something they could easily remember . . . something hip . . . something fun. Nat recalls how a family collaboration inspired the famous opening rap.

Nat Morris: "My nephew Felix had a record called 'Flame Thrower Rap.' He had a couple of [lyrics] that we decided would help the record if I included them in the script of my show. His hook was 'Are you ready to throw down? Yes we are!' So, I wrote a new opening, which became very, very well known . . . I was relaxing on a Saturday night, and it came to me.

Well, it's six o'clock and it's time to rock.
We rock nonstop till seven o'clock.
We don't stop, we don't stop.
We rock, rock, rock all around the clock.
Hip hop, hippity hop,
We jam, jam, jam on.
Dancers come from all around
To throw down in this here Geektown.

The latest steps, the latest styles,
Pretty faces and pretty smiles.
It's six o'clock and time for *The Scene.*

Then I would come out, do my little monologue, which basically included a hello and say something to the kids and tell who's coming up on the show if we had a guest. Then I closed it by saying, 'I will change the name of the town from Motown to Geektown so that everybody can throw down. Are you ready to throw down?' And they would say, 'Yes, we are!' We had it all choreographed that the dancers would yell back at me. So I would say, 'Okay, enough has been said. Let's go to the opening spread,' which was that 'take the floor' segment."

Following the Scene Circle was an established *Soul Train* segment that featured a "Nat Morris" innovation, which, oddly enough, *Soul Train* later adopted. Nat and LaWanda spell out the details.

Nat Morris: "We stole a dance line from *Soul Train.* [Don Cornelius] had the *Soul Train* line, so we thought it natural to showcase our dancers with the dance line. We started the men's and women's line, and Don probably picked up on it later. I think he had couples because of the fact he had one line. By us being on daily, I thought it would be cool to have two lines: a boy line and a girl line. We also choreographed the dancers who were standing on the sides."

LaWanda Anner: "When I got there, the dance line was already in effect, and that was the ultimate because everybody didn't get to come down the line . . . To start the line off and be first, you either had on a really nice outfit or you were getting ready to dance your heart out for your 10 seconds of fame. The boys would line up for the girls to come down and then the girls would line up for the boys to come down in between them."

Another newly implemented feature, the Triple Spotlight, quickly made its appearance at the bottom of each hour. This added bonus would showcase three dancers at once on separate risers under individual spotlights. Only the hottest moves and/or outfits qualified for the bright lights. With chic moves and clothes on the rise, *The Scene* was no longer a traditional teen show of simple music and dance; it was rapidly evolving into an intriguing social statement.

Dancers Come from All Around

Since the dancers are the most important ingredient in the success of any dance show, just how did *The Scene* go about assembling its troupe? Nat

Morris interviews Motown artist Kim Weston. (Courtesy
Nat Morris.)

Morris, along with *Scene* cameraman Wally Harrison and LaWanda
Anner, describe the method.

Nat Morris: "They tried to do the show properly with a dance coordinator at the beginning. WGPR is located in Downtown Detroit in close
proximity to the Martin Luther King homes. From what I heard, the original first dancers were recruited from those areas close to the station. Just
by people knocking on doors, telling them that WGPR was moving down
the street and was going to be doing a dance show and wanted to get
some dancers on. The other dancers came because they saw it on the air.
Once I took the show over, I began to hold auditions."

Wally Harrison: "They had a little process where you'd send your
name in and they'd call you down. Then, I think, after it really got flowin'
and became popular, it was more of who you knew. Somebody might
bring somebody down and say, 'Well hey, you know, this is my friend or
family member, can they dance?'"

LaWanda Anner: "I had a neighbor [named Randy] who appeared
pretty regularly on the show. I saw him walking down the street one day
[in 1982] and said, 'Randy, I would really like to go on there.' He said,
'Oh, they'd like you . . . you're tall and all.' So I went down, and at that
time you would sit in the lobby and they would come out and choose you

to go on the show. Eventually everybody got to [dance] in the back, but they would come out first and pick you to dance on the risers. The young lady came out, and she looked around; it's really like trying to get into Studio 54, where people would be lined up, hoping they would get picked to go in. Then the young lady looked over [at me], and she goes, 'Okay, you.' After that, I didn't need anybody to bring me. I just started going on my own and became a regular and reported every Friday for tapings till it went off the air."

Wally Harrison: "You even had some people out there that shouldn't have been there . . . [people] with two left feet . . . like I could never be on *The Scene*. I got two left feet; I'd just make a fool of myself. And you'd have some people down there that would do that, but the energy was— you didn't care. They were on *The Scene* for an hour . . . 15 seconds of fame . . . that's the way it was."

Unlike Motown's previous dance shows, where all the dancers appeared in nice suits and dresses, indistinguishable, *The Scene* established recognizable personalities. The WGPR studio on Jefferson became the local headquarters of a youthful bandwagon of unforgettable originators and imitators. Wally Harrison and LaWanda Anner introduce us to a few of them.

Wally Harrison: "You had Fast Freddy, he was a wardrobe master. He did his own little dance with the shoulder and shooting the coat over it and laying it down, doing the splits. You had Giselle, she was like Miss Energy, this girl was a dynamo! Her body was unbelievable, so you know it drew attention, and she had moves that a person half her size couldn't do, but Giselle could do them. Everybody had their own little gimmick. A lot of people became known just for that."

LaWanda Anner: "By the time I got there, you were either a Michael Jackson look-alike or a Prince look-alike. And I mean they would adopt movements, personalities, clothes . . . And then the girls wanted to be Vanity, then I think Madonna one time, and then it changed. Even when we left we still had the Prince people, [and] their girlfriends walked around like Apollonia. I mean it was just like they were reenacting *Purple Rain;* they were really into it. Then you had your characters. You had Diaz, he would wear shorts, fishnets, and boots . . . and always doing something crazy. You had Moses, who was very popular on the show, who imitated Morris Day to a tee. They took on these personalities, these characters on the show. We had an older guy, J. B. [which stood] for James Brown, so you know he wore a cape on the show and slid across the floor every time he came [on]."

Wally Harrison: "There were tons of regulars. It was comical because after a while you knew everybody by name. It was more of a family thing,

Fast Freddy. (Courtesy Nat Morris.)

like a big party, because everybody knew everybody . . . everybody knew everybody's routine. You knew who was gonna couple up, so it became a little clique."

Artists Paint *The Scene*

Even though the dancers were the focal point of the show, *The Scene* drew the attention of many musical acts, both locally and nationally. When it came to major artists, many appeared as a result of being in town to promote a record or perform at a nightclub. Nat Morris remembers how one particular club practically hand delivered some of the recording industry's biggest names.

Nat Morris: "GPR radio at the time was known for advertising nightclubs. So during the beginning of the show the nightclub Henry's on Fenkell was bringing in acts like the Manhattans, the Whispers, blues artists like Johnny Taylor . . . So all of the acts that came into Henry's, Henry brought down to the show for that exposure for his weekend business. So we had the Dells quite a bit out of Chicago; we had all of the Jacksons that put out a record except for Michael. Prince was broken [in] on the show because he had videos that MTV wouldn't play at the time; he never came on, but he had his artist Morris Day on. We had the Spinners on quite frequently, George Clinton without the Parliaments, Gladys Knight, Mary Wilson . . . Anita Baker was on the show as Chapter 8, she was the lead singer; she never came and did it as Anita Baker."

And the list doesn't stop there. Here's Nat, LaWanda and Wally with a few more.

Nat Morris: "Some of the biggest stars we ever had were Luther Vandross once he left the group Change, [and] Teddy Pendergrass when he separated from Harold Melvin and the Blue Notes and went solo. One of the first groups we had that was big was the Silvers. They were like a follow-up act to the Jackson 5, a family group. We had them on in 1976. We were around at the beginning of rap. We had the Fat Boys, and Curtis Blow. I think we were the first media outlet in Detroit to play rap."

LaWanda Anner: "Vanity 6 came one time, and that was really a big deal, you know. Vanity 6 . . . that was as close to Prince as you were going to get."

Wally Harrison: "I was asked to do a personal [security] detail with Vanity. Before the term *diva* was out, she was the ultimate woman. We took her out to a nightclub on the East Side. She goes in [and] it's like no women in there, just her . . . all the rest were men. She pulls all these guys out on the dance floor and starts dancing. And she can dance; she had an unbelievable body. The guys were starting to get a little bit too crowded around her and touchy-feely . . . I gotta go in there and get her now. And she was like, 'I'm having fun.' I'm sweating because this is about to be a problem. So we get her out. She understood when I told her, 'If I gotta move you, there's a reason.' Once we got in the limo, she was glad to be out of there because she could see that the tension was building. But she really set her market in Detroit after that . . . That was because she came down to *The Scene* and did her thing and did all the clubs while the dancers were there, so it was like one big circle."

As exciting as it was to see some of the music's top stars perform on

Dressed to kill: *Scene* regulars Pam Thomas (*left*) and LaWanda
Anner. (Courtesy LaWanda Anner.)

the program, it was equally exciting to see some of our homegrown acts
get their big break courtesy of Mr. Nat Morris and *The Scene*.

LaWanda Anner: "The majority of the guests were local acts really
trying to promote themselves, promote their records, and I loved that
about Nat . . . because if you had something and he listened to it he
would give you a chance to come on. It was an avenue to get your stuff
out there. One group I remember was Al Hudson and the Soul Partners,

[and] they had records that went farther than Detroit. Then you had your groups around the corner, who sounded like they may have done their recording down in their basements."

Nat Morris: "That was the prerequisite for coming on as a guest: you needed uniforms and a record out. So we were bombarded with new groups with records out . . . we did quite a number of local artists. We helped break this group out of Flint called Ready for the World. They went on to go gold . . . they really went big on MCA Records."

The Latest Steps, the Latest Styles

Shaun Robinson: "You tuned in to see what everybody was wearing, how they were wearing their hair, who was dancing with who. And I'm telling you we thought the guys were hot and we thought the girls were beautiful."

LaWanda Anner: "We set the pace. As far as fashion, everybody tried to have their own thing happening so you could be an individual. I remember one girl used to love to have her hair just standing straight up, and, you know, some of that stuff caught on. It set the trend for a lot of the fashions and definitely the dances! You could tell if somebody watched *The Scene* because if you went out they were doing the dances that we were doing on the show. And we would make them up! I know I would stand at the mirror and think of a move and then go and try it out. If it was good, the next week somebody was doing it right there on the show, too.

"You had a couple of people, Cheryl Peoples and Bobby Johnson, go national on *Dance Fever* and win. We even had one young man, Lorenzo, go to *Star Search,* and he made it for a few weeks. We had this one young lady from a very large family, her name was Yvonne. She had a dance that I happened to see on *Soul Train* one day—somebody was doing it! The dance went worldwide, it was the Snake. Everybody, black, white, young, old, knew about the Snake, and [Yvonne] was the originator of it."

So what would happen when dancers copied each other's moves? Unlike the confrontational shouting matches and backstabbing betrayals seen on reality television today, *The Scene* found a more constructive way to settle scores, one that was tailor-made for the fiercest rivals.

LaWanda Anner: "They used to have this thing where they would create a battle. You would holler 'battle,' and you would know two people were gonna dance against each other. Yvonne was very good at making up dances, and Cheryl was, too. So I don't know if there was a real

The Brothers Johnson take a moment to pose with Morris on the busy set. (Courtesy Nat Morris.)

rivalry or if we just created it because they both could dance well. We'd pit them against each other."

The countless number of dance battles throughout the history of the show were some of its finest moments. Dancers really went to town when called to the floor to strut what they got! Without trophies, cash, or prizes, winners would walk away with nothing more than bragging rights and 10 seconds of fame. Why not have some sort of prize for a winning performance? It was felt that *The Scene* wasn't about monetary gain; it was about feeling the momentum that built when these kids hit the floor.

As with Newton's law of physics, for every action there's an equal and opposite reaction. Morris had his own principle to help balance the intensity—even if it was only "for show."

Nat Morris: "We put in the format a slow record—a ballad—because that was something Don has never done to my knowledge, played a ballad on *Soul Train*. When I put the slow record on, it was because 'he' wasn't doing it."

LaWanda Anner: "Some people were really good at acting, and the slow dances were acting. They would tell you to look in his eyes . . . so people who could really do that didn't mind whoever they were with because the camera would always do a close-up. It was always on the girls, to tell you the truth: she would be looking at him like she adored him. Most times it was to zoom in on your face and get that dreamy-eyed look . . . that's what the slow dance was.

"I always slow danced with the same person because I was tall and there weren't a lot of tall males on the show. So I would always dance with Fast Freddy. I danced with him so much that people began to say, 'Oh well, that's his girlfriend' because I never danced with anybody else. But there was no one else tall enough to dance with me. The other couples, if they didn't come together, they would pair you up by the color of your clothes. He has on red and she has on red, so that's a couple for the slow dance."

What about those who didn't have a partner?

Wally Harrison: "They'd twirl around in the corner . . . but it would add to that effect. If you had somebody there doing a little fan dance or something, we could use that to play off the shadows on the wall. Just a shadow of a female dancing. People would be like, '*Who* was that?' Some mystery woman . . . well, you can find out who she is next [time]."

It was that kind of spontaneous creativity from the crew and Morris that fueled another innovation that set this dance show apart from its predecessors.

Booty Shots!?

Already renowned for its music, fashion, and dance, *The Scene* also deserves a lot of credit for rewriting the rule book on how to shoot a high-energy dance program. The only way to get the home audience to "throw down" with the action in the studio is through the lenses of the cameras. Air personality Greg Russell of WDWB, Wally Harrison, and Nat Morris look back at the roving "eyes" behind *The Scene*.

Greg Russell: "Nat Morris would have guys on the floor shooting up. I think he might have been, as far as local TV, one of the first to ever have it where they'd have a camera just walk through and shoot the audience. It wasn't like everything was locked down. He had all these innovative things going on. That was a show that invented new camera angles."

Wally Harrison: "I started out in stage and props, and then [Nat] put me on a minicam to just shoot stationary shots of certain girls . . . it was a small camera on a big tripod. It was stationary, and I was like, 'Nat, can I put this on wheels?' And Nat was like, 'Show me what you got.' I'm always the type to be inventive: the slow zooms, fast zooms, rack [focus] in, rack out, or the low angles coming off the lamp. Once [Nat] moved me to another camera, one of the big studio cameras, [and] I started riding it. I would push it—it had a big wheel on it—so that's when you could dart in and dart out. I did a lot of handheld, too, and I would go real low, come up and spin around and twirl it. If it looked good and fit the atmosphere, Nat was like, 'I want it.' So he let you be creative."

Nat Morris: "Because we had four-foot risers, the camera could shoot upward or between the legs. We didn't concentrate on booty shots, but how can you shoot a dance show without somebody shaking their behind; that's part of it. We tried to keep it moving; we didn't want to stay on a dancer unless the dancer was really doing something."

Wally Harrison: "It was a lot of fun because you had all the guys that were down there on the production team, they were all eager to show their skills. Everybody had different ideas . . . everybody wanted to [say], 'If you see this . . . that's my work.' So there was a lot of energy put into it."

Technical Difficulties Cause Embarrassing Scenes

The ability of the crew members to utilize their factory of ideas was often disrupted by the limitations of the equipment. The experience of technical difficulties became so commonplace that the production often suffered and looked amateurish, contrary to the professionalism that guided it.

Nat Morris: "The production values weren't there—ever! When GPR signed on, it had brand new cameras. Those cameras quickly deteriorated from a lack of maintenance and money. They [had] tubes . . . and so the tubes would go out, that's 3,000 dollars, and I guess it took 9,000 dollars or so a year to keep them up. The cameras went out about 1976, 1977 maybe 1978, then it was down from two cameras to one good one and one bad one. As chip cameras became available and cheaper, GPR switched over to some small, really not broadcast [quality], but professional cameras. And that really helped the show out . . . the picture all of a sudden got clearer."

Wally Harrison: "The equipment wasn't top of the line, so you would have situations where your monitor would all of a sudden show three images. When you would call back for one of the techs, he would say, 'Hit it on the side.' You'd hit it and it straightened up."

Nat Morris: "The sound system was always terrible down there; that was one of the biggest flaws of the show. It never did get corrected till the final days, and it still wasn't right. That kept us from doing live tracks."

LaWanda Anner: "I got to the point where I recognized editing: I just did that step, [then] next thing you know I'm doing the same thing again. When they had a show with a lot of editing, you knew there were a lot of mistakes."

Nat Morris: "It seemed like every time we'd have an opportunity to bust wide open, something would happen. I had this sponsor, Brady Keys, who had brought in Kentucky Fried Chicken. He had a number of Kentucky Fried restaurants in the black community, and so he benefited tremendously from his advertising and exposure. So I got him to sponsor a dance contest. The show *Dance Fever* was out, and so dance contests became hot. I wrote one called Swing Fever. The day we had our final presentation, [Channel] 62 kept doing things like moving their news around the show. And it so happened on my championship day we had to prerecord it. So I got Kentucky Fried in there, people from the front office there . . . and the recording of the finals had bad tracking on the two-inch tape and would not play back! It killed me that day."

But not all the bloopers on the show were due to technical difficulties; some of them were human.

LaWanda Anner: "[On] the live shows, which would air on Friday at six, anything could happen. Live television is scary, especially with a bunch of teenagers. I remember an incident [when] one of the guys was coming down the dance line and he flashed open his coat and he had on a G-string! What can you do? It was live, it was seen, we were right there looking at it."

Nat Morris: "I remember having the Spinners as guest hosts one day; they were going to host the show for me. Our script was an ad-lib script, and I had mentioned this to one of the lead singers, who was going to do most of the talking: 'Hey, when I point to you just start talking and go to the record.' We counted him down, we go live to him, and he freezes! Totally embarrassing for me . . . that was another moment I'll never forget."

Colorful Scenes

Nat Morris: "We started off with a cartoonish type set with some flats with drawings on them—different colors, multicolored—it kind of looked 'kiddish' or 'bubble-gummish.' But that was the first set, it was really inexpensive. We had 'The Scene' in Styrofoam letters. When the show started, the logo wasn't even hung, it was just sitting on a table or platform. I was kind of brokenhearted the day I saw it. I said, 'Aw, this will never do *Soul Train*.' And I really had big, big thoughts about not doing it because it didn't even look close to *Soul Train*."

By the 1980s, the simplistic set of the 1970s had undergone a facelift.

Wally Harrison: "We had the different stages of risers, and then we had the different curtains that had a lot of Mylar and a lot of mirror effects and a disco ball. You had to set the lights to hit the disco ball and put the cookies in the gel. It was a full stage production on a small scale coming out of [Channel] 62. You did all of the big stage things in a limited amount of time."

LaWanda Anner: "At home, it looked like this really big place with these nice props, and when you got there it was a small place with holes in the stuff and the mirror broke, but you don't really see that on TV. It was low budget, and when you're there that's what it looks like. You had maybe five or six risers that you would position some dancers on. Then you had the dance floor and a little stage where Nat stood and sometimes people would dance there. But if you were put on a riser it was because you were gonna really dance well or you were dressed really nice. It was always color coordinated; all the blues were up on the risers or the reds. Most times people were just extras for real. If you don't really do anything to stand out, they don't search for you."

Wally Harrison: "We had to set 'the set' up every Friday. They had the news and everything else that was going on back there, so at 5:30 or whatever time it was we'd jump into action mode and put *The Scene* together . . . *The Scene* was in a box."

Fame! Remember My Name

For a little program that was produced "out of a box" on a shoestring budget, the exposure was enormous! Thanks to the immense popularity of the show, audiences overlooked the technical faults and budgetary restraints to concentrate on what was most important to them . . . the dancers. Because of that, an appearance on *The Scene* was more than a privilege; it became an honor. Shaun Robinson remembers the day she was in the studio with her classmates dancing the Robot.

Shaun Robinson: "*The Scene* had, during one part of the year or something, High School Day, and I think it was every Friday a different high school was featured. I was going to Cass Tech, and I got to dance . . . and I remember I wore a white dress. It was a white wrap dress, white shoes, and I had a white flower in my hair. My hair was curly, and I was just so excited. And I remember after dancing on *The Scene*, I think I got to dance on a little platform or something, I remember everybody going, 'Hey Shaun, we saw you on *The Scene*, you were great . . .' That was like 'our' Oscars, appearing on a show like that!"

As for the regulars, they ultimately became the toast of the town.

LaWanda Anner: "It was like once you started dancing and people started recognizing you, you were a local celebrity. They would point and

ask you for your autograph, and you really felt like a star. At first, I
didn't know how to react to it: *my* autograph? I got fan mail, bags and
bags of fan mail. We were always asked to model for people that were
sponsors, do little commercials and stuff like that. You really didn't get
money, but you got recognition, and if you were doing a clothes commercial you could keep some of the stuff that you modeled. It was an
experience, and I wouldn't have traded it for anything!"

In the summer of 1987, Detroit became the location for the production
of the feature film *Collision Course*. During the shoot, it was Hollywood's turn to roll out the red carpet for the local stars of Motown.

LaWanda Anner: "*The Scene* was invited down to be in a Jay Leno
movie with Pat Morita. We were the dancers in a club scene. The saxo-
phonist was Norma Jean Bell. Her group was the group playing at the
club, and we were just like the patrons in the club. I never knew until
then that you danced and there was no music playing if the actors were
speaking their lines."

And, with the hometown fanfare blazing, when the clock struck six
there was one particular audience bloc that always tuned in religiously
from a state of captivity, literally.

Wally Harrison: "There was a thing where they were getting letters,
fan mail—I even got fan mail—but it was from some of the correctional
institutions. And it was like guys had their favorite dancers, and they
would say, 'You know our situation. We're locked up this and that.
Show more of her, show more of this . . .' So it was like a little following
. . . and guys would write me and say, 'Could you show this girl or could
you get her to send me a picture.' So it's like, do you answer them? I'd say
to Nat, 'What do you want to do?' He'd say, 'Well, they're fans.' And we
would show . . . this is for the brothers that are locked up . . . if it helped
them—hey! If it stopped them from doing something they weren't supposed to do for that hour, more to it. It was an experience."

The Social Scene

With all of the hoopla generated by *The Scene*, what kind of social
impressions did it succeed in making? Did the show serve Metro Detroit
well? Let's ask the experts.

Nat Morris: "It captured on videotape the culture of black Detroit. It
was amazing that some people thought *The Scene* was a disgrace to the
black community while others praised it. It inspired other African Americans in the Detroit area to want to become involved in television. When
we came out, we were like an oddity. It was rare to see something like

that other than *Soul Train* on the national level or black comedy shows. So being local it inspired local people."

Shaun Robinson: "Back then the only dance shows were obviously *American Bandstand* and *Soul Train*. That's all I really remember . . . and obviously on *American Bandstand* we didn't see many people of color. On *Soul Train* we did, but that was a national show and so we didn't have any real connection with those people. Here for us, with *The Scene*, you got to see people you knew from school or there was a chance you would run into them at the mall. So it was a real sense of community."

Wally Harrison: "It was a lighter side of Detroit because that was back in the time when they were still having some gang problems. At Friday from six to seven, it was *The Scene*. I've met guys in gangs, and once they found out I worked for *The Scene* they were like, 'Look man, we could be doing something that's probably wrong, but at six o'clock, we stop to go watch *The Scene*.'"

Another important social milestone is that *The Scene* was very successful in bridging the racial barriers that often divide a community. The universal language of music and dance speaks volumes amongst teenagers, regardless of their neighborhood or skin color, and so *The Scene* dispelled the myth that it was only a black show by opening its doors to suburban performers and dancers. Scott Gordon, the son of Detroit talk show host Lou Gordon, reinforces the point from personal experience.

Scott Gordon: "It had a lot of impact on me as far as being a deejay and being exposed to music that I wouldn't ordinarily be exposed to . . . and incorporating that into my own shows at the weekend teen clubs I was playing for. All these very lily-white kids from neighborhoods like Waterford and these far outlying suburbs at the time loved the stuff that they had never heard before. A lot of subcultured white kids were affected by *The Scene*, and I was one of them."

Sugar, Sugar

Nat Morris: "At the end of [each] show, I closed it by changing the name of the town back from Geektown to Motown."

Shaun Robinson: "I remember standing behind Nat Morris when he said at the end of the show, 'Sugar, sugar, salt to salt, if you didn't get off . . . it ain't our fault.'"

Nat Morris: "I'm still remembered by that line."

By 1987, Nat Morris felt he had reached his pinnacle with the show.

The pizzazz topped out, and the ratings began to fizzle. As fate would have it, while Morris was looking to end his association with the program, the hierarchy at WGPR was, too.

Nat Morris: "The president and general manager came in with his staff, and they decided that they should be the ones producing the show. I had a couple of meetings with him about selling the show; he talked about buying it back from me. They thought that my price was crazy and ridiculous. So at the end of 1987, that last day of the year, December 31, the show was canceled. They had already cut a couple of episodes and were pretty much on the air, pretty quick, in January 1988 with a show called *Contempo*. And I think that lasted six months or so."

Today's Scene

Although we may never get to see a *Scene* reunion on television, the "family" bonds that came out of the program still exist.

Wally Harrison: "I still see some of the dancers, and we just sit back and laugh. They've straightened up now, they're older, and I'm like, 'I remember you when you thought you were Michael Jackson.' I'll see them at a Home Depot or out somewhere with their families now; these were kids then. Now they have their families, and I'm like, 'Have you ever seen tapes of your daddy? He was a fool. I'm sure he probably still has it in him, but I could tell you some stories.' And kids just fall out laughing. Some of them don't have any of the tapes to show their families: this is how silly I was back then."

LaWanda Anner: "The majority of the people I still talk to, and it's been [over] 20 years, I'm still friends with them. We had our kids together, and we still laugh and talk about *The Scene* and how much fun we had. We still sit around, watching our *Scene* tapes, and just pass out because then it wasn't funny, we were serious. But now when we look at them we just crack up."

Thus, what started out as a small dance show on a new local TV station in 1975 went on to revolutionize the culture of a teen generation by becoming a trendy culture in itself.

Going to the Movies

5

Bill Kennedy

From the time motion pictures were developed in the mid-1915s up to about 1950, there wasn't a question that you could ask that Bill Kennedy couldn't answer.
—SONNY ELIOT, Detroit TV icon

For every Hollywood success story, there are a thousand failures. Since the advent of the motion picture, people from all walks of life have flocked to Tinseltown with their suitcases packed full of dreams of stardom in the movies. And for all the ambitious souls yearning to see their names on a marquee in bright lights, many return home broke and busted after years of rejection. But, unlike all of the failed celluloid wannabes who came back dejected, Bill Kennedy was one actor who turned his bigscreen disappointment into a small-screen victory in the Motor City.

Sporting loud plaid jackets and never without a cigarette, Bill Kennedy epitomized the stereotype of Hollywood's yesteryear. Appearing in 60 films, many of which were B movies, along with a number of early television programs, Kennedy had firsthand knowledge about the ins and outs of the "dream factory." He didn't just have brushes with the stars; he rehearsed, worked, and socialized with them. His behind-the-scenes accounts relating to a movie weren't just idle gossip because he had been there. He could tell an infinite number of stories, answer almost any question, and produce a photograph from almost every motion picture imaginable. The credentials that Bill Kennedy brought to Detroit placed him in a class by himself and earned him the reputation of being Motown's undisputed movie king.

Beginning in 1956, Kennedy hammed up his showbiz persona in front of the local TV cameras every afternoon at one o'clock Sunday thru Fri-

Bill Kennedy in his early days at CKLW-TV. (Courtesy Matt Keelan.)

day. For the first 13 years, audiences tuned in to CKLW, Channel 9, to watch *Bill Kennedy's Showtime,* and later they switched to WKBD, Channel 50, for *Bill Kennedy at the Movies,* which ran for another 14 years. Whether you saw him on Channel 9 or on Channel 50, the program format was always the same: countless old movies and lots of trivia from Bill! Local television personality Greg Russell recalls the role Bill Kennedy played in his life.

Greg Russell: "Very close to my heart was *Bill Kennedy at the Movies* . . . everybody loved that show. He would always show a lot of the B movies. You knew you were never gonna see *Gone with the Wind,* but you might see "Blown with the Wind" or something like that! Bill would always have these interesting movie tidbits and guest stars like Jimmy Stewart. He had the Supremes on, and he even had Ron O'Neal promoting his new movie [in 1972] *Super Fly.* Bill was also good for showing movies in which he had walk-ons or bit parts, and he made sure you knew it, too: 'My part's coming up next!' He was fun. It was a very innovative show, and it's something that I wish, honest to gosh, we could bring back today."

A Hollywood publicity still with Laura Elliott for the 1951 release of *Two Lost Worlds*. (Courtesy CBC Windsor.)

Hooray for Hollywood!

Willard A. Kennedy was born on June 27, 1908, in Cleveland Heights, Ohio. When Bill was expelled from a Cleveland high school in 1925, his father, W. B. Kennedy, a Great Lakes coal supplier, negotiated a deal with one of his customers, Father Nicholson of Assumption College in Windsor, Ontario, to admit Bill as a student. His tuition was taken out of the purchase price for the many tons of coal the college needed for heat in the winter. During his three-year stay, young Kennedy used to pray for bitterly cold winters—the colder the winter the more his standard of living improved.

In 1935, the year he would turn 27, showbiz called, and Bill was happy to oblige. His first media job was in his hometown of Cleveland, where he became the sports announcer at WTAM radio. A year later he traveled northwest to the Motor City to be WWJ radio's Hollywood commentator. By 1940, talking about Hollywood didn't seem as glamorous to Kennedy as being *in* Hollywood. With lots of stars in his eyes and little in his wallet, he packed his bags and headed west in pursuit of fame and fortune.

After arriving in Southern California, the 32-year-old aspiring actor landed a radio gig at KHJ in Los Angeles as the host of a program called *Broadway Hollywood*. It wasn't long before legendary producer Hal Wallis (of *Casablanca* fame) heard Bill's distinctive voice and offered him a screen test for Warner Bros. Shocked and thrilled, Kennedy was determined to give Wallis a performance he'd never forget. Less than a year after his arrival in a town where many dreams are broken, Bill Kennedy was signed to a contract with Warner Bros. Studios! In his first big-screen appearance, he had a bit role as a cop in *Highway West* (1941), an ironic title for a man who had just taken the highway west a year earlier.

Over the next 15 years, much of Kennedy's movie career was spent playing minor characters that appeared on screen for a scene or two. Avid Kennedy fan and friend, CKWW air personality Wayne Stevens, describes a scene that became one of Bill's favorite cinematic moments.

Wayne Stevens: "He had a bit part in *Now, Voyager* [1942], where he played Hamilton Hunneker, a famous polo player, in one scene. Looking very dapper, he escorts Bette Davis off of a cruise ship. She introduces him to her girlfriends, who are waiting on the dock: 'This is Hamilton Hunneker.' One of the girls, who appears to be captivated by Bill, says, 'You're Hamilton Hunneker, the famous polo player?' Bill answers with a smile, 'Is that a question or an accusation?' Then he has a few more lines and he exits."

Although he could masterfully add some degree of distinction to his characters, the hope of becoming a leading man in his own right began to dwindle by the time he reached his mid-forties.

Wayne Stevens: "It just wasn't happening for Bill. He'd get bit parts here and there, and he'd have auditions all over the place. One of his few starring roles was *Web of Danger* [1947], which was a picture he was very proud of. He had some good parts, he had some bad parts, he had a lot of parts in B movies with the Bowery Boys, and he worked on TV doing some *Lone Ranger* episodes and some other westerns. But I think when he realized it really wasn't happening for him he decided to come back here."

From Tinseltown to Motown

Since the day he debuted on CKLW in 1956 until the day he left the studios of WKBD in the early 1980s, one of the props on Bill Kennedy's set that never changed (and there were many), was a photograph of a dark-haired woman wearing a smile and holding a cigarette. Always hung somewhere behind Bill's desk, this mystery woman, to whom he religiously waved goodbye at the close of his show before disappearing into the shadows during a piano rendition of "Just in Time," would become the single most important and influential person in his life. It wasn't his mother or his first wife or a famous actress. Her name was Anastasia Buhl.

When Kennedy returned to Detroit in early 1953, he became *Your Hollywood Host* on WWJ-TV, Channel 4. In April, while the rest of the print media wrote poor reviews about Bill and his afternoon movie show, one columnist took note of his talents and gave him his very first compliment. The favorable critique was written by A. Pryor of the *Grosse Pointe News*. Wishing to express his thanks to the columnist, Kennedy wrote a letter to A. Pryor and soon discovered that it was a pen name for Anastasia Buhl, the owner and publisher of the paper.

Unfortunately, Buhl's positive review wasn't enough to stop WWJ from canceling *Your Hollywood Host* in May. After unsuccessfully pitching the program to WJBK and WXYZ, Bill returned to Hollywood for "take two," and this time it looked like he had hit the jackpot. He was signed to a three-year contract with CBS to anchor the 11:00 p.m. news on KNXT. Not having to report to the station until six in the evening allowed Kennedy to moonlight during the day in bit parts on such TV shows as *The Lineup, Burns and Allen,* and *I Married Joan.* He was at last on top of the world . . . at least for a little while.

In an undated letter to Wayne Stevens, reprinted with permission, Kennedy explains the turning point in his career that brought him home to stay at the insistence of Ms. Buhl.

Bill Kennedy: "My big disaster came in early 1955. CBS decided they wanted a commentator type reporter and dumped me for Clete Roberts who was a news analyst. The three year contract meant nothing—CBS lawyers laughed at it! Career-wise, everything came to a crashing halt! Stasia Buhl and I had been writing each other and when she was told of the KNXT debacle, she urged me to return to Detroit—this was early 1956.

Motown legends Bill Kennedy and the Supremes at Christmas
1964. *Left to right:* Diana Ross, Bill Kennedy, Florence Ballard,
and Mary Wilson. (Courtesy Detroit Institute of Arts, Bill
Kennedy Collection.)

"Stasia insisted that I come back and sent me a ticket on the 'Chief' for
the ride back. I lived in the guest house on the Buhl estate and it wasn't
until August 10, 1956 that I appeared on Channel 9. She was the greatest
person to me and without her faith I never would have made it!"

It's Showtime at the Movies

By 1956, CKLW had purchased a movie package consisting of old B
movies and a few classic A-list pictures. It was an era when current A-list
features were only available to the networks for prime-time airings, thus
giving the local TV stations the old and lesser-quality movies. Reluctant
to repitch his movie show to the Detroit stations due to his prior rejec-
tions, Bill crossed the border to the town he had once called home—

Charlton Heston pays a visit in the 1970s. (Courtesy Detroit
Institute of Arts, Bill Kennedy Collection.)

Windsor. The timing was right, as CKLW was looking for a venue to
showcase its new afternoon movie package, and Bill felt comfortable presenting his ideas without any fear of preconceived opinions about him.
Wayne Stevens paraphrases the scenario.

Wayne Stevens: "I believe in his heart he thought 'I've been in Hollywood and I know some of these actors and directors, so I can do more
than just say "Here's *Now, Voyager,* starring Bette Davis, take it away
. . ." I can go on and tell people what it was like to be in that picture.' He
wanted to translate that intimate Hollywood knowledge into 'I can come
on TV every day and tell you what was going on behind the scenes. I can
give you a little bit of dirt on some of the stars . . . I can tell you about a
scene they shot 14 times because they just couldn't get it right . . . .' There
wasn't another movie host who could do that."

Kennedy's unique spin on hosting such a program persuaded the station management to give him the job. Retired CKLW director Matt Keelan remembers the impression Bill Kennedy made on his first day.

Matt Keelan: "I can recall Bill walking into our studio with his briefcase, which read, 'Bill Kennedy—Hollywood,' and we thought, 'Who the hell is this guy?' He looked like some big shot."

And a big shot he was. The master storyteller had just arrived to dazzle audiences with showbiz news and personal memories of Hollywood during the movie breaks. His stories seemed endless and always had a touch of gossip and enough detail to make the viewers feel they were there, too. A wonderful example comes from the man himself in a letter to Wayne Stevens dated November 18, 1990, reprinted with permission.

Bill Kennedy: "I had the pleasure of working on one episode of *The Jack Benny Show*. I played one of a group of tourists going through the CBS studios who was completely unimpressed with Jack Benny & Co. And of course this theme was a great foil for Jack's attempts to impress us. Gisele MacKenzie was the guest star—she is from Canada [and] her big song on that particular program was 'Fascination.'

"By happenstance I rode in an elevator with Jack and Gisele. Just the three of us. It was only five floors down, but the elevator was very slow and it seemed we were closed in for hours! Not one word was spoken!! Jack stared straight ahead and Gisele seemed tense—and I felt like an interloper! I heard later that they were having an affair—as Jack was a not so well known womanizer.

"On the set, Jack was aloof from all—of course his coterie Dennis Day, Don Wilson and Mel Blanc were close to him. He was not gregarious. I was paid $300 for that appearance and I only had two or three lines. Jack was not a miser as he pretended to be."

Movie Trivia

In addition to telling tales about the movies or his experiences in them, Bill Kennedy made a significant connection with his audience by devoting a large portion of his program (primarily the daily version) to answering trivia questions. Viewers would often call or write in with questions, asking, "Whatever happened to this actor? Is this actress still alive? Who played the part of the sheriff in this movie?" And for every question that came in, the cigarette-toting host always seemed to have the answer on the tip of his tongue . . . or did he?

Matt Keelan: "Bill gave the impression that he was off the cuff, but in reality he was a very prepared person. He prepped himself by studying clipped articles and notes he made relating to the films before going on the air."

Having that special interaction with the audience is one of the elements that drew people closer to Kennedy. Longtime fan Jim Humlong, who watched the program from 1959 until the final show in 1983, remembers how his own deluge of questions led to a personal nickname, compliments of his favorite cinema host.

Jim Humlong: "I'd write him a lot, and there'd be about 20 questions in each letter. I also called in a lot over the years, in fact, it was so much that Bill gave me a nickname on the air . . . he started calling me 'Hummer.'"

Most of the time when Kennedy took calls they were off-camera during the movie run or a commercial break; he seldom took them on the air live. He didn't like to be caught off guard or at a loss for an answer. Anytime he was thrown off or stumped, it was obvious, as local TV fan Larry Dlusky remembers.

Larry Dlusky: "One afternoon this guy calls up and asks about [the musical group] the Byrds. He asks, 'Do you think the Byrds will ever get back together again?' And Bill Kennedy said, 'Alfred Hitchcock directed *The Birds,* and Tippi Hedren was in it. I know some movies have sequels, but Hitchcock has never made a sequel to any of his movies. So if you're looking for a *Birds II,* I don't think that will happen.' The guy then says, 'No, man, the Byrds . . . you know, David Crosby . . . "Mr. Tambourine Man" . . . do you think they're gonna get back together again?' Kennedy replied, 'Like I said, Alfred Hitchcock directed *The Birds,* and I don't know about the people you mentioned being connected with the movie. I don't know those names, and I don't know of any plans to make a sequel.' The caller says, 'No, no, man . . . I'm talking about the group . . . you know, the songs . . . "Turn, Turn, Turn" . . . the Byrds broke up. Do you think they're gonna get back together?' Kennedy goes, 'I'm sorry. I answered your question twice . . . I don't know what you're asking, but you have my answer and good day.' After the caller hung up, Kennedy looked directly into the camera, totally bewildered, and said, 'What was he talking about?'"

The Fabulous Files

Jim Humlong: "I loved to see him get up and go to his file cabinet and bring out his pictures. Somebody would call in and say whatever happened to whomever and he'd show the audience a picture of that person. When it came to Hollywood memorabilia, he just had everything!"

Wayne Stevens: "He always had in his Fabulous Files a million stills from movies. He wouldn't just say, for example, Margaret Hamilton was the Wicked Witch of the West in *The Wizard of Oz;* he would show a photo and say, 'Here's a picture of Margaret Hamilton, and you can see in the picture she's . . .' whatever. And that's the kind of thing he would do with stills. It was great."

With a collection of approximately 300,000 photographs, Kennedy's files were indeed fabulous! His vast accumulation of photographic memorabilia started out as a hobby dating back to his childhood, when he sent away for an autographed picture of silent film comic Fatty Arbuckle. After receiving the signed photo, young Bill sent for more. Once he made it to Hollywood as an actor, he continued to collect stills from the publicity offices of the studios. Exactly how his movie anthology grew to such enormous proportions can only be answered by Bill, but, regardless of the "how," Detroiters were glad that he "did." The Fabulous Files were an added bonus to watching the program. Nobody else could whip out a photo at random to help answer a question or explain a movie scene like Bill Kennedy.

On June 12, 1987, Bill donated his treasured files, which were valued in excess of $230,000, to the Detroit Institute of Arts. At the late morning dedication ceremony, in front of a large audience of fans gathered in the museum's recital hall, the master showman couldn't resist telling a tale that put a humorous twist on a very serious film. Wayne Stevens recounts the story.

Wayne Stevens: "He recalled a movie he was in with Ingrid Bergman called *Joan of Arc* [1948]. Joan of Arc [Bergman] was burned at the stake, and Bill Kennedy was the executioner in this picture, setting the fire. He said, 'I had a line to deliver and I couldn't believe the line I had to do.' He then interrupts himself and says to the DIA audience, 'Do you know what a small bundle of kindling is called? Do you know the proper term? It's a fagot!' He goes back into the story: 'My script called for me to yell, THE FIRE'S NOT GOING . . . WE NEED MORE FAGOTS OVER HERE!' So I go to the director [Victor Fleming], who was a real prima donna, and I said, 'Sir, I have this line, and nowadays the word *fagot* has a different connotation than what it had in medieval France.' The director barked, 'DO THE LINE!' Bill says, 'So I had to do the line, and I felt totally stupid.' And then they shot the scene and the picture was done.

"He continued, 'The picture was terribly boring. I remember when it had its premier in Hollywood. I went to it, and all of Hollywood's elite turned out for this Ingrid Bergman picture and it's boring. Finally, we get to the scene where she's burned at the stake, and my line comes up: 'WE NEED MORE FAGOTS OVER HERE!' Suddenly the whole theater blew up with laughter!' The director was there and realized *then* it was a mistake and later cut the line out."

Touching the Stars

As much as Bill loved to talk about the stars, he loved to interview them even more. Any celebrity in town, whether it was to promote a new film or appear at clubs, such as the Elmwood or the Top Hat, entertainment's top stars of yesterday and today appeared on the Sunday edition of *Bill Kennedy*. Everybody from Buster Keaton to Jayne Mansfield, from Hedda Hopper to Duncan Renaldo, and even oddities such as Colonel Harlan Sanders, sat down to chat with Bill.

Wayne Stevens: "I remember him interviewing these big stars. I was kind of a showbiz kid, and I would be thrilled because I would be thinking, 'That's Jimmy Durante!' Now I'm only a kid, and I don't know Jimmy Durante that well, but I know he's a really big star and right now he's at 825 Riverside Drive down by the river! So it was fun for us to watch this local guy interviewing these huge celebrities."

Having the entertainment world's aristocracy in the studios of Channels 9 and 50 not only authenticated Kennedy's credibility, but it gave Motown audiences the sense that they, too, could touch Hollywood.

Matt Keelan: "The stars liked Bill. I've witnessed tons of interviews where the celebrity's reaction is, 'Here's another local who's going to ask me stupid questions.' But with Bill, he was knowledgeable about the movie business because he had worked in it himself and he could speak their language. Bill was gossipy but not in his interviews. He delved more into the person than the gossip. His questions were winged, they developed during the course of the interview, and sometimes they were funny.

"I remember he was interviewing Phyllis Diller one time, and she was boasting about how she really knew her way around town. She said, 'I stayed here and I stayed there,' and Bill asked, 'Did you ever stay at the Hotel Dieu?' And she says, 'Yes, I stayed there.' Then Bill said, 'Really!? That's a hospital.'"

According to Kennedy's widow, Suzy, Bill's finest moment as an interviewer took place in 1971 when a spaghetti western actor rolled into town to promote the film that marked his directorial debut: *Play Misty for Me*.

Suzy Kennedy: "He thought his best interview was Clint Eastwood. He always said it was his favorite."

When it came to publicizing local talent, Kennedy was equally as proud to interview the best and brightest of the Motor City, from television stars such as Rita Bell, Johnny Ginger, Soupy Sales, and Sir Graves Ghastly to radio personalities such as Lee Alan and Brace Beemer (the original Lone Ranger on WXYZ), athletes such as Joe Louis, and the recording artists of Motown. Tony Micale, lead vocalist of the Detroit

Chatting with actress Arlene Dahl in the late 1970s. (Courtesy Detroit Institute of Arts, Bill Kennedy Collection.)

quintet the Reflections, reminisces about how Bill Kennedy drafted his group to appear on the show.

Tony Micale: "Back when we were doing *Swingin' Time,* we used Bill Kennedy's dressing room. Being that we were young kids, we were in awe of Bill Kennedy and thrilled to be given his dressing room to use after he left the building. I remember seeing this big case that looked like a fishing tackle box, so we opened it up and it was full of makeup. And, being prone to using makeup when we went on television, we helped ourselves. He had some tan stuff in there, so we looked like we had suntans. From that moment on, every time we went on *Swingin' Time* we used his dressing room and his makeup.

"Well, one time he caught us! He came in and said, 'So you're the guys that have been using my makeup.' We apologized and offered to pay for it. He said, 'Oh, you're gonna pay me for it all right . . . you're gonna be on my show.' He was just a gracious guy; he had us on for an entire show as cohosts. I was just totally in awe of this man's stories about the movie stars he knew and worked with. He was a part of Detroit who had a bigger history than anybody else I knew, even in the record business."

Highs and Lows

Wayne Stevens: "One story that was a high point, but it ended up as a bit of a low point for Bill, was when he told me about the day he recorded the opening for the *Adventures of Superman* TV show with George Reeves. It was recorded onstage at the Desilu studios in Hollywood in a theater setting. He said, 'I'm up there, and I know I've got the part, but we had to do it over and over again to get it right. While I'm doing this, I looked out into the audience . . . the place is completely empty, but sitting there alone in the audience section along the aisle is Charlie Chaplin!' He continues, 'I found out that Charlie Chaplin was going to use this studio just as soon as we finished. Now, I'm thinking here's my chance to be discovered by Charlie Chaplin.'

"So he really gave it his all! 'Faster than a speeding bullet! More powerful than a locomotive! Able to leap tall buildings in a single bound!' He said, 'I really pitched it, and we finally got it right after doing it forever! When it was over, Charlie Chaplin gets up, and he starts walking toward me on the stage. I just thought, this is the moment I'm going to remember the rest of my life . . . I know he's gonna offer me something! He came up, he shook my hand, and he said, "Young man . . . you have a very big voice." Then he turned and left.' Bill was so crushed because he really thought Chaplin was going to offer him something and he got nothing. However, he was very proud of that *Superman* intro because that was a major television show."

There were those who loved Bill Kennedy, and there were those who couldn't stand him. Kennedy possessed a cut-and-dried personality that was either likable or intolerable. Many of his critics thought him to be egotistical, arrogant, and vain (perhaps because he often spoke of his two hair transplants), but the truth of the matter is there was a whole side to Bill Kennedy that his faultfinders never saw . . . and that was his kind-hearted nature and diverse sense of humor, as depicted by former WKBD director Bill Murray, Suzy Kennedy, retired CKLW production manager Frank Quinn, and Wayne Stevens.

Bill Murray: "Kennedy was not dictatorial. He was very polite to everybody. He was gentlemanly to any woman who showed up on the set. When he passed people in the offices, he had a friendly greeting for each person. He liked the idea that people in Detroit thought of him as a movie star, even though he knew and we knew he wasn't. He seemed genuinely happy—the smile on his face was seen often!"

Suzy Kennedy: "He had a marvelous sense of humor, and sometimes it would be ridiculous. He would tell a story where you would be so enraptured by it and the whole thing would be a big lie. He would do stuff like that to see people go 'What . . . what?' That was a joke to him. He liked to catch people off guard with ridiculous stories that he made sound so serious you'd believe them."

Frank Quinn: "When he came back from having his appendix out, all the crew guys went into his dressing room to see how he was doing at various times. He showed off the stitches to the guys as they came in at random. After showing the stitches for the third or fourth time, he took off all his clothes and went into the studio with only a towel around him. This was on a Sunday, so the only woman in the building was the switchboard operator. In the studio he yells out, 'Whoever wants to see my operation . . . here it is!' He whips off the towel and stands there stark naked! Much to his embarrassment, when he looked up into the control booth, there was a guy with a group of old ladies who had just come from church to tour the station. For the next week, Bill thought those ladies were going to petition him off the air."

Wayne Stevens: "Bette Davis appeared at one of the theaters in Detroit late in her life. And it was just her onstage showing some old movie clips and speaking to the audience . . . so of course Bill went. When the question and answer period came, Bill said, 'This was my moment to stand up and renew our acquaintance.' He said, 'I stood up and said, "Ms. Davis . . . do you remember an actor who was in a few of your pictures playing small parts . . . an actor by the name of Bill Kennedy?"' And all of Detroit is in this theater. She went, 'I don't remember such stupid players like that!' Bill was just so crushed and deflated. But when Bill told these stories of being made to look dumb the audience thought he was fabulous. It was just like Johnny Carson, he was funnier when he bombed with a bad joke."

A Hollywood Ending

By 1981, Bill Kennedy was 72 years old and preparing for retirement. That year he said goodbye to the staff at WKBD, who felt the same loss as the folks at CKLW did in 1969. Bill and his wife Suzy purchased a home in the ritzy community of Palm Beach, Florida. Prior to his departure from Motown, Kennedy negotiated a deal with Channel 50 to continue his Sunday editions. The daily show was taken over by Bill's friend and Detroit TV star Sonny Eliot and renamed *Sonny Eliot at the Movies*.

At first, Kennedy made weekly commutes to Michigan from Florida, but the stress of having to travel on schedule every week took its toll. Consequently, Bill finagled a remote broadcast from Channel 5 in West Palm Beach until the fall of 1983, when he decided to call it quits after 27 consecutive years on the air. Suzy Kennedy relives the taping of the final show from the estate her husband named "The Villa."

Suzy Kennedy: "The station [WKBD] wanted to tape the last show from a studio, but we said no, people wanted to see where Bill ended up. So I suggested that we shoot it in our backyard around the pool. The weather was beautiful that day. Bill sat in a wicker fan chair, and a good friend of ours, Howard Davidson, dressed in a tuxedo and carried a silver tray, posing as a butler. Bill said he wanted to create the illusion that he's going out in style! When they did the final shot, Howard poured champagne for Bill and Bill took a sip, then flipped the glass into the pool. The glass landed upright and was floating—you couldn't have planned a better ending! So the camera zoomed in on the floating glass, and that was the end."

After years of battling emphysema, the man who had shared a scene with Cary Grant in *Destination Tokyo* (1943) and was one of Bette Davis's lovers in *Mr. Skeffington* (1944) on the silver screen, and who rode into the sunset with the Lone Ranger and the Cisco Kid on the small screen, passed away on January 27, 1997, at the age of 88. In Tinseltown, Willard A. Kennedy was one of a million bit actors who graced the studio back lots, but in Motown he was the leading man he always dreamed of becoming. . . . He was one in a million!

Rita Bell

Rita Bell—schoolteacher type, attractive lady, wonderful human being . . . She was important in Detroit television.
   —RON DAVID, former director, WXYZ-TV

If you're the type of person who turns the television on first thing in the morning and you lived in Motown during the 1960s and 1970s, odds are you'll recall a perky lady hosting an interactive movie show on Channel 7. From 1960 to 1977, Rita Bell was a regular fixture in Motor City living rooms every weekday morning between breaks in old B movies to give away cash prizes on WXYZ's popular *Prize Movie*. Contests varied from Name That Tune to trivia questions to revealing celebrity photos by removing pieces of a jigsaw puzzle. Whatever the quiz of the day was, the

Rita Bell on the phone with a contestant on *Prize Movie*. (Courtesy Jerry Hansen.)

contestants were always contacted by telephone. Other than the contests and the movie, there wasn't much else to the show except for its glamorous hostess . . . Ms. Rita Bell.

Born in 1925, Rita was a native Detroiter who began her show business career at the age of nine singing every Sunday on WXYZ radio's *Children's Theater on the Air*. After she enrolled at Marygrove College in 1944, her father passed away, leaving her mother to struggle financially. Nineteen-year-old Rita offered to quit school and get a job to help out, but at the insistence of her mother she stayed at Marygrove and obtained a bachelor of arts degree.

The following year she married her first husband, John Connolly, and later gave birth to a son, Michael. Professionally, she sang with several Detroit orchestras, performing all over the state of Michigan. In 1952, she was employed as a public relations specialist at the United Foundation (now the United Way) and taught speech classes at Detroit's public schools and Marygrove College.

While attending a corn roast put on by Wrigley grocery stores in 1956, Bell was asked to sing a number with the strolling orchestra. In the audience that day was WXYZ vice president and general manager John Pival, who was mesmerized by her voice and enchanted with her beauty. He quickly approached her to request an audition for television. After consulting her coworkers at the United Foundation, Rita went to the audition, unaware that she was about to embark on a whole new career and make local history. Bell's second husband, Jerry Hansen, explains.

Jerry Hansen: "Pival put her on as the first woman weather person in Detroit at 12:30 at night. She worked at that for a while, but she was still working at the United Foundation and it just got to be too much for her. She went to Pival and told him, 'I'm going to quit, I can't work two jobs at the same time.' He said, 'You're quitting? Nobody quits television!' She said, 'Well I'm one that's quitting . . .' and she did. She was off for about two or three weeks when [Pival] called her up and said, 'Would you come back if I put a show on with you in the daytime?' Well, she was very lucky at that point because they had a big shakeup at the United Foundation and she got fired!"

Prize Movie

In the summer of 1959, Rita Bell was handed the reins to a show that aired weekday mornings at 8:30 a.m. called *Stage Three*, which was soon renamed *Prize Playhouse*. Retired WXYZ stage manager Art Runyon describes the concept of the show.

Art Runyon: "On *Prize Playhouse*, they'd maybe run a couple of sit-coms back-to-back and they went to running regular hour-long shows, old network shows. I don't know whose idea it was, but Pival really pushed it, and it was adding phone calls. At first, it was to answer a question about what was showing and it worked out pretty well. They'd have a bunch of prizes they'd give out, hence the name *Prize Playhouse*. Well, then the idea came to expand it a bit so it was at least an hour and a half and they'd run movies."

With the addition of movies in 1960 came yet another name change to *Prize Movie*. Along with the title change came a new game plan as well.

Contests were now open to a wider variety of trivia questions along with the most popular and frequently used game of all: Name that Tune. Former WXYZ stage manager Chuck Derry remembers how Rita went about picking her contestants.

Chuck Derry: "She used to get them out of the phone book. Some people were not too happy about that because she was just calling random people. So then they got the idea that you send in a card. People would send in postcards with their names on them, and she would shuffle up the cards and draw a card out and call that [person]."

Art Runyon: "It was very popular . . . it was the most popular morning program on Channel 7. She dominated that time period. Finally, they didn't bother with the prizes, it was just money."

And the dollar amount, whatever it started out at, would always increase by seven dollars for every wrong answer until somebody won. Why only seven dollars? Would the fact that it was Channel 7 have anything to do with that . . . hmm?

Name That Tune

As mentioned, winning the cash jackpot often involved naming a mystery tune. The person largely responsible for selecting the tunes was the ET (electrical transcription) operator. One of the ET operators during the 1960s was WXYZ news anchor Erik Smith.

Erik Smith: "My first steps in Broadcast House were to the set of *Prize Movie*. When I was hired full time as an ET operator, Rita gave me full rein to select the *Prize Movie* song . . . that melody that she would play a couple bars of for the audience. I chose the music, and it was kind of a challenge to musically find something that was probably fairly familiar to most people. But you didn't want it to be too familiar because, after all, it was a game. Sometimes I would do an easy one, and sometimes I'd do one that was really, really difficult . . . 'Fly Me to the Moon' or something, but it would be done on a harmonica or something just a little peculiar. That was the challenge of selecting her music."

One of the many fans stumped by Smith's choices of music was the future host of WDWB-TV's *The Movie Show Plus*, Greg Russell.

Greg Russell: "Rita Bell's *Prize Movie*, I think that's where all of us who were kids at the time in the 1960s learned about big band songs. It seemed like you'd always be sitting at home when the song would come on, and you're going, 'Ah . . . I don't know what that song is . . . I wish I knew what that song is . . .' And somebody on the phone would say, 'Oh, that was Benny Goodman . . . da-da-da-da . . . .' But it was cool!"

Erik Smith: "They were pretty familiar tunes . . . I would say they were tunes reminiscent of the 1940s and 1950s largely. They were not contemporary songs . . . we might do 'Mockingbird Hill' or something out of the 1950s. It was not classic rock and roll. We had a whole library of music that was purchased by the station [with] the rights to use it. We used very little outside music because you had to pay royalties for it, so the tunes that had been licensed to the music suppliers were all paid for and then nobody was being doubly paid."

Guests

Every once in a while *Prize Movie* would feature an in-studio guest. They ranged from Hollywood A-listers such as Lee Marvin to local public officials. Since guest appearances were infrequent and subsequent to the contest, they were often brief but memorable. Tony Micale, lead vocalist of the Reflections, recalls the experience.

Tony Micale: "When we sang on [*Club*] *1270*, I remember being asked if we would make an appearance on Rita Bell. Rita was beautiful; she reminded me of Arlene Dahl, the actress. I remember meeting her, and you kinda look at her a little differently because she was a real fox for an older lady, I mean a real pretty lady. She was very nice, treated us very nice . . . but it was a quick on and off. We sang a cappella, so we were able to do a quick song. We got in there and sang a song, she introduced each of us, we talked a little bit, she announced where we were gonna be in town, and it was over—that was basically it."

But not every appearance went as smoothly as Micale's. Chuck Derry reminisces about the day Sheriff William Lucas stopped by.

Chuck Derry: "We had the Wayne County Sheriff come in; he flew in by helicopter. I start convincing him, 'Well you ought to do the dialing and let Rita fly in the helicopter.' She had never flown in a helicopter before, and she really wanted to go fly in the helicopter. So, okay, she gets in and flies off.

"The only people that knew what was the tune on the tape, unless you knew the tune, was the guy that cut the tape—the ET operator—and Rita Bell. Well, on this day the guy upstairs was a substitute ET operator, so he didn't know what was on the tape. Rita was the only one that knew. The movie runs out—so the sheriff's gotta do [the contest] himself. Here's the sheriff dialing for dollars. As he's doing this, we suddenly realized that nobody knew the name of the song but Rita . . . and she's up in the air! The sheriff had absolutely no clue what the song was; fortunately the lady caller says, 'I don't know the name of that song.' Had she guessed a name, we wouldn't have known whether she was right or wrong!"

Lovely Rita

Regardless of what movie was featured, the contest jackpot, or the guest, at the heart of *Prize Movie* was the elegant charm of Rita Bell. As lady-like as she was, she had some idiosyncrasies, which are well remembered by retired WXYZ director Chris Montross and her husband Jerry Hansen.

Chris Montross: "I used to zip up the back of her dress. When I was doing the show, she always had clothes from an outfit that got credit on the show. She would show up in her regular clothes, then she would change, and she could never zip up the back of her dress. So it got to be a habit for good luck [that] I would zip up the back of her dress.

"She used to say some dumb things sometimes. She was talking about thunderstorms once. She said, 'Thunderstorms are isolated. Sometimes you're in a thunderstorm and the sun is shining five blocks away. That happened to me just the other night!' I remember that since obviously the sun wouldn't be shining at night. She would say some odd things."

Jerry Hansen: "She had a commercial on her show, Amy Joy Donuts. And she always fouled it up, saying, 'Amy Doy Jonuts.' She could say it very well when she wasn't on the air, but if she was on . . . that was it, she'd blow it."

Retired WXYZ art director Jack Flechsig and Chuck Derry comment about how much Rita loved a joke . . . especially when it was on her.

Jack Flechsig: "She was the subject of many, many, many practical jokes. The stagehands couldn't leave her alone. There was one stagehand by the name of Jack Brock, and [he and Rita] would chat while the movie was on. I remember one time they had Peter Pan Peanut Butter for a sponsor. And Jack Brock said to her, 'Now Rita, be careful so you don't say "penis" butter.' He would always plant something like that, and she said it right on the air. Another one, she had either Silvercup or Wonder bread for a sponsor and Jack would say, 'Now Rita, be careful during the commercial. Don't say it's the "breast in bed."' And she'd say it right on the air. Looking back now, I wonder if Rita didn't do it just to go along with the gag and be one of the guys. She loved the jokes, and she loved when they played jokes on her."

Chuck Derry: "When they would do stuff like that, people laughed about it. It wasn't something terrible that happened then . . . now that would be terrible."

On the Set

Chuck Derry: "The desk was probably six feet across, so there was enough room to put two people there. One day she was interviewing [local businessman and advertiser] Mr. Belvedere. That was a funny bit. She was interviewing Mr. Belvedere and he was saying 'we do good work' and he kinda slid back on his chair. It wasn't a big platform, but it was raised off the floor. The chairs had wheels on them, and this guy rolled right off the back of the set! On the air, all of a sudden he went, 'OOH-AHH!' . . . he was just gone."

Jack Flechsig: "She had many sets. I know on one of them she wore real glamorous clothes and had a long cigarette holder, and I think she reclined on a chaise longue for that one. But the most recent one, the one that ran the longest, [was] she sat behind a desk and the walls behind her were panels with an overall telephone motif. It was built around the concept of a telephone dial. That one was specially made for her."

Throughout the years, the telephone on the desk would change, too. There was the ever-popular princess phone of the 1960s and the French-style phone she had in the 1970s. Does anyone remember what she did for the American bicentennial in 1976? Stars and stripes were added to the dials on the set wall and the phone was replaced with an old-fashioned "star-spangled" candlestick telephone.

Remembering Rita

Although Rita Bell was most recognized for hosting *Prize Movie*, WXYZ managed to keep her busy in the 1960s with two other shows called *Starlit Stairway* and *Hollywood News*. She also appeared on an episode of the ABC network's western series *The Big Valley*, starring Barbara Stanwyck.

In September 1977, WXYZ pulled the plug on *Prize Movie* to pave the way for a new morning talk show, *Kelly & Company*. Under the assumption that viewers still wanted to see Rita Bell in the morning, the station management assigned her as John Kelly's original cohost, the "company" part of the program. When the pairing failed due to a lack of chemistry between Rita and John, she was replaced with Kelly's wife—Marilyn Turner.

Returning to the news department, where her television career began so long ago, Bell's last days at WXYZ were spent reviewing movies during the 6 p.m. newscasts in a segment called "At the Movies with Rita Bell." After 21 years at Channel 7, Rita left the station in 1978 to focus all of her energies on an advertising business she formed with her husband, Bell and Hansen, Inc. In 1987, the couple moved to San Diego, where Rita lived until she lost a two-year battle with cancer on December 9, 2003, at the age of 78.

Looking back at the legacy of Rita Bell with a few thoughts are retired WXYZ director Mason Weaver, Detroit TV fan Marci Wojciechowski, and Jack Flechsig.

Mason Weaver: "Rita and I were very good friends for many, many years. She was just a lovely person. What you saw was what you got with Rita. She was just a real down-to-earth, nice lady. Everybody just loved her"

Marci Wojciechowski: "She was a lady. The generation that I am from, we took sewing. We weren't taking shop class, we weren't doing auto mechanics . . . we were training to become housewives and moms. [Rita] was someone who worked for a living and still was a lady. She was something that I think a lot of little girls wouldn't have minded growing up to be."

Jack Flechsig: "She was so refined, demure, and fun loving. She was the glamour gal of Channel 7."

Sir Graves Ghastly

I would paint a tiny face on my chin and then hang upside down on my bed to mimic the Glob. My parents would have their friends over and I would cover the rest of my face so you would just see the chin and I would sing. I used to imitate what Sir Graves Ghastly did, and I would even try to sound like him—I just loved him!
   —LINDA LANCI, air personality, WMGC Radio

When it comes to the wackier side of local movie shows, *Sir Graves Ghastly Presents* sits at the top of the list. Through the graveyard gates of WJBK-TV, Channel 2, viewers were led by the hand to a coffin for the awakening of a campy vampire who showcased horror films every Saturday afternoon at one o'clock. With an exaggerated English accent and a sinister laugh that echoes in your head, Lawson Deming created the perfect kid-friendly persona to entice Motor City audiences with chilling

Detroit's favorite vampire, Sir Graves Ghastly (Lawson Deming). (Courtesy Lawson Deming.)

monster "stories" about such classics as *Dracula, Frankenstein,* and *The Wolf Man;* sci-fi mutant features such as *The Creation of the Humanoids* and *Tarantula;* and all of the hokey British fright flicks starring Christopher Lee and Peter Cushing.

Hailing from the days of William Shakespeare, Sir Graves was sentenced to death after infuriating Queen Elizabeth I. He was hanged in the Tower of London but cheated death to emerge as one of the living dead, condemned to a personal mausoleum where a moon that is always full shines through the evening fog. Craving a twentieth-century audience, the theatrical count penetrated Motown television in 1967, where he staged comical cryptic antics with the assistance of his gruesome cohorts until 1982. Although he originally sought to capture the attention of teenagers and young adults, the night walker's whimsical charm made him a favorite among the children of Metro Detroit. So when the immensely popular Sir Graves Ghastly beckoned, "Turn out your lights, pull down the shades, draw the drapes, and cuddle up in your favorite spot by the telly for today's tale of terror . . ." thousands of youngsters, including Shaun Robinson and Mark Nowotarski, found themselves glued to the tube for an afternoon loaded with spooks and fun.

Shaun Robinson: "On Saturday afternoons, I religiously made myself a pot of Chef Boyardee ravioli right before *Sir Graves Ghastly* would come on. I'd pour myself a bowl and go down into the basement and watch *Sir Graves* crouched underneath a blanket. I'd peek through my hands and just be scared for the entire program. That was my Saturday afternoon—I absolutely loved that show!"

Mark Nowotarski: "Sir Graves Ghastly gave me some of my most pleasant memories. He was in a world of his own that, as a child, you wished you were in, too!"

A Vampire Rises from the Woods

Possessing a beautifully rich baritone voice, Lawson Joseph Deming was born in April 1913. Growing up in Cleveland, he studied theater acting before prospering in radio broadcasting in the 1930s. In 1949, when an exciting new medium called television was in need of an afternoon movie host, Deming decided to take the plunge and cross over like so many other radio professionals in his day. Years later a local actor by the name of Clay Conroy portrayed a character known as Woodrow the Woods-man on the popular children's program *Barnaby the Leprechaun*. When Woodrow was spun off into his own show in 1961, Deming was employed to voice all of the woodsman's puppet pals on Cleveland's KYW, Channel 3.

In 1965, station KYW was sold and the new owners announced their plan to ax *Woodrow the Woodsman*. Concurrently, Storer Broadcasting in Detroit began to shop around for a program to replace its recently canceled *B'wana Don*. *Woodrow* was a perfect fit, and so Conroy and Deming headed up to their new home at WJBK, Channel 2, in 1966. While Clay Conroy viewed himself as the star of the show, his audience, along with the station management, took more of a shine to the talents of the unseen Lawson Deming. His versatility and charisma prompted the brass at WJBK to make him an offer that would lead to immortality. Former WJBK director Dick Dietrich and Lawson's son, Dave Deming, recount the evolution of Sir Graves Ghastly.

Dick Dietrich: "Everyone liked Lawson personally to begin with; he really worked hard. And, as I remember, the station had bought a series of old horror movies. So we needed a guy to bridge in and out of the commercial breaks during the run of these movies."

Dave Deming: "The station indicated they wanted a vampire. At first, my dad thought that was something he really didn't want to do, but they convinced him to do it for a month. Immediately he and my mother started to think about what the character should be like. Dad was always a tongue-in-cheek guy and a punster; he loved Shakespeare, he loved Basil Rathbone, and he loved a lot of the English plays. He decided this character would be a friendly vampire. And because he wanted to be proper and dignified he chose 'Sir' as part of his title. 'Graves' was his [spin] to being a vampire."

On the day Lawson suggested the name Sir Graves to his wife Mary Rita, her immediate reaction was, "That sounds ghastly!" Hmmm . . . ghastly, hah! Why not? The word *ghastly* became the icing on the cake for Deming. And so the name Sir Graves Ghastly was officially christened. The next question Lawson had to answer was: what should a Sir Graves Ghastly look like? Drawing on his theater background, he played around with different kinds of makeup and hairstyles until he achieved a look reminiscent of Bela Lugosi's Dracula but with a sixteenth-century twist. A false, upturned mustache and a goatee were added to his pale face, as well as slick, center-parted hair, to evoke the Elizabethan period when Sir Graves would have roamed the Earth as a mortal. Once the show got under way, Deming made minor alterations to his appearance. The first was to apply heavy makeup to his eyes, followed by layered hair swirls on his forehead and temples. Dapperly dressed in a black suit and draped with a shiny black cape containing a deep red lining, he now projected an image of a suavely sophisticated count who'd been washed up for centuries. Was there anything else you could think of to add to the mix, Lawson?

Lawson Deming: "Sir Graves was very melodramatic because after all he was British, you know. I could do a pretty good English accent, and I figured I might as well get paid for doing it."

The Haunted Graveyard

To further enhance the horror motif for the presentation of *Sir Graves Ghastly* as well as the movies, it was imperative for Channel 2 art director Jim Mackey to design a set that coincided with Hollywood's perception of the living dead. Retired WJBK stagehand Errol Fortin, who constructed the set to Mackey's specifications, explains the origin of a few key ingredients.

Errol Fortin: "The station bought the cheapest casket it could find. It was bare wood covered with a blue-gray cloth [and a dark red lining]— the kind that's typically used for a potter's field [poor people's] burial.

Outside the coffin in the late 1960s. (Courtesy Dave Deming.)

We had previously done a show called *Morgus the Magnificent,* which had a whole bunch of Frankenstein laboratory props. So we recycled many of the laboratory props, like Morgus's old-fashioned rolltop desk, into the *Sir Graves* set. We filled the desk with burned-out candles and cobwebs and painted huge gray boulders on the walls to simulate an old castle type of decor."

With sawhorses serving as a makeshift casket bier, Sir Graves's "bed" was placed outside the facade of a creepy Old World mausoleum enclosed by two large wrought iron gates bearing his initials. The haunting set where the made-for-TV vampire would spend eternity was ready for its unveiling. The program's unforgettable opening, developed by former WJBK director, Marshall Slocum, painted a creepy "enter if you dare" scenario to set the mood for Sir Graves Ghastly's grand rising. Former WJBK and current WXYZ director Jerry Rimmer, one of the few local African American directors in the 1970s, describes the memorable sequence.

Jerry Rimmer: "The opening was on tape and ran for about 25 to 30 seconds. It started with a smoke effect to simulate fog, and there would be all kinds of eerie sounds [taken from the Disneyland album *Chilling, Thrilling Sounds of the Haunted House*]. The camera would close in on the gates as they opened and then continued to float through the grave-yard, passing a few headstones, until it zeroed in on a stone that read, 'Sir Graves Ghastly.' From there, we would cut to a live studio shot of the casket, where a bat would fly by before Lawson would rise up as Sir Graves and begin the show. He would establish his identity as Sir Graves [and] talk a little bit about the movie, with a few chilling lines like 'Have you ever seen a werewolf at night? What would you do if you were con-fronted by a monster?' And then he'd say something like 'Now here's my good friend Lon Chaney or Boris Karloff in . . .'

"From there, he'd go into his dialogue about 'turning out the lights' and he'd do his laugh. The line about turning out the lights was a takeoff on the old *Scream Theater,* and there was a movie called *The Tingler* that contained similar verbiage . . . so Lawson was doing his own kind of par-ody of it."

Neeeyaaahh!

Lawson Deming: "It took me about fifteen minutes to get into the makeup and costume."

Despite the relatively short time needed to assume his alter ego, Law-son Deming was very much a perfectionist when it came to his transfor-mation. The actor would not go on unless every detail was precisely cor-rect. After all, his reputation was at stake.

Jerry Rimmer: "I remember him looking at his makeup and saying, 'Does that look okay? I think that's all right . . . no, wait a minute . . .' We couldn't tell the difference. He was very particular about his makeup; he wanted to see how he looked on-camera before we'd roll tape. So by the time he was made up he was *that* character! He moved very, very quickly as himself, Lawson Deming—he was a very busy man—but when he became Sir Graves Ghastly he slowed the pace down dramatically, with flowing movements involving the cape. The camera would be posi-tioned behind him. Then he'd turn his head over his shoulder and raise his eyebrow to speak in that deep Shakespearian voice: 'Have you ever seen a hand by itself or an eyeball rolling down the road?'"

Lawson Deming: "Very often what I thought was funny was very dif-ferent from that of other people."

Dave Deming: "Even though he played this character, his character was actually a reflection of his own humorous personality. My dad was always a lot of fun. He was always joking and punning, and he was an awesome storyteller."

Jerry Rimmer: "He would make comments about the movie such as 'Did you see how Bela Lugosi changed into a bat? I taught him how to do that!' If the movie was campy, then he would be campy along with it: 'Can you believe how they made that bat fly? No self-respecting vampire flies like that!'

"Then there were times during production when the stagehands would lock the coffin on Lawson. We'd roll the tape, and when the cue came for him to open the coffin you'd hear this thumping noise followed by, 'Hey, I can't get outta here!' totally out of character. Then, when we'd open the lid, he'd say, 'Whew, it was getting a little cloister phobic in there.' Lawson had a great sense of humor, and he loved to laugh."

And if there's one element in the aura of Sir Graves Ghastly that's permanently tattooed on the brain of every Metro Detroiter, it's his signature "NEEEYAAAHH!" The laugh that Mary Rita Deming described as annoying became the most distinctive and beloved attribute of her husband's character. In fact, it went on to become the most widely imitated gimmick of any local television personality to date. Deming's personal appearances often evoked shrieks from hundreds of kids and adults from all walks of life attempting to emulate his devilish guffaw.

Lawson Deming: "I remember one day during a personal appearance at one of the Catholic schools a voice comes up from behind me and it was a perfect mimicry of the Sir Graves laugh . . . when I turned around, it was a chubby nun! I said, 'Where did you ever learn that?' She said, 'I learned that from you, and I use it when I want to get the kids' attention!'"

The Chamber of Horrors

Dick Dietrich: "Lawson had so many different characters and bits that there was never a dull moment. He was extremely innovative."

Fearing that audiences might grow bored with a vampire commenting on the movies between commercial breaks, Deming cleverly devised a diverse cast of characters to interact with Sir Graves in corny satirical sketches, all of whom he portrayed himself. Dick Dietrich recalls the first character: Baruba.

Dick Dietrich: "Baruba was supposed to be a medieval caretaker who did Sir Graves's bidding. He dressed up in a dark brown, hooded robe similar to [that of] a monk, and all he did was grunt."

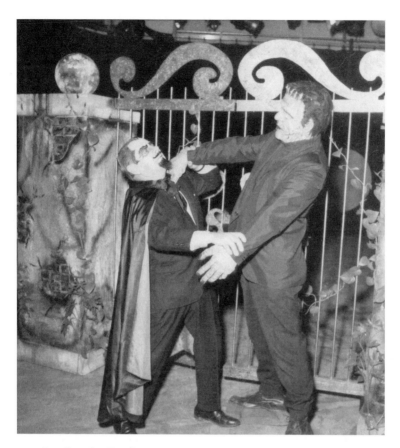

Battling the Frankenstein monster. (Courtesy Dave Deming.)

From Baruba, the depths of Lawson's imagination spawned a series of morbid misfits that included Reel McCoy, a gnome in overalls who dug up the film reels for the featured movie; the Cool Ghoul, the decapitated head of a 1950s biker dude sporting a pair of shades; a talking skull dubbed the Voice of Doom; Walter, Sir Graves's wicked alter ego; Baron Boogaloff; and Ivan Awfulwitch, just to name a few. He also created a series of puppets, including the soft-shoe Dancing Skeletons, which were dangled by the stagehands, and a Señor Wences knockoff fist puppet with a little goateed face drawn on his index finger and thumb.

But within the Sir Graves ensemble the two favorites among the production staff and home audience were undoubtedly "That Georgeous Cookie" Tilly Trollhouse—Sir Graves's girlfriend whose name was a wordplay on Nestle's tollhouse cookies—and of course the infamous big-mouthed Glob! Dave Deming and Jerry Rimmer describe the feminine poise of Sir Graves's better half, both on- and off-camera.

Dave Deming: "Dad would dress in drag with a blond wig and tight dress and lip-sync to Jo Stafford songs. Jo Stafford sounded like she always sang a little off key, so when Dad did exaggerated pantomimes to cuts from her albums it was hysterical!"

Jerry Rimmer: "Tilly Trollhouse was just totally outrageous! Off-camera Lawson had a lot of fun being in drag. He would kid with the stagehands, 'Hello big boy . . . are you new in town?' And their reaction was, 'Whooo! That's an ugly broad!' He would also joke about being ready for his close-up as Tilly. He would look right into the camera and say, 'I'm ready for my close up Mr. DeMille.' 'Yeee . . . yikes! Man, that's nasty!'"

As big a hit as Tilly was with the viewers, she had to take a backseat to the Glob, a giant, upside-down mouth tightly superimposed on the full moon. With a miniature face printed on his chin, Deming's ghoulish creature lip-synced to everything from Spike Jones to horror novelty songs such as the "Monster Mash" and the "King Kong Stomp." Jerry Rimmer and Dick Dietrich recall the Glob's melodic intros.

Jerry Rimmer: "The Glob was just cool! It would come on: 'Ba-ba-bla-ba-bla-ba-bob-ba-bla-bla-ba-bob-ba-blaaaab!'"

Dick Dietrich: "Sir Graves would sit and look at the Glob in his easy chair and say, 'Hit it, Glob!'"

Jerry Rimmer: "I remember once we accidentally rolled the Glob at the wrong time and he covered by saying, 'No, no, no . . . not now; shut up . . . go away, go away, Glob!' Afterward he came into the control room and we were ready to apologize for the mistake, but he said, 'Hey, I liked that! Let's use it.' From that point on, he let us roll the Glob in at these bizarre times, and his reaction would be, 'Oh, look, the Glob is here . . . he's got something to saaay!'"

Given the sheer funkiness of the Glob's appearance, fans may wonder whether Lawson Deming actually hung upside down during the segment tapings. So for those who wish to know, here's the answer from the director who recorded them.

Jerry Rimmer: "As I remember [it], he was never upside down. He lay sideways on a table, and we tilted the camera sideways but in the reverse direction. So when the tape was played back it gave the illusion that he was upside down. We had to get the 180 degrees this way because there weren't any digital effects available in those days that allowed you to rotate the image and we couldn't have him stand on his head or hang upside down."

Conception and Execution

Dick Dietrich: "Lawson commuted to Detroit from Cleveland every week for the entire tenure of the show. In the early days, when he came up on Fridays, before he rented an apartment, he would sleep on a couch in the prop room. He would either stay in there or go to the office across the hall and write out all of his bits for the next day."

Dave Deming: "Sometimes he took a bus, now and then he flew, but most of the time he drove to Detroit. And, knowing him, he spent much of his commute developing his ideas for the show. That way when he got to Detroit he was ready to put the ideas into motion."

Lawson Deming: "When I'd get an idea, I'd talk to myself about it, and it worked pretty good."

Since boyhood, Lawson Deming had been an actor. His many years of training in the theater proved invaluable at this juncture in his career. Already in his mid-fifties at the onset of *Sir Graves Ghastly,* the preparation needed to pull off such a complicated production required his entire life's work as an actor in all three mediums: theater, radio, and television. He would have to conceive, write, stage direct, and produce the entire program single-handedly every week for 15 years consecutively. Even more challenging for Deming than the number of hats he'd have to wear was developing his ability to execute comedy. Although he was a comedian at heart, prior to this show everything on his showbiz resume was of a serious nature. *Sir Graves Ghastly* was his first true attempt at comedy.

When WJBK initially launched the *Sir Graves Big Show,* before permanently renaming it *Sir Graves Ghastly Presents* in 1970, the family vampire played second fiddle to the featured movie. But as time went on and his celebrity grew, as in the case of other local hosts, the films became a backdrop to Sir Graves. Movies were edited down to fit his time, allowing all things to be possible.

Jerry Rimmer: "There would be about six to eight bits per show. Lawson's dialogue during the bits were always ad-libbed. We would do a walk-through, but we never knew exactly what he was going to say until the cameras were turned on and tape was rolling."

Errol Fortin: "All of his characters were prerecorded and inserted into the format as complete segments. But if Sir Graves wanted to talk to a character from his casket or chair the pre-recorded bits were chroma keyed electronically into his live segment."

Dick Dietrich: "Another fun thing we did with the chroma key was to cut out Sir Graves's head and move it around the TV screen."

No other Detroit TV show utilized as many special effects as *Sir*

Graves Ghastly Presents. For the crew at WJBK to assemble a final one-inch tape master to broadcast around movie breaks, the Saturday shooting schedule usually took a full eight hours without the prerecorded bits. The dramatic lighting and spooky effects necessary to sustain a scary presentation became much more time consuming than what's needed for a normal production. Thus, many of the prerecorded bits had to be taped either the day before or during the week, depending on the complexity of the setup. And because the program had such a wide range of complicated effects the margin of error could easily be fatal without teamwork.

Jerry Rimmer: "Lawson would come in after we taped a segment and would watch a clip of it. And, like most perfectionists, he would ask us, 'How'd that go? What did you think of that? Did you like it?' And we'd say, 'That looked great . . . you were fine.' Then he'd say, 'You really think so?' He needed that affirmation. It was important to him that others approved of his performance."

Errol Fortin: "If anybody had a good idea, Lawson latched onto it, and he listened intently. He was a very good guy when it came to somebody making a suggestion."

For All the Little Goblins

Mark Nowotarski: "Sir Graves had an art segment, similar to Oopsy's, where kids would send in homemade drawings to be displayed in his Art Ghoullery. Only these drawings were of Godzilla, Frankenstein, the Wolf Man, and other scary creatures. I remember that I sent in about nine drawings all at once, and four of them were featured on the program, all at the same time. The one that I can recall most readily was of an electrical Cyclops monster battling Frankenstein. And even though the drawings were shown for just a fleeting moment . . . man, that made my day!"

Jerry Rimmer: "We played music and panned the camera across the board. Occasionally we'd stop on a drawing and key in Sir Graves's face so he could say, 'That's a nice one here.' But he would always mention the kid's name and age, and he would describe the picture, too: 'This one has the Wolf Man and Frankenstein fighting, and you can see the Mummy is over in the corner.' He covered everything that was in the drawing. Even if he didn't know exactly what the picture was, he'd say, 'This looks like it might be the Tasmanian Devil . . . I'm not sure, but let me know. Write me and tell me who that is.'"

Along with the Art Ghoullery, Sir Graves Ghastly catered to his number-one fans by announcing their birthdays and reading their letters from his overflowing mailbag.

Jerry Rimmer: "The kids would write in questions like: Do you live in the coffin? What do you like to eat? What's your favorite drink? And his answers were thematic and funny: 'I like spaghetti, but no garlic . . . garlic is bad . . . no, no!' Or 'My favorite drink is Type O . . .' which he made sound like it was a drink you could order on tap. He was very good at presenting a friendly vampire to the kids; he separated himself from the blood-sucking and religious aspects of being a vampire. He always made the cross out to be like an X in tic-tac-toe as opposed to [having] any religious significance."

Because of Lawson Deming's love of children, not only did the show shift gears to accommodate them but he devoted an enormous amount of his free time to public appearances at schools, fairs, shopping malls, hospitals, and anywhere else the kindhearted creature of the night was welcome . . . especially around Halloween.

Mark Nowotarski: "One appearance that I dragged my mother to was at the Gateway Theater around Halloween time in the late 1960s. Sir Graves was hosting a spook show filled with scary characters that came out into the theater while a movie was playing, so it had a haunted house kind of effect. The featured movie that afternoon was *The Ghost and Mr. Chicken* with Don Knotts. And I remember not liking the movie because I wanted to see more of Sir Graves. So after the movie Sir Graves came out onstage and stayed there for almost two hours because there were about 300 kids and about 100 parents all wanting to meet Sir Graves Ghastly. It was absolute chaos!"

Lawson Deming: "My favorite memory of being Sir Graves Ghastly comes from the crowds—kids by the droves with their arms around my knees, shouting, 'I love you, Sir Graves!' I'd look down and say [in character], 'I love you, too!'"

Vamping Out

Lawson Deming: "I remember once there was a young guy who tried his damnedest to copy my character and take it over. He showed up in crowds dressed like me, and people were laughing at him, so he didn't last too long."

Dave Deming: "When I was a graduate student at Cranbrook, my wife and I lived in the gatehouse of a retired Ford vice president in Bloomfield Hills. On this one particular Saturday, while I was doing the gardening in the courtyard, the lady of the house was out showing me where she wanted the plants to go. And this 68-year-old woman always hated it when people came into her courtyard unexpectedly, using the service drive as a turnaround. Well, a car pulled up the service drive, and she muttered while I was on my knees, 'Why do these people keep doing this!?' I looked up at the car and saw my dad sitting in the passenger seat in his full costume; he had just come from an appearance. And just as she turned around Dad jumped out of the car flashing his cape open and said in the character voice, 'Good afternoon!' And this lady screamed so loud I thought she was going to have a heart attack! Later she said to me, 'You know, your father scared the pants off me, but I enjoy watching him on TV.'"

Dick Dietrich: "When WJBK was still on Second Avenue in Detroit, across the street on Second and Bethune was Momo's Bar. There was a brief period when the show first started when we ran it on Friday nights. After Lawson did the opening, there was about twenty minutes of down-time. He came into the bar in full costume while I was in there with some people from the news department. We would sit there and never acknowledge him, and the guy who owned the bar would never acknowl-edge him either. He would sit at the end of the bar, and we'd hear people saying, 'Get a load of the guy at the end of the bar' as they were pretend-ing not to look. And of course Lawson picked up on what was going on. So when he walked toward the door to exit he'd let the Sir Graves laugh go and then leave. It was always interesting to see how people who didn't watch the show reacted to him."

Dave Deming: "One of the things I always appreciated about my dad was that despite his love for attention when he was done with the char-acter he became very private and liked to be alone with his family. Because he was in show business for so long, he was famous most of his life, and I never ever had an inkling that his fame went to his head. He was always gentle and personable with people.

"I remember once when I was a kid we went to Chippewa Lake Park. Now my dad was only 5'4" and some guy who stood 6'5" comes up to my dad and says, 'Are you Lawson Deming, that guy on TV?' My dad smiled and said, 'Yes, I am.' And the guy goes, 'Well, you're just a little shrimp!' My dad laughed and said, 'I can see from your perspective I am.' The guy asked for an autograph, and my dad gave it to him. Somebody else might have been totally offended by that opening remark, but Dad wasn't at all; he loved people. He handled being a celebrity very well!"

Entombment

When Sir Graves fever ran high in the late 1960s and early 1970s, thanks in part to the widespread appeal of the horror genre, the eloquent count enjoyed brief TV stints in Washington, DC, and his hometown of Cleveland, where he was acknowledged as Count Alu Card (Dracula spelled backward). By 1982, with the improvement of animated special effects and the rising interest in a new media—video games—there was a growing feeling among the suits at Channel 2 that the old scary movies stored in their film vault had become a novelty of yesterday and that the audience for Sir Graves had changed.

Unbeknownst to fans (as well as Deming himself), November 6, 1982, marked Sir Graves Ghastly's last rising before he spent five months of seclusion in television purgatory. In April of 1983, the very month in which Lawson Deming celebrated his seventieth birthday, WJBK officially laid Sir Graves Ghastly to rest. After a 15-year stretch of colorful comedy, musical parodies, and eerie madness, Lawson Deming retired from television, retreating to his home just outside of Cleveland. Over the next several years, he would reprise his beloved character for Detroiters by honoring requests for appearances around Sir Graves's favorite day of the year—Halloween. For all of the Motown fans who embraced the vampire, the delightful memory of Lawson Joseph Deming shall live forever!

Lawson Deming: "I never had one bit of hostility directed toward me. The press was always very kind to me . . . I was lovable, and I really had fun doing Sir Graves Ghastly."

The Ghoul

One thing about *The Ghoul* is that it didn't require you to think too much. But it didn't insult your intelligence, either. It made you laugh—the theater of the absurd. It was the state of mind that was different about it.
—FRANK GADWELL, Detroit TV fan

He epitomized our dark side while elevating bad late-night horror flicks to alarming heights of weirdness in the 1970s and 1980s. Costumed as an off-color counterculture beatnik, the Ghoul spawned a strong cult following among Motor City kids, teens, and young adults, whom he branded his Ghoul power generals. Sporting a fright wig, a false mus-

The Ghoul (Ron Sweed) trashes another bad film in 1977.
(Courtesy Water P. Reuther Library, Wayne State University.)

tache and goatee, sunglasses with one lens missing, and a lab coat covered with buttons, this figure of sheer madness was known for blowing up food, model cars, dolls, and of course his arch enemy, a rubber frog named Froggy!

Although most adults, especially parents, found him to be disgustingly offensive, it was the anticipation of his taboo antics every Saturday night at 11:30 that beckoned Detroit's children to stay up past their bedtime and for teenagers and college students to end their dates early. Ghoul fans Mark Nowotarski, Greg Russell, Marci Wojciechowski, and Joe Humeniuk describe the Saturday night ritual.

Mark Nowotarski: "The Ghoul was totally irreverent; he was just absolutely wild! He had an odd-looking outfit that nobody in the Detroit area had ever seen before . . . so nobody knew where the heck this guy was coming from. He would do pretty much whatever he wanted and say whatever he wanted. It was a pretty wild affair . . . I mean, this is a grown man coming in on one of those giant bouncing balls . . . it was like, 'wow,' this is something new."

Greg Russell: "The Ghoul was almost the complete opposite of Sir Graves Ghastly. Sir Graves was the nice guy, the fun guy . . . the Ghoul, on the other hand, was always blowing up frogs. And all the hippy stoner kids would go, 'Yeah, man . . . the Ghoul . . . yeah . . . .' *The Night of the Living Dead* was more of his genre, the kind of movie he would show."

Marci Wojciechowski: "He was bizarre! It was more of a fad to like him. Groups of kids would watch him because it was the cool thing to do, like with the TV series *Dark Shadows,* but you also had to be in the mood for the Ghoul. The movies were okay. They were your typical bad scary movies."

Joe Humeniuk: "He was always doing these parodies that were rude and obnoxious. He was kind of a loudmouth, but that was the 'Ghoul' way. He would always either burp in the middle of a [movie] scene when something funny or weird was gonna happen . . . or he'd have these crazy voices come in, 'Hey, hey, hey, HEY, HEY!!!' He was cool, and I looked forward to watching him every Saturday night. *The Ghoul* was definitely my favorite show when I was growing up!"

The Ghoulish Beginning

Behind the Ghoul's disguise was the very mild-mannered, soft-spoken Ron Sweed. The foundation for his alter ego goes all the way back to his early youth in Euclid, Ohio. While most young boys were out playing sports, Sweed remembers how he divvied up his spare time between the library, his basement, and scary movies as he journeys back in time to a "horror-filled" childhood.

Ron Sweed: "I just always, from very early memories, have been interested in monsters and that type of genre. By the third or fourth grade, I was reading Edgar Allen Poe. I was a voracious reader at the library and got everything on Poe. I discovered *The Screaming Skull,* which turned out to be one of my favorite movies as a kid, but I read the book first. And long before haunted houses were big I was building stuff in my basement for the neighborhood kids. I had kooky things set up to frighten them, so I loved that sort of thing.

"In 1958, the first wave of 'Chiller Theater' came out across the country, where the all local stations got the Universal horror movies: the *Dracula* and *Frankenstein* films. I asked my dad who Frankenstein was and who Dracula was, and he explained them to me. My parents let me stay up late to watch them. They were hosted on Friday nights by a local called 'Mad Daddy,' who was Pete Myers, a deejay who did one of the early rock shows with Alan Freed on Cleveland radio. He would wear a death cowl—the black-hooded robe type of thing with bat wings on the arms—and he said everything in rhymes: 'Little Jimmy peachy-keen, built himself a time machine . . . set a dial, pushed a button . . . poof—there was nuttin'! Ah-ha-ha-ha . . . hey! Now back to the movie, gang . . . *Dracula*.'

"One of my best movie memories is of the Boris Karloff Frankenstein monster. That scene where you hear him shuffling down the steps and he comes in backward and slowly turns to face the camera . . . man, that was just the greatest. A lot of times, as you get older, you forget the impact that certain things have, like the first time you held a bug in your hand, just simple things like that. I always try to hang on so I don't get jaded and let the years make those things commonplace. And [*Frankenstein*] is one of the things I hung onto . . . that Jack Pierce makeup and Boris Karloff's interpretation of the creature, it was just a killer! It was really good."

Ghoulardi

The powerful imagery of Boris Karloff's Frankenstein monster that so influenced Ron Sweed's childhood was about to be overshadowed by an offbeat movie guru sporting a fright wig, a fake beard and mustache, and a pair of single-lens sunglasses. Tuning in to *Shock Theater* on WJW, Channel 8, the adolescent Sweed was about to see the face of his future.

Ron Sweed: "In 1963, when I was in junior high, this great movie host started in Cleveland named Ernie Anderson, and his character was Ghoulardi. He was phenomenal. He was the first guy to be completely honest. Mad Daddy, along with other first-wave hosts, would say, 'Ooh, it's a spooky one tonight,' that kind of thing. So in the second wave of Chiller Theater came films like *Attack of the Crab Monsters,* that type of stuff. Ghoulardi would come on and say, 'Hey, group, do you believe tonight's movie? We have 17 cents tied up in this piece of celluloid trash!'

"Plus he would do inserts into the movie with sound effects, and he would also chroma key himself into the movie. For example, in the Lon Chaney *Caveman* movies, where he's sitting in front of a fire with a piece of meat on a stick, roasting it, you'd see Ghoulardi looking at him and saying, 'You're not going to eat that stuff are you? Oh man, there's a good burger joint right around the corner I can take you to . . . it'll taste a lot better than that garbage you're about to ingest.' His timing was just impeccable. There was a lot of adult humor, and he wasn't talking down to kids either."

Radio and television announcer Ernie Anderson ignited a ratings frenzy for Channel 8 with his edgy character, Ghoulardi. All of Cleveland embraced this radical departure from the traditional horror hosts. Within months, Anderson became the hottest and highest paid local performer in the city's history! His fan base was huge. Teenagers would cut their Saturday night plans short in order to catch the next installment of Ghoulardi's shenanigans. And among those hooked teens who religiously watched him was Ron Sweed.

In July of 1963, Ghoulardi announced that he would appear at the Euclid Beach Amusement Park. Sweed aspired to meet his new idol but just for an autograph. Hoping to draw Ghoulardi's attention and get the coveted signature, Sweed showed up in a gorilla suit that he had permanently borrowed from a movie theater. The scheme worked, as Ghoulardi invited the "gorilla" onstage with him. The chemistry between the two sparked, and Sweed became a part of Ghoulardi's show. One day, after a few weeks on *Shock Theater*, Ron arrived early and was afforded the chance to wait in Anderson's office. Noticing how cluttered and disarrayed the desk was, the teenager offered his services to Mr. Anderson, thus becoming his gofer.

Reincarnation

By the fall of 1966, Ernie Anderson's best friend, comedian Tim Conway, invited him to join the cast of a new sitcom called *Rango*. Anderson packed his bags and headed for Hollywood, leaving his Ghoulardi costume with Sweed. WJW replaced Anderson with station engineer Chuck Schodowski and Bob "Hoolihan the Weatherman" Wells. Together they became *Hoolihan and Big Chuck*. Schodowski, who in Sweed's eyes had become his big brother at Channel 8, offered the high school senior a job on the program behind the scenes.

Taking the advice of Tim Conway, whom he had met through Anderson, the following year Ron Sweed chose to attend Conway's alma mater, Bowling Green State University, as an English major. While going to school Monday through Thursday, he commuted back to Cleveland on Fridays to continue his work on *Hoolihan and Big Chuck*. By his junior year in 1970, Sweed had grown bored with Big Chuck's conservative humor. He longed for the unpredictability that had made Ghoulardi a local legend. His prayers were answered when he received a surprise phone call from Anderson. Since his sudden departure from Cleveland, Ernie Anderson had found fame and fortune as the voice for the ABC network. He notified Sweed of his return to host an hour-long special for Cleveland's Channel 5 and reprise Ghoulardi in a few segments.

When Anderson asked him to prepare the old set and revive the costume for the special, Ron was thrilled! It was during the preparations for Ghoulardi's homecoming that he figured the time was right to approach his mentor with an idea. He hoped to convince Anderson to fly into town once a month and tape a month's worth of shows as Ghoulardi. That way Anderson could stay out on the coast, Cleveland would get Ghoulardi back, and everybody would be happy . . . right? Wrong! When Anderson declined, Sweed quickly proposed plan B.

Ron Sweed: "I said, 'Would you let me re-create the character of Ghoulardi?' Ernie said, 'Why? What's with all this Ghoulardi stuff?' I said, 'Your comedy was so much edgier and that's how comedy should be and people here miss it. If you won't do it, I think I might be able to re-create it.' He squinted his eyes at me and said, 'If you're gonna do something, you gotta do something that you can relate to, and you're such a nice, quiet, Dick Cavett kind of guy. Ghoulardi is just so wild, maybe you should do something more Ron Sweed.' I said, 'There's a side to me that you don't know about, and I think I can pull it off.' He says, 'It seems to me you won't be satisfied until you give it a shot. I personally don't think it's going to work. But since you have your head set on it and you're asking my permission to do the character . . . yes, you have my permission. The only thing is, Storer Broadcasting owns the name Ghoulardi. So knock off the "ardi" and call yourself the Ghoul or some other stupid thing.'"

After getting the blessing of his hero, Ron Sweed donned the famous costume and wasted no time in producing a pilot.

Ron Sweed: "I made it in the basement of Channel 8 and then took it to Kaiser Broadcasting, which owned Channel 61 in Cleveland and Channel 50 in Detroit. My spiel was, number one, I would give them something that the city wanted; number two, I would give them something that would beat Channel 43 [their biggest competitor] in the ratings; and, number three, I'm so confident about this that I will generate mail by the bag."

More Ghoul garbàge. (Courtesy Dave Riley.)

In 1971, *The Ghoul* made its television debut on Channel 61 in Cleveland. Appearing before a black curtain on a darkened stage with a scoop light at his feet aiming upward, Sweed introduced rock-bottom sci-fi horror flicks as a reincarnated Ghoulardi. But after a month of playing it safe he realized he couldn't imitate Anderson forever; someday he would have to make the character his own. The moment arrived with the addition of stage flats and a pair of roller skates.

Ron Sweed: "I said, 'I'm gonna come in with a pair of roller skates this week.' I just wanted to come screaming in from point A to point B. When I came through, I tripped over the camera cables and tumbled into the set and the flats came down on top of me. The camera guys are just laughing with tears in their eyes, and so I started to feed off them by laughing and kicking all the crap off me. 'Hey, gang, you're not gonna believe tonight's show. The movie is . . . .' And that was the birth of Ron Sweed as the Ghoul, not Ron Sweed as Ghoulardi."

Ghoul Power

Slapstick with a bang separated the Ghoul from Ghoulardi. The societal and pop culture changes in the early 1970s fueled an endless number of explosions on the show . . . literally! Blowing up everything from toys to food became a new pastime on the set of *The Ghoul*. A new generation was now hip to the late-night hysteria that had appealed to Ron Sweed eight years earlier. Pushing the envelope generated bags of mail, just as Sweed had promised. In fact, Channel 61's general manager, Art Hook, whom the Ghoul referred to as Captain Hook on the air, was pleased with the amount of mail derived from the station putdowns alone. The more the Ghoul slammed the station, the more mail came in. Within a matter of months, the ratings tripled, and the Ghoul became the new face of Channel 61. "Ghoul Power" was on the rise!

Ron Sweed: "It just became so big that Dick Block, the CEO [chief executive officer] for Kaiser and the brother of the guy who did H&R Block, said, 'Let's put *The Ghoul* on in all the cities of the seven markets that we're in.' So 1971 hadn't even ended yet and I went on Channel 50 in Detroit, on Channel 44 in Los Angeles, a station in San Francisco, Boston, Chicago, and Philadelphia . . . seven of the Top 10 markets. And we did really well in all of them except for Boston. For some reason, they decided to put me on prime-time Saturday against CBS's *All in the Family, The Bob Newhart Show,* and *The Mary Tyler Moore Show.* 'Well, he isn't so good . . . he's not doing much here in Boston.' Oh, I wonder why. *Attack of the Crab Monsters* against three of the biggest comedies in television history? So I did my run in Boston a lot quicker than in the other six markets . . . but Detroit just went bananas over it!"

Motown's horror genre in 1971 was dominated by Sir Graves Ghastly on Saturday afternoons. Exhibiting the more serious Universal and Hammer classics, *Sir Graves Ghastly Presents* made light of the genre with innovative, kid-friendly sketches filled with fun-loving characters; all of which were played by Lawson Deming. With the arrival of *The Ghoul,* Detroiters were given an alternative to the traditional vampire, one that was demented, sinister and much more puzzling than the happy-go-lucky Sir Graves. Mark Nowotarski elaborates.

Mark Nowotarski: "Nobody ever saw this before in Detroit on late-night TV, so nobody really knew exactly how to take the Ghoul when he first arrived. He was something new because he would show these horror films, not the classics like *Sir Graves* would show, but you knew they were some sort of scary films. So kids or young people would want to check them out if they liked scary movies and the Ghoul was just an added bonus. But then, as time progressed, it was reversed: the Ghoul was the best part of the show, and the movies were crap."

Joe Humeniuk and WXYZ engineer Dave Riley, the webmaster of ghoulfan.com, recall their first Ghoul sightings.

Joe Humeniuk: "I discovered the Ghoul when I was a kid. One night I woke up from my sleep and I went into my older brother's room to watch TV with him. He had *The Ghoul* on, and I was wondering, who the heck is this guy? So I got sucked into *The Ghoul,* and I was just intrigued; like, who's this guy—he's great. And being a kid I thought he was hysterical."

Dave Riley: "I first saw *The Ghoul* in the fall of 1972 during my freshman year in college. At that time, I remember being home most Saturday nights watching it, and I thought it was rather interesting. Here's this wild guy on TV being a movie host and doing wild stuff. I just found it totally amusing. When I first started working at Channel 7, I used to race home on Saturday nights to watch *The Ghoul.*"

Although *The Ghoul* was part of a syndicated package from Cleveland in 1971, the very Ghoul-friendly Motor City would become his exclusive home four years later. In 1975, Kaiser Industries liquidated its broadcasting properties, and subsequently the Ghoul was edged out of Channel 61. The Ghoul's chances of survival hinged on relocating to the city with his largest audience—Detroit. During this hiatus, Ron Sweed negotiated a deal with CKLW, Channel 9, to pick up the show. A few weeks before production was to commence, WKBD, Channel 50, threatened CKLW with a lawsuit over ownership of the program. Even though Sweed owned the show outright, the hassle of clearing his props through customs coupled with a possible legal battle forced him to reconsider his prospects with Channel 9.

Over the next 10 years, *The Ghoul* bounced around the Detroit UHF dial like the giant rubber ball on his show. After finishing out 1975 and most of 1976 at Channel 50, he moved to WXON, Channel 20, where for the next two years management kept a tight rein on his antics. Dave Riley describes an ongoing bit about a Cleveland suburb, Parma, Ohio.

Dave Riley: "He had some run-ins with the Channel 20 managers because they wouldn't let him say 'Parma.' Most of the time he would make a crack about Parma, which was a carryover from *Ghoulardi.* Parma has a primarily Polish population, like Hamtramck does here. So he would make Polish jokes and play the "Parma Polka." For some reason, Channel 20 didn't want him to say anything about Parma; they felt it was wrong. So when he left 20 and went to Channel 62, on one of his first shows he belted out 'PARMA!' I think he was waiting to say that."

In 1979, the Ghoul checked into the Jefferson Avenue studios of WGPR, Channel 62, where he aired in prime time on Friday nights. When a change in management occurred at WXON in the beginning of the new decade, Ron Sweed was welcomed back to Channel 20, where he stayed until Ghoul Power declined in the mid-1980s.

Sci-Fi Horror

In the 1950s and 1960s, the motion picture industry in both the United States and Japan turned out an onslaught of cheap sci-fi horror flicks, which local TV stations were able to purchase for next to nothing. Television stations saw them as fillers, but to the Ghoul they were an endless source of comedic material.

Dave Riley: "He'd come out and say something like, 'We've got a really bad movie for you tonight . . . it's another 17-cent movie. I don't know why you're wasting time with it . . . get out the air freshener and squirt it all around . . .' I remember one show started with an empty set. There was no Ghoul around, just music playing, and suddenly a door opens and there's the Ghoul with a gas mask on. He had a long rope tied to a garbage can on a cart with a film in it and a lot of smoke coming out of it. And as he's pulling it he says, 'Here's tonight's movie, gang . . . it really stinks!' At the end of the show, he might say, 'That was a really bad movie, and we're gonna make sure nobody sees that one again if I can help it.' The film would be in a big piled mess, and he would destroy it."

Frank Gadwell: "On *The Ghoul* you saw things like *Psychomania* [1971], which was one of his classic films, or *The Giant Gila Monster,* both of which were really bad, bad B movies."

And long before there was ever such a thing as *America's Funniest Videos* the Ghoul invited the viewers at home to send in their own 8mm films to be shown on the program and subjected to Ghoulish commentaries!

Don't Think, Just Watch It!

Frank Gadwell: "His set [a collage of memorabilia plastered over six-foot-tall flats] was always something really wild to me in trying to figure out all the different things on it. You'd want to send something in, as a lot of people did, because he'd put them on his set. One of the biggest things I remember about his set was when he had the people from Lynch's or the Hollywood Costume Shop in Dearborn come there and give him a Darth Vader mask."

As previously mentioned by Mark Nowotarski, the films became secondary to the Ghoul. It was his raw sense of humor wrapped in twisted "no-brainer" skits that captured the attention of his youthful audience. Joe Humeniuk highlights a few of them.

Joe Humeniuk: "He had this little crazy car that he'd drive around in the studio and out in the parking lot. He was as big as the car, so when he sat in it almost all of his body stuck out of it. It was like a little van, and he was always running over stuff. He'd run over Froggy a million times.

"He did parodies that were really bad, but they were funny to a kid. He would imitate people like Peter Falk and pretend to be in a scene from a Columbo episode, but as 'Ghoulumbo.' There was the 'Little Rasghouls,' which was kind of an odd twist on *The Little Rascals.* And there was his spin on *The Galloping Gourmet,* a popular cooking show in the late 1960s and early 1970s, [which] he called the 'Galloping Ghoulmet.'

"My fondest memory of the 'Galloping Ghoulmet' was when he broke out a bunch of tomatoes and he pulled off his shoes and socks and then squished the tomatoes with his bare feet, like you would do with grapes to make wine. Juice from the tomatoes was flying everywhere in the studio, and it was just hysterical! And this was something he did long before Gallagher became famous for smashing food with his 'Sledg-o-matic' hammer."

When the Ghoul wasn't ragging on Hollywood, he turned to the Motor City for inspiration.

Mark Nowotarski: "The Ghoul would take humorous and critical shots at other local TV personalities: Bill Kennedy, Sir Graves Ghastly, Lou Gordon, Bill Bonds . . . He would attempt to mime them but not insultingly. Whether it was [local advertisers] Mr. Belvedere or Ollie Fretter, he would try to do a line on just about anybody in the local market."

Ron Sweed: "When I did Sir Graves Ghastly, I called myself Sir Greasy Gravy, and I used to turn my mustache upside down and laugh, 'Naaaah-hhh.' I parodied *Bowling for Dollars* as 'Pitching for Pennies,' and I used to call Lou Gordon 'Old Leather Lungs.' I appeared on Lou's show when I first came to Channel 50. They wanted me to be on the show after I had established myself, and I came bouncing in on my bounce ball. I threw a string of firecrackers onto the riser with him and Jackie . . . it was a lot of fun. Usually when you suck people of status into a little bit of lunacy you find out if they're pretty good sports . . . and Lou was one. So was Bill Kennedy."

Ghoulicious!

Frank Gadwell: "Another thing I really liked about the Ghoul was when he had the Big Boy Battles. It was an eating contest where he allowed people to come on the air to see who could eat the Big Boy [hamburger] the fastest. It started out with just two people doing it, but eventually, since the Ghoul couldn't get a second person all the time, he became the one you challenged."

Mark Nowotarski: "The Ghoul had the Pizza Battle of the Century where he'd get a bunch of people and they'd go nuts on large pizzas—this was *Animal House* 10 years before Hollywood did it. He would take Cheese Whiz and spray it all over the place, like under his armpits. He was absolutely nuts! Critics of *The Ghoul* would say the show was in bad taste. People would write in to the Ghoul to say how bad he was, and he would respond to them on the air by saying something like, 'There's a dial, change the channel—hurry!'"

KABOOM!

Perhaps nothing was more controversial than the Ghoul's notorious blowouts! For all the late-night couch potatoes surfing the dial in search of an action-packed explosion, *The Ghoul* quenched their appetite for fancy pyrotechnics with spontaneity and simplicity.

Dave Riley: "Generally, the explosions almost always came up by themselves. You'd hear some rock music playing away while the picture was still in black. Then they would fade up, and there was the object of destruction. Sometimes there would be a little card right in front of it, saying something like, 'Hey, Ghoul, this movie really stinks!' And it might be a Frankenstein doll that's holding the card up, but you'd always see an M–80 planted right in front of it. The Ghoul would be yelling something off-camera, like, 'This movie's sooo bad, we're gonna do something about it now . . . we're gonna blow this thing up!' Then you'd see his hand come into the shot with a lighter, clicking it several times . . . or sometimes when the lighter didn't work he'd toss it away and grab another one, saying, 'Don't worry, we'll get it going—Oh, there we go . . . I'm getting outta here!' And then BOOM! The explosions were usually self-contained segments."

Blowing up objects at random was not only the Ghoul's grandest exploit, it became his signature shtick. While critics deplored the destruction, especially when it came to food, the Ghoul power generals revered it.

Dave Riley: "People would make things, particularly model cars, and send them to the Ghoul, asking, 'Can you please blow this up on camera?' Since people would send him stuff, there was no shortage of things to blow up. Whenever he would do Halloween theme shows, he blew up a pumpkin. He would hollow them out and put M–80s inside, and BOOM! The thing would blow into a million pieces."

Froggy (*Ghoulus nemesis*)

Mark Nowotarski: "The Ghoul's biggest foe was a little squeezy frog. As I became older, I found out this frog was featured in the old Andy Devine shows, the western star Andy Devine. So it had a certain amount of history. And the Ghoul was always battling with Froggy."

If you thought Wile E. Coyote had it rough every time one of his ingenious schemes to capture the Roadrunner backfired, then consider his local counterpart, Froggy. Resembling a waiter in his red blazer, black pants, and bow tie, the wide-grinning amphibian with a gravely voice relentlessly antagonized the Ghoul to the point of no return. And, just like Wile E., Froggy was a glutton for punishment.

Joe Humeniuk: "Sometimes they'd segue from the movie to a white screen, and then you'd see Froggy swinging in the middle of the screen, and he'd say something like, 'Hey, gang, hi ya, hi ya, hi ya . . . Froggy's the name and messin' with the Ghoul is my game!' Then you'd hear the Ghoul yell something back, and then Froggy would get blown up by a firecracker. He would blow up Froggy at least two or three times each show."

The Ghoul on the Hill

Joe Humeniuk: "I distinctly remember him showing Beatle clips all the time because I was an absolute Beatle nut! And that's one of the things that hooked me. I just knew he had something to do with the Beatles . . . I didn't know in what way or form, but he kept showing these rare clips of the Beatles at an airport. He always showed them arriving at the airport, getting off the plane, going into a press conference, and concert clips.

"I don't know where he got them, but he had all this footage that I'd never seen before. When you thought he was going to a commercial, suddenly you'd hear a Beatles song, and then all this footage appeared. It looked like it all came from a handheld camera. Sometimes he'd cut them into the movie. You'd watch the film, and then it would go into these clips of the Beatles getting off of a plane with their music in the background . . . And this would go on for several minutes before the movie continued or they'd cut to the Ghoul, and he'd tell a story about the Beatles. He said that he had met them and that he got some footage of them and what an awesome experience it was for him. He was absolutely enthralled with the Beatles."

Ron Sweed: "I was lucky enough to meet the Beatles three years in a row on their American tours. I was working at Channel 8 [in Cleveland] for Ernie Anderson when he was doing *Ghoulardi*. And because of him I'm at the CBS affiliate when I was just a kid of 14 in 1964. All of the photographers and news people were just very nice to me and they took me under their wings, so I'm getting access to places that other kids my age weren't getting. So when the Beatles were coming to town it was like, 'Holy crap—the Beatles!' I mean besides Ghoulardi, in my life the Beatles are the next-biggest thing. I asked the news guys if I could tag along. Ernie Anderson had given me an 8mm film camera for Christmas, so I slapped some Channel 8 stickers on it. The cops didn't know the difference between a simple 8mm and professional equipment . . . and I did look older; I knew how to act accordingly.

"So when I went to their hotel I was alone, and I said, 'I'm just here waiting for our [Channel 8] guys.' And then I thought to myself, I've got to get to their room! So I got up to their seventh-floor suite outside the door, and when they came around the corner there they were! And there I was taking my 8mm movies of them. I talked my way into the room because it was WHK disc jockeys who brought them there and they knew I worked for Ghoulardi . . . and Ghoulardi was an icon among professionals, so they said, 'Hey, Sweed works for Ghoulardi, come on in.' And so I got to meet the Beatles all three years, one on one, sitting next to them just talking.

"The first time I met them, in case I got kicked out of the situation I went to John Lennon first and asked, 'Can I shake your hand?' He said, 'Well it's a little bit sweaty, but go ahead.' Then I shook hands with Paul McCartney, then George and Ringo. And they were just the nicest bunch of guys. I literally was the closest one to their age. I didn't tell them I was 14, but they could tell because everyone else was in their late twenties and thirties. I could really talk music with them, and we did. They were just the biggest things in the world, and they knew it, but at the same time they were such down-to-earth, cool guys!

"The last year I got to be with them was in 1966. I had never asked for their autographs or anything because I didn't want to be a pest. But I had my press pass, and that year I thought, I may never meet them again, so I asked Paul to sign it first and he wrote, 'Best wishes—Paul McCartney.' Then John signed it, then George and Ringo. I remember John was smoking Marlboros that year, and I saw him crush one out at a press conference in one of the hotel rooms, so I picked that up and I have his cigarette butt saved. Then the Red Cross ripped out the carpet and sold each square inch for a dollar. Ernie Anderson promoted that on the *Ghoulardi* show and then gave me a huge piece of the carpet. So I have that, John's cigarette butt and my autographed press pass, plus . . . since it was my third year in meeting them, they let me take 35mm pictures of them. I have the 12 photos I shot of them in 1966 and my 8mm film, so I have a pretty comprehensive documentation of my meetings with them. The only thing I regret I don't have was in 1966 I was sitting next to John on a couch in the hotel suite and a photographer shot a photo of John and me sitting [together]. It occurred to me a couple of days later, there's a photo now of John Lennon and me sitting next to each other. I tried to track it down, but I never did get it . . . But, hey, I can't complain."

Ghoulmania!

Ron Sweed: "Detroit has the best fans I could ever ask for . . . they always have been from day one!"

Frank Gadwell: "I remember for years trying to get my parents to take me to the Tel-Twelve Mall to see the Ghoul. He'd do things like a March of Dimes benefit, where he would swim in Jell-O in a Jell-O pool."

Ron Sweed: "When I did mall appearances, the typical situation was six- or seven-hour-long lines, and I have a firm policy that I'll stay until the last autograph. They supported the character that much, so I'm gonna support them. That's the ongoing love relationship that the Ghoul and the Ghoul power generals have for one another out there.

"In 1972, I did a thing with the Harlem Globetrotters at Olympia [Stadium]. They promoted the heck out of the thing, so it was sold out for the Globetrotters; there was just a mega crowd. So I was supposed to come out at halftime. They announced, 'Now that you've seen the Globetrotters, here's our special guest . . . the Ghoul!' I came out to the middle of the court, and everybody started running down from the stands. Before I knew it, I was in the middle of Detroit humanity on a basketball floor. First my fright wig went, then my sunglasses, then my beard, then my mustache, the buttons on my lab coat . . . and there was nothing I could do. I called out to the security guards, who brought me out: 'Hey, try to get me back to the dressing room.' I can't do anything in this situation.

"They got me back there, and here I am with just my Ron Sweed face on in a lab coat with no buttons. All of a sudden the door opens and the promoter, who was immaculately dressed in a suit, comes in like he was shot out of a cannon. His tie's all askew, his suit coat is ripped up, and he says, 'This is great! I haven't seen anything like this since the Beatles were here! C'mon, you gotta get back out there.' I said, 'I can't go out there, I'm not the Ghoul anymore.' I didn't have extras of anything. He says, 'Where's your stuff?' I said, 'It's out there somewhere.' He says, 'Let me go out there and make an announcement.' So he made an announcement to the effect that the Ghoul would like to come back out, but throughout the crowd are pieces of him. Please return them if you'd like to see the Ghoul come back out. It took about six different knocks at the door; just unbelievable . . . first my mustache showed up from a fan, then my fright wig came, the beard, the glasses, a couple of buttons . . . and I put them back on. They announced, 'The Ghoul wants to come out and entertain you, but you have to stay in your seats now . . . promise you'll stay in your seats . . . here he is, the Ghoul!' That was the power of the Ghoul in Detroit, and it's been like that ever since."

Stay Sick and Turn Blue

Dave Riley: "In the 1970s, he would close his show by saying, 'We're gonna wrap this thing up . . . I got just enough time to go down to the bar and get a couple last rounds . . . at home to Queen Barbara [his first wife], love ya baby . . . stay sick, turn blue, scratch glass, climb walls, and, most important of all, do it all you can but don't get caught.' Then he'd have one of his exits where he'd ride off on a little tricycle or on a bounced ball or he'd do something stupid in the studio. There'd be fake credits that would come up, too, like 'Special Electronic Effects by Wildlife Transmitter' or 'Echoes by M. T. Chambers.'"

In the mid-1980s, the Ghoul advised his Motown audience to "stay sick and turn blue" for the last time on Detroit TV. But after more than a decade of public appearances at local events in and around Detroit and Cleveland Ron Sweed returned to television in full costume in 1997 on WBNX, Channel 55, in Cleveland. An attempt was made in 2001 to bring him back to his old battlefield at Channel 20, which had since become Detroit's WB. However, a conflict between the sales and programming departments terminated his much-anticipated renaissance.

Hopeful that he'll one day recapture his glory as the Motor City's prime mischief maker for one last hurrah, the Ghoul, love him or hate him, will go down in history as an influential symbol of local pop culture. And on that note avid Ghoulites Mark Nowotarski, Frank Gadwell, and Dave Riley sum up the impact of the man who showed all of us how to have fun living life on the edge!

Mark Nowotarski: "*The Ghoul* hit fans on a number of different levels. First of all, it was pure entertainment, pure escapism . . . but basically he's just another guy who gets to do some of the things we'd like to do."

Frank Gadwell: "Watching a horror movie and seeing him joke around a bit became a mental purge. It was a good stress reliever to watch *The Ghoul,* to sit back and, like he used to say, 'Tune out your mind,' because that's what you end up doing and sometimes you need that. He's somebody that everybody can laugh at because he makes you laugh at him."

Dave Riley: "He had a positive impact on his fans. Here the guy was on TV 30 years ago, and today the people that watched him are in their thirties or forties and pushing into their fifties, and if they had a chance to see the Ghoul again they'd go see him. The memories are fond memories of the guy. You don't hear anybody saying, 'There was somebody on TV once who did bizarre stuff' . . . no, they remember the Ghoul!"

Can We Talk?

6

Kelly & Company

One time John came in, and I can remember him talking about the dinner Marilyn made, but didn't make—so he would tease her about cooking. And Marilyn would kind of banter back about John and his absolute lack of knowledge about dressing. They would make fun of themselves, but they did it with a twinkle and with caring; it was never mean-spirited.

   —LYNDA HIRSCH, soap opera columnist

If ever there was a real-life love story made for local TV, it was that of John Kelly and Marilyn Turner. The Channel 7 news anchor and weather girl who fell in love and tied the knot spent nearly 20 years playfully sharing their marital ups and downs in front of live television cameras every weekday morning at nine on Detroit's number-one talk show, *Kelly & Company*. As America's first husband and wife team to cohost a morning program, John and Marilyn brought a freshness to daytime television that was part real and part fantasy. Audiences could identify with the day-to-day chatter about the couple's quirks, yet they could also admire the glamour attached to their profession.

And, speaking of glamour, no other local program was as successful in rivaling the national shows in celebrity interviews, fashion shows, makeovers, gourmet cooking, and remote broadcasts than *Kelly & Company*. Thanks to the magnetism of John and Marilyn, WXYZ's Broadcast House literally became the entertainment capital of the Midwest. Their open set, with only a few chairs facing the 100-plus audience section under a grid of studio lights, was *the* place to see and be seen from 1977 to 1995. The man and woman who Detroit saw reporting the news and weather . . . the man and woman who Detroit saw fall in love,

Detroit's power couple, John Kelly and Marilyn Turner. (Courtesy John Kelly and Marilyn Turner.)

embraced their community and audience with daily doses of lighthearted fun, gossip, and self-help by simply letting their hair down and being themselves. Media professionals Linda Lanci of WMGC radio, Shaun Robinson of *Access Hollywood,* and former WXYZ producer Chris Stepien provide insights regarding the popularity of the program and its cohosts.

Linda Lanci: "I really enjoyed *Kelly & Company.* I always felt when watching the show that John and Marilyn had a good rapport, and I always felt comfortable with them. It was nice having the live studio audience, and you also got the feeling when they showed the audience that everyone enjoyed being there—it was a great local variety show."

Shaun Robinson: "I remember being in the audience for *Kelly & Company,* and I was ecstatic about being there and meeting John Kelly and Marilyn Turner. I watched them when I was growing up, and I really, really admired them because I used to say, 'That's what I want to do one day!' They were an inspiration to me."

Chris Stepien: "*Kelly & Company* was basically a conversation with the city! It was every day for 90 minutes, and it was NOT the news that comes off as a monologue. There was interaction with a live studio audience, and the viewers at home could call in when the show was on the air."

News + Weather = Talk

On Labor Day 1966, WXYZ began an early morning talk show at seven o'clock to run ahead of *Prize Movie* called *The Morning Show,* hosted by Bob Hynes. After a five-year tenure, Hynes left and the program was handed to local deejay Tom Shannon for a brief period. By 1972, the management at Channel 7 looked to mirror the success of Chicago's, *Kennedy & Company* with a "company" program of its own. The person they believed was best suited for the job in the market was WJBK news anchor John Kelly. Kelly came to Detroit from Peoria in the mid-1960s, and within seven years he became a hot enough commodity for the executives at WXYZ to consider luring him away from their competitor.

After agreeing to host the show, which would bear his name, the newsman turned in his resignation to Channel 2 in July, thus leaving the studio on Nine Mile Road to settle into his new home on Ten Mile. It wouldn't be long before a good friend from WJBK, Marilyn Turner, would join him at Broadcast House. In the fall of 1972, *Kelly & Company* made its debut with John as the new host. Art director Jack Flechsig designed the set to accommodate Kelly's preference for casual conversation in an informal environment to create intimacy with the viewers. Although the show was doing well in the ratings, the powers that be at Channel 7 decided to make a change after a mere five months.

In early 1973, John was pulled off the morning show in favor of Dennis Wholey—the host of Channel 7's new *AM Detroit.* Sadly for Kelly, the days in the newsroom that he thought were behind him suddenly became his only alternative to unemployment. While coanchoring the 6:00 evening news with Bill Bonds, he resumed his working relationship with Marilyn Turner, who had joined the *Action News* team a few months earlier.

A native of London, Ontario, Marilyn Turner arrived in Detroit in the late 1950s to become one of four "Miss Fairweathers" at WJBK. Looking to freelance her talents by the dawn of the 1960s, she left Channel 2 to contract her services for Drewry's Beer, which sponsored the weather at WXYZ. Working as a freelancer at Channel 7 allowed Marilyn the flexibility to pursue her ambition to act in films and commercials. In the mid-1960s, she returned to WJBK until September of 1972, when she, like her friend John Kelly, said goodbye to the station on Nine Mile and headed up to Broadcast House.

Off-camera, both Turner and Kelly had suffered failed marriages with children. Divorced and over the age of 40, the two began to date. The speculation among *Action News* viewers that there was a little more than a mix of news and weather going on between John and Marilyn proved true. On December 27, 1974, John Kelly at 47 and Marilyn Turner at 43 said "I do," unaware that one day their marriage would be the talk of the town for many years to come—literally!

When the ABC network, which owned WXYZ, announced in late 1975 that it was going to compete against NBC's popular *Today Show* with a new production, *Good Morning America,* the days of *AM Detroit* were numbered. More than a year later, with *Good Morning America* occupying the seven-to-nine time slot, the audience for Rita Bell's long-time *Prize Movie* began to decline. At the same time, the news department was grooming their top female reporter, Doris Bisco, to become the coanchor of the 6:00 p.m. newscast with Bonds. Examining all of the pieces in the Channel 7 puzzle, program director Bob Woodruff proposed a brilliant solution to the vice president and general manager, Jeanne Findlater, that would pump new life into the sagging morning ratings and relieve Kelly of his duties in the newsroom. John Kelly and Marilyn Turner discuss the rebirth of *Kelly & Company.*

John Kelly: "In 1977, I was called into the boss's office and was told that the station was going to launch a big morning show. I was told they were going to revive *Kelly & Company* and that it would be 90 minutes again. But this time there would be a studio audience and a big budget for it. They were going to do away with *Prize Movie,* so this show would air from 9:00 to 10:30. I was essentially told, 'You can do this or goodbye' because they were making room for somebody else [Bisco] in the news department."

Marilyn Turner: "When John said that he was going to do the show alone, I told him that they were going to pair him with Rita Bell. He said, 'That's never going to happen,' and I said, 'Yes it is . . . she's going to be your cohost.' Now, I wasn't even thinking of doing the show. I was still doing the weather and I was doing film work, so it hadn't even crossed

Marilyn has fun with *One Life to Live* star Judith Light. (Courtesy Chuck Derry.)

my mind because I was quite happy with my little life. And, sure enough, I was right . . . Rita Bell became John's cohost."

Unlike Marilyn, Rita Bell wasn't able to bounce off of John's humor and lead-ins very well. Together the two lacked the chemistry to sustain a live show every day for an hour and a half. A change needed to be made if the show was to survive. One of the biggest obstacles to John was Rita's popularity with the housewives he was trying to win over. So let's see, what to do? Suddenly it hit John that he was married to a woman in showbiz who was already an established personality on the payroll at Channel 7. Why not have Marilyn replace Rita?

John Kelly: "I went into Jeanne Findlater and said, 'It would be more natural to have Marilyn on the show with me.' Apparently, Bob Woodruff was working quietly to get Marilyn on the show, which I knew nothing about. Marilyn didn't know anything about it either."

Prior to becoming the program director at WXYZ, Woodruff had produced *The Lou Gordon Program* at WKBD, Channel 50. Part of Gordon's show included a well-received question-and-answer segment in which Lou's wife Jackie joined him on the set and subsequently became a significant element in the show. Regardless of whether the experience of working with Jackie Gordon fueled Woodruff's plan to incorporate Marilyn into the morning gig or not, doesn't matter, by the fall of 1977 *The Lou Gordon Program* was off the air. . . .

Marilyn Turner: "There wasn't another man and wife in the whole country hosting a show together. And Bob thought that was a great idea! He's really the one who put that package together. So in an attempt to appease all of us in the beginning they put Rita on for three days and then had me on for the other two."

John Kelly: "It was Monday, Wednesday, Friday for Rita with Tuesday and Thursday for Marilyn. That lasted for a short while. Then it flipped: Marilyn was on Monday, Wednesday, and Friday with Rita on Tuesdays and Thursdays. Eventually, Rita was gone [by early 1978] and it became Marilyn Monday through Friday."

Live with John and Marilyn

For all of the pizzazz exhibited on-screen, it was the engaging personalities of Kelly and Turner that always outshone the brightest stars. The colorful banter between Regis Philbin and Kathie Lee Gifford (and now Kelly Ripa) that has charmed America since 1989 is the same concept that John and Marilyn began in 1977. Standing in the midst of a live audience and holding a single microphone, Detroit's TV couple routinely opened the show with a humorous ad-libbed monologue that poked fun at their personal whims, habits, styles, you name it . . . And in doing so they revealed just enough of themselves to bond with their audience in a nonegotistical manner. To better elaborate on the appeal of John and Marilyn, here are two individuals who knew them well: former *Kelly & Company* producer Dan Weaver; and a regular guest, soap opera columnist Lynda Hirsch.

Dan Weaver: "John and Marilyn were absolute originals. There was something about the two of them that other markets tried to duplicate and failed . . . They were really kind of Detroit's Sonny and Cher in that they were a real-life couple that had a very successful show by working well together. People were intrigued with them because they knew John and Marilyn were a married couple. There was a dynamic element in knowing that when your hosts go home at night they fight, they have sex, and so it presented a 'realness' that was intriguing to the viewer. If John was talking and Marilyn looked bored, she really was bored and you got to see it. So it was very much a show where people were enamored with them and also felt that they were the couple next door. It was a very special show in that respect."

Lynda Hirsch: "Even though there was a lot of playful banter between them, they never did the 'Kathie Lee' thing of constantly talking about their private home life. You knew they loved each other, so they didn't talk about themselves to the point where you wanted to hit yourself in the side of the head. What they concentrated on was the guests, and they were great at interviewing because they let the guests talk!"

Dan Weaver: "John was very much a newsman. He was so well read and he had a style that was warm, but he was also about getting the information and putting some perspective on it. He could take any topic and give it some importance and relevance. With Marilyn, there was rarely a question that she wouldn't ask; she was always very curious. She loved any kind of topic—she was very good at sexual topics, very good at probing people—and she was great at personally connecting with people who'd suffered some sort of traumatic experience; she could really find the heart of the matter. And Marilyn was not above giving it to John on the air, which is something women really liked about her because she stood up to him."

Lynda Hirsch: "As a guest, you knew that if John was going to make a jab at you, twenty seconds later he'd make fun of himself. He also allowed you to crack a joke about him and have great fun. Even during the commercial breaks, a lot of hosts change their personality, and not for the better, but John and Marilyn continued to joke with the audience and tease the crew. In all the years I did the show, I never saw either of them say anything derogatory to a cameraperson or anybody else on the crew. They understood that they're on the air because of those people . . . [that] their faces aren't going to be seen unless those folks show up feeling appreciated."

Young, Fun, and Number One

Marilyn Turner: "We had very little input regarding the content of the show, not because the production staff didn't want us but because they did such a wonderful job. We just loved our producers!"

Throughout most of *Kelly & Company*'s long run, John and Marilyn were midlife adults (both over 45 in 1977), but any time the audience saw John horseback riding or Marilyn up and away in a hot air balloon you'd swear they were still in the prime of their youth! And in spirit they were. Much of their vibrancy stemmed from their young production staff. Although there were a few seasoned pros, such as Nancy Lenzen, who, like Woodruff, had produced *The Lou Gordon Program*, many of John and Marilyn's beloved producers were in their twenties when they were hired to work on the show, hence the official *Kelly* slogan: "Young, Fun,

John steps into the kitchen for a cooking segment. (Courtesy
John Kelly and Marilyn Turner.)

and Number One." Dan Weaver and former stage manager Chuck Derry
describe some of the factors that propelled *Kelly & Company* to the top
of its game as the highest-rated local talk show in the country.

Dan Weaver: "*Kelly & Company* was an amazing talk trendsetter. We
were one of the first local programs to really 'travel' the show. We did
live broadcast remotes from places like Sea World. And there were fans
who actually traveled to those destinations to be a part of the audience
for those shows—that was incredible! We were also one of the first shows
to do live weddings, which have now become a staple for *Good Morning
America, Today,* and *Regis and Kelly.* We also did some of the first audience giveaways. Oprah now gives away cars to her audience, but in the
days when we were starting it, it was a huge deal to the entire audience
to get a book by the guest author.

"Detroit at that time was the seventh-largest market in television, but
it was the fourth-largest market in book sales. And since it was an enormous place to sell books we would literally get calls from virtually every
publisher in New York, looking to include Detroit as part of their
author's tour. So we got almost every best-selling author on the show and
we had the luxury of picking and choosing the authors as well.

"We'd also try to find some of the quirky local news stories. I remem-

. . . and they called it puppy love! (Courtesy John Kelly and Marilyn Turner.)

ber one of the first guests I booked was a man in Michigan whose company made a new kind of port-a-potty called 'Here's Johnny!' He was actually being sued by Johnny Carson to stop selling Here's Johnny port-a-potties. So we had him on, bringing his port-a-potty with him, and we did the interview from his port-a-potty . . . and it was very funny!"

Chuck Derry: "We were the only local show to beat Phil Donahue, who was on top of the line all the time, and finally we beat him! Then we invited him on the show!! A lot of talk show hosts at the time, including Oprah, came in to find out what John and Marilyn were doing because their reputation was well known in the talk show circuit. And none of them could figure out what we were doing, but they noticed that everyone was having a great time. But that's because the crew, the producers, and John and Marilyn just loved the show and what they were doing, so it was infectious!"

The Stars Call Us!

Chuck Derry: "*Kelly & Company* was a great place to go if you had friends or family coming in from out of town. You got to see a free show with big stars showing up . . . and we did have all the big stars coming in one after the other every day!"

Chris Stepien: "It was the heartbeat of the station in the morning! There was so much activity backstage: there were guests gathering in the greenroom, hair and makeup was being done, and production people were running in and out. When we did fashion shows, models were everywhere. If you were just walking down the hall, you might bump into a major celebrity coming out of the restroom. We saw people like former president Jimmy Carter there all the time. There were so many different kinds of people in and out of that studio, it was almost like a carnival atmosphere. *Kelly & Company* made Detroit like a New York or Los Angeles during its time, and it really was *the* place to be in the morning."

Like so many other local programs, especially in the talk genre, *Kelly & Company* reeled in the prime talent. But unlike most of the other shows, where the bookings were limited to a weekly schedule, John and Marilyn showcased them to the Motor City daily. Where else could you tune in on the local dial to see a movie star like Michael Douglas on Monday, a comedian like David Brenner on Tuesday, a pop singer like Marilyn McCoo on Wednesday, a TV star like Robert Urich on Thursday, and a supermodel like Cheryl Tiegs on Friday . . . all live and in person and right in your own backyard? Nowhere! The sheer range and number of the celebrities that appeared on *Kelly & Company* was unprecedented. John and Marilyn, along with Dan Weaver, look back at a few favorites.

John Kelly: "I liked the musicians and the comedians. Some of them absolutely blew my socks off. Henry Mancini once sat down and played the piano for us."

Marilyn Turner: "Alan Alda was just a sweetheart! The funniest moment came when I asked him [at the height of the popularity of *M*A*S*H*] about being a sex symbol. He looked at me and said, 'I'm not a sex symbol.' I said, 'Okay then . . . a modified sex symbol.' And everybody in the audience roared in laughter, and then Alan started to laugh, too. That interview always stands out in my mind."

Dan Weaver: "We had so many people from the early days of television: Art Linkletter, Imogene Coca, Sid Caesar, and of course Soupy Sales. It was such a kick to watch Soupy Sales come on and see the Detroit audience embrace him in a fashion that was like going back in time . . . And it was fun to see Soupy hit John in the face with a pie!"

Because of the friendly, comical aura surrounding the show, comedic personalities such as Red Skelton and Motown's own Larry Thompson (Mr. Whoodini from *Bozo*) felt comfortable enough to perpetrate some harmless gags.

Actor John Forsythe works the audience with Kelly. (Courtesy Chuck Derry.)

Chuck Derry: "This one day when Red Skelton came on, Gundella the Witch was the next interview, which was the last segment of the show. While Gundella's on, Red approaches the stagehands and asks for some wood. So he gets a big armful of kindling wood and just at the end of the show he gives me the high sign for me to give him a minute before the closing. John has Gundella standing by the door with a minute to go, and in walks Red. He drops the whole pile of wood in front of Gundella, then turns to the audience and asks, 'Does anybody have a match?' And the whole audience went into hysterics!"

Larry Thompson: "Art Cervi [Bozo] and I were on *Kelly & Company* one time after our show went off the air. When they had us come on, I did my old routine of taking half a dozen watches from the unsuspecting female audience. Then I went back and said, 'By the way, I found this and this and this' as I'm holding up the watches. Then the camera swung over to the audience, and they're going, 'Ahhh!' It was a good bit because they didn't expect me to lift their watches. And John, while he was talking to Bozo, I was right behind him pretending to curl his hair and he didn't even know it!"

In addition to interviewing and indulging their guest's pranks, *Kelly & Company* also became the quintessential public relations machine for promotional tours that included Detroit.

Dan Weaver: "Lou Rawls called me after appearing on the show and said, 'I want to thank you for having me on your show. My theater performance is now sold out and we were behind in ticket sales before I came on your show.' And this happened a half hour after *Kelly & Company* went off the air. Actor Peter Strauss from *Rich Man, Poor Man* was in a TV movie called *Heart of Steel*. For some reason, the promotional tour he was on didn't stop in Detroit, and he told the promoter, 'You have to include Detroit. I want to do *Kelly & Company*.'"

John Kelly: "The show developed such a good reputation that the stars would call us! They would say that they're going to be in town and they wanted to be on our show."

And, as John Kelly also recalls, there was one man in particular who always aspired to be a guest on the show back when nobody knew his name.

John Kelly: "Tim Allen used to hang out on our show during the time when he was really struggling. Some mornings I'd come in and there was Tim standing around backstage jiggling his pennies and coins [and] trying to get on *Kelly & Company*. So when we did have him on the show I thought he was hysterical, and Marilyn loved him, too, but we never saw him again. We had a boss at the time who didn't like Tim. We finally got it out of one of the producers that this boss didn't want Tim back because he belches all the time.

"When Marilyn and I moved into a house in Farmington Hills, we were looking for a place to work out. When we went to check out the YMCA, there was Tim's wife on an exercise bicycle. So we went to talk to her and asked, 'Where's Tim?' She said, 'Tim's going to give comedy another few months. This is his last shot before he gives it up and gets a real job. He's out in LA appearing at the Comedy Store right now.' And the rest, of course, is history."

Love in the Afternoon

One of the largest troupes of actors that became a smash hit with the *Kelly & Company* audience came from the soap pool. In the early to mid-1980s, ABC daytime's "Love in the Afternoon" ad campaign boosted the network's serial dramas to number one. *All My Children, One Life to Live,* and *General Hospital* were at the top of the daytime ratings. Soap columnist Lynda Hirsch explains how John and Marilyn understood the impact those programs had on their own show.

Lynda Hirsch: "Some talk show hosts made fun of the genre, but the truly smart ones didn't. John and Marilyn never made fun of the soap media; they understood that [it] was a large part of their audience. The same people who watch daytime dramas also watch the talk shows. So John and Marilyn were very smart in understanding that making fun of the genre was the same as making fun of the audience that watches them."

Realizing just how important the soap market was to their fans, Kelly and Turner devoted a number of their shows, and in many cases a week's worth of programming (remember Soap Opera Week?) to getting up close and personal with daytime's finest!

Marilyn Turner: "I really liked having the soap stars on . . . Kim Delaney was on a lot, more than any of the others."

Lynda Hirsch: "That was when Kim was playing sweet Jenny Gardner on *All My Children,* before she went on to *NYPD Blue* and other prime-time network shows. They also had Larry Lau [*All My Children*] on a lot and Michael Knight, who's still on *All My Children* as Tad Martin. John and Marilyn knew which actors were important in relating to the audience."

Marilyn Turner: "We got to know a lot of the soap stars quite well. When we went out of town, they often substituted for us. They liked to come and do our show, and because of that we could take long vacations—sometimes three weeks at a time."

Not only did the soap actors get to host *Kelly & Company,* but in turn, out of ABC Daytime's tremendous respect for the program, John and Marilyn were invited to make a couple of appearances on the dramas. Do you recall the time they played talk show hosts on *All My Children* and interviewed Pine Valley's most notorious home wrecker, Erica Kane (Susan Lucci)? Or how about the day they portrayed airport attendants on *General Hospital,* assisting Robert and Holly Scorpio (Tristan Rogers and Emma Samms) in a missing-persons search?

Equally important to *Kelly & Company* was a fledgling prime-time serial on ABC—*Dynasty.* Many of the cast members, including John Forsythe, appeared on the show, along with their fashion designer, Nolan Miller . . . which reminded John Kelly of a time when Marilyn critiqued one of Joan Collins's dresses.

John Kelly: "Marilyn has not, nor will she ever, master the art of understatement. We were in Nolan Miller's studio when we were out in LA doing one of our specialty shows. And Marilyn, with the cameras rolling of course, had one of Joan Collins's dresses he designed specifically for *Dynasty,* and she says, 'Well . . . it's too loose in the waist and too tight in the bust!' I'll never forget that."

The Look of the Week

Along with Soap Opera Week came an abundance of other theme shows aired at random. Every premise, from fitness to cooking to westerns to shopping malls to "What ever happened to . . .?" was either tagged with a week's worth of guests or styled into a special-interest show of its own. Given the nature of the *Kelly & Company* demographic, it's not surprising that two of the most popular themes were makeovers and fashion.

When it came to makeovers, the ladies of Motown were treated to A-list hairstyles from the likes of famed Hollywood stylist José Eber and makeup from the cosmetologist to the stars, Jeffrey Bruce (who occasionally substituted as a guest host). Just as stunning were the many fashion shows presented by acclaimed designers Halston, Bill Blass, Ralph Lauren, and even the risqué lingerie architect Frederick Mellinger, better known as Frederick of Hollywood. But for every face that was fortunate enough to be made over courtesy of the show, the elegant clothes that were modeled in the fashion segments often exceeded the budget of the average housewife. In this instance, local knockoff artists visited the program to demonstrate how high fashion could be copied and sold for less. However, as Marilyn Turner learned on a cold wintry night, imitation isn't always the sincerest form of flattery.

John Kelly: "One of the [knockoff designers], out of the goodness of his heart and as a great sweeping gesture, copied and sent a dress to Marilyn. It was a gorgeous, sexy, black dress with all sorts of netting on it. We had to go to this huge affair at the Ritz-Carlton, and in those days we had a limo that was paid for. So we get there, and we're there five minutes when Marilyn says, 'This dress is driving me crazy!' And because of that we cut our appearance short and left early."

Marilyn Turner: "The problem was the designer didn't put any lining in the waist and bustline and it had a very stiff neck. I was so uncomfortable that when we got back in the car I said, 'John, I'm taking this dress off now!'"

John Kelly: "I put the separator up between us and the driver, and the next thing I knew there's my wife taking her clothes off in the back of the limo."

Marilyn Turner: "It was in the winter, so I had a coat that I could wrap around me. That dress was so scratchy and horrible that I gave it to a resale place, and I'm sure they just threw it away."

Playing to the Audience

Lynda Hirsch: "John and Marilyn were great at handling the audience because they had such personal contact with them. For example, John would touch them on the shoulder and he would joke with them . . . and that has become such a lost art."

Without question, the most vital aspect attributed to the success of *Kelly & Company* was the audience. As far as the cohosts and producers were concerned, if the audience reaction wasn't good on a given day the show had been a failure. Fortunately for the crew, they never experienced a shortage of ticket holders or a lack of excitement. The house was full every morning for 18 consecutive years—audience wranglers needn't apply.

Dan Weaver: "One of the things that I've come to learn about Detroit, especially after leaving to work in other markets like Los Angeles and New York, is that the audience in Detroit was extremely loyal. Most of the time we had well over 100 people in the audience, but depending on the guest we'd sometimes get more. For instance, the soap stars were always a big draw, and there was a psychic called the Incredible Elizabeth that when you mentioned she was going to be on an upcoming show we were almost guaranteed a line of 200 at the door."

Chris Stepien: "That line was there if you had 12 inches of snow or if it was the hottest day of the summer; they always had an enormous audience turnout."

Of the more than 100 ticket holders standing in that long line, rain or shine, less than 10 percent were male. The vast majority of the audience, not only in the studio but at home, too, was female. Regardless of the gender imbalance, John and Marilyn showed their appreciation by affirming their gratitude to each and every member. At the end of the day's show, before the audience exited the building, John would pass out small "Kelly bags" filled with goodies to everyone as they departed. Meanwhile, Marilyn would retreat to their tiny office at the station to accept telephone calls. Former *Kelly & Company* producer Ellen (Kennedy) Stepien comments about the attempts made to accommodate those unlucky audience seekers who had been left standing at the end of the line beyond the cutoff point.

Ellen Stepien: "Sometimes we had overflows. When that happened, John would go out and shake hands with them and politely apologize and give them tickets for the next show. A lot of times those people were allowed to stay and watch the show from the cafeteria or some other place inside the station."

Good Afternoon Detroit

In 1983, ABC sought to expand its prosperous morning magazine, *Good Morning America,* by adding an afternoon edition—*Good Afternoon America.* But rather than risk the hefty investment of producing a full-blown network show, the brass at ABC opted to test the concept in key markets via the local stations the network owned and operated. Their first stop was Motown.

John Kelly: "Dick O'Leary was the president of ABC's owned and operated division. It was his idea to create one of these afternoon shows for every one of the O&Os and eventually put it on the network. We understood at the time from Dick that we would eventually be the cohosts of the network version and that it would be produced in Detroit."

Chris Stepien: "*Good Afternoon Detroit* was developed by Bob Shanks, who created *Good Morning America* and *20/20,* and he was brought in from New York by ABC to launch the project. It was a big surprise at the station that they were going to have John and Marilyn host it because a lot of people thought, how are they going to do two shows a day? Is the market going to be over saturated with John and Marilyn? Are they going to have the energy? And why do an afternoon show with the same hosts who are on for 90 minutes in the morning? But it turned out to be a brilliant decision. Even though they were under a lot of added stress, they managed to succeed! Their morning show didn't suffer, the afternoon show took off, and their celebrity grew!"

Marilyn Turner: "A lot of money went into that show. We had two to three crews out on the streets all the time because it was more of a news magazine kind of show."

Chris Stepien: "The afternoon show was heavily based on tape inserts, but there was still a significant live aspect to it. The opening and in betweens were live, and there were live interviews."

John Kelly: "There was a staff of about 50 people, and they put up a couple of separate buildings and expanded the main building so they could have *Good Afternoon Detroit* offices. The set was designed and shipped in from New York. The New York people came in to assemble it, and then our stagehands had to correct the mistakes they made. As important as the show was to the network and to us, what we didn't realize was that the idea of us doing the national version upset every station manager in the country. All the program directors said, 'We don't need those hosts, we got our own people, blah, blah, blah.' So we ran almost five years until ABC sold Channel 7 to Scripps-Howard, which then canceled us."

There's No Place Like Home

While John and Marilyn's celebrity soared to heights beyond their wildest dreams in the mid-1980s, in part resulting from exposure that totaled two and a half hours a day, opportunities to syndicate the Motor City's supercouple without the aid of ABC came knocking on their door. One of the offers was from the television industry's largest syndicator, KingWorld. The TV distributors were in search of a plan B regarding their ailing afternoon talk show in Chicago. Kelly and Turner were asked to wait in the wings should their plan A—Oprah Winfrey—flop. As everyone knows, *Oprah* skyrocketed, nixing John and Marilyn.

The other deal was proposed by a repeat guest on *Kelly & Company*, famed Hollywood producer and personal manager Jay Bernstein. Known for discovering Farrah Fawcett and recognized by his trademark walking stick, the persuasive Mr. Bernstein convinced Kelly and Turner that he could put them in every living room from coast to coast. The chance to become household names across the country sounded too good to be true . . . because it was. John and Marilyn were told that if they wanted to be syndicated they would have to host the show from Los Angeles—NO Detroit!

Marilyn Turner: "We really didn't want to go and live out in Los Angeles because we loved Detroit! Everybody and everything is so transient out in LA; the same is true with New York. Especially in our business, you go out there and you think you're going to be a big star. If nobody likes you in two or three months, they just drop you . . . it's not a loyal market like Detroit. The viewers here are the most loyal of any audience anywhere; they really know their television people."

John Kelly: "The loyalties in Detroit are extraordinary, and we're glad we stayed!"

Seriously Speaking

Marilyn Turner: "We had more stars on the earlier shows because there weren't that many syndicated talk shows around. Why would a star need to go to Detroit when they could be on *Oprah* and be seen everywhere? So after *Oprah* came in all the talk shows suddenly became very popular. That's when our show became more subject oriented than celebrity interviews. We got real serious in the later years . . . it was like we had to get into the depths of somebody's mind."

Dan Weaver: "We were one of the first shows to talk about AIDS when it was thought to be a rare gay cancer. We also did some of the first shows on bulimia. And the calls that we would get during the program when we covered these topics would just break your heart. It was a phenomenon at that time to even be able to talk about something like anorexia, so we became a tool for social change; we weren't just about fluff."

Ellen Stepien: "We had an author coming to promote a book about cesarian sections. So I thought maybe we could do a live C-section. The biggest issue was finding someone who'd agree to 'bare their soul' on TV. They loved the idea at Oakwood Hospital because this was a time when hospitals didn't get this kind of PR [public relations]. Well the PR director, Pat O'Dowd, was able to find a pregnant nurse on staff that was going to have a C-section. Marilyn did a predelivery interview with the mother and father before the surgery, then the camera crew went into the OR [operating room] with the mother. Meanwhile, John is interviewing the book author live in the studio back at the station. The operation was performed by Dr. Sami Guindi, and he was wonderful about explaining every procedure. And of course Marilyn cried when the baby came out, along with every other viewer at home."

Chris Stepien: "*Broadcasting Magazine,* the bible in the broadcast industry, declared it as the first known live C-section in the history of broadcast television."

John Kelly: "The show changed because the research indicated that trends were going in a more serious direction and we also had a complete creative management change at the station. Most of the creative staff that was there in the beginning had left, and the show started to slowly go down hill from there."

Company without Kelly

Marilyn Turner: "*Kelly & Company* was, I believe, the last talk show that was locally produced in the country because everyone else was going to the syndicators for talk—the Oprahs and the Jenny Joneses."

By 1993, the talk show genre had exploded with a fleet of nationally syndicated shows flashing a lot of trash and controversy with hosts who seemed to have come from nowhere: Jerry Springer, Ricki Lake, Montel Williams. . . . Over the next year, a new executive producer was hired to take over *Kelly & Company.* She was a woman with very different ideas and concepts of how a local talk show should be administered. Part of the new philosophy called for a reduction in airtime from 90 minutes to a standard hour and for the replacement of the original host, John Kelly.

John Kelly: "I left the show in 1994, and it continued for another year with Marilyn and Nikki Grandberry under the name of *Company.* I returned to the news for about six or eight months, then I decided it was time to retire."

Nikki Grandberry was an African American advertising professional who stood over six feet tall, towering over the petite Marilyn Turner. Grandberry was handpicked by the new executive producer to fill the shoes of John Kelly. The new combination of Marilyn and Nikki got off to a rough start, one that would never smooth itself out.

Chuck Derry: "As hard as they tried, the pairing really didn't gel that well. Nikki was a very unique lady, and I thought she was wonderful, but the mix with her and Marilyn wasn't wonderful. For almost 20 years, Marilyn played 'cutesy wootsy' to John with their bantering, and she couldn't do that with Nikki—they had to be equals. So for another mix to work there needed to be a guy for Marilyn to play against. Marilyn and Nikki got along well, but they struggled to make their pairing work on the air."

By late May 1995, it was apparent to WXYZ's vice president and general manager, Grace Gilchrist, that the strategy of *Company*'s executive producer wasn't paying off. It was time to put an end to the long-standing morning show.

Marilyn Turner: "My agent and I had lunch with Grace Gilchrist about four weeks before the end of the show. I could tell by the way Grace was talking that she was going to cancel the show. We did a show on Friday, the twenty-third of June, and afterward Grace came to my office and closed the door. She said, 'I'm going to tell you first because you've been here the longest. I want you to know that this has nothing to do with anything you're doing; we're just going to close the show down.' And that was the last day of the show."

Channel 7 news anchor Erik Smith, who appeared on that final show, and Chuck Derry relive that summer morning when Gilchrist delivered the startling news.

Erik Smith: "Chad Myers, who was our weatherman at the time, and I did a cooking segment. It was an outdoor show on the station grounds, and Chad and I barbecued a lobster of all things. After the show wrapped up, the boss came down and said that was the last show. We were all shocked because there had been no hint whatsoever that the end was near."

Chuck Derry: "The day the show folded, nobody had a clue . . . I mean, NOBODY had a CLUE! We all thought we were going into a meeting for next Monday's show, and we were told that the show had been canceled and today's was the last one."

And so the husband and wife team that fed us every morning with spoonfuls of Hollywood stars, showbiz gossip, beauty secrets, fashion tips, celebrity look-alike contests, and ordinary folks with stories of heartache and inspiration in between fun-loving tales of their marital woes, John Kelly and Marilyn Turner, will always be looked on as the mediators that brought the very best of America to Detroit and used it to bring out the very best in all of us!

John Kelly: "Once when I was out getting a newspaper, long after the show ended, a lady came up to me and said, 'I never missed a morning!' "

Sonya

Because of Sonya's background and her private practice, it wasn't so much just interviewing Q&A to get the facts out; it really was wrapping the whole interview around to what the viewer can learn from it—what they can take away for their own life. And as a psychologist, a licensed academic, she had the credibility to do it.
—TERI KNAPP, former producer, *Sonya*

When you think of daytime television, three things come to mind: soap operas, game shows, and talk shows. While the networks and syndicators were distributing soaps and games nationally in the early 1980s, the locals were generating talk based on the tastes of their communities. In Detroit, John Kelly and Marilyn Turner were the king and queen of local talk with their morning entertainment program, *Kelly & Company,* on WXYZ-TV, Channel 7. But in 1981 John and Marilyn's exclusive chat room was about to be invaded by a radio doctor named Sonya.

Before Americans heard the names Oprah and Dr. Phil, and long before the explosion of syndicated talk shows in the 1990s, WDIV-TV, Channel 4, gave audiences, not just in the Motor City but all across the country, one of the first psychological self-help programs ever produced on television. From 1981 to 1985, Dr. Sonya Friedman took viewers into the depths of societal issues (particularly those concerning women) by analyzing the real-life experiences of her guests. Detroit TV fan Mark Nowotarski and former WDIV program director Henry Maldonado outline the objective of *Sonya*.

Mark Nowotarski: "Her show had a groundbreaking premise in that you had a psychologist bringing various people on, both famous and infamous, checking their expressions, and then giving her own analysis of

On the sofa, Dr. Sonya Friedman listens intently in 1981. (Courtesy Walter P. Reuther Library, Wayne State University.)

that. And then, at the end of the show, [she presented] a recap of the discussion in one or two statements. I can't recall a show doing that previous to hers, and of course now all the talk show hosts are 'psychologists' in one sense or another."

Henry Maldonado: "Sonya always threw the spin of 'What was it in your life that made you a success?' or 'What was it in your life as a woman that helped you make it in a man's world?'"

As a couple of women in the media who made it in a "man's world," soap opera columnist Lynda Hirsch and WMGC-FM air personality Linda Lanci highlight a few traits belonging to the woman in front of the camera.

Lynda Hirsch: "I think she was a combination of Dr. Phil and Oprah, which is a good thing. She was beautiful, intelligent, and there was always sympathy in her voice. She was helpful, and she had fun."

Linda Lanci: "I think Sonya was definitely someone that women especially looked up to. She paved the way for women in media in a big sense. I believe she was somebody that women respected."

TV Psychology 101

With a master's degree in educational psychology and a doctorate in psychology, both from Wayne State University, Dr. Sonya Friedman was destined to be in the public eye as early as the late 1960s, when a young WXYZ news reporter named Erik Smith needed an expert opinion for an exposé.

Erik Smith: "I was doing a series on prostitution around 1968 or 1969, and I needed a psychologist to explain to me the drug addictions and other obvious things that force women into prostitution. I had heard about Sonya from someone, and so I called her and asked if she would undertake this project with me . . . not only to psychoanalyze but to also get into the sociology of the world's oldest profession. She was glib and smart and attractive on camera. I liked Sonya very much; she was just wonderful. And to my knowledge that was her first real brush with television."

Continuing on the path of "public" psychology, Dr. Friedman became a special correspondent for ABC News in 1976 and two years later a daily talk-radio host on WXYZ. By the time she reached her early forties in 1981, Sonya was already an established lecturer, writer, and media celebrity; the perfect candidate for a brand new TV show that was brewing at WDIV. Henry Maldonado, Dr. Sonya Friedman, and Teri Knapp recount in detail the evolution of what was to become a landmark in local television.

Henry Maldonado: "I came in after *Sonya* was already on the air. She had just started some months before. The way it came about from what I know is that Post-Newsweek had taken over the station a few years earlier [in 1978]. And one of the things going on in the market was *Kelly & Company*, which was a very successful show. Alan Frank [the program manager at the time] and I came from Westinghouse, where we all had morning shows. As a matter of fact, Alan Frank had started a morning show in Baltimore called *People Are Talking* and the first host was Oprah Winfrey. He gave Oprah her first job. And because most of their successful stations had as part of their arsenal a morning show I don't think it was necessarily a major decision [for WDIV] to consider doing a morning show.

"They did one with Gene Taylor called *Taylor-Made* while they were trying to figure out what they wanted to do. At the time, Sonya had a very successful radio show. It was one of those self-help shows like what *Dr. Phil* is now. It was ahead of its time, but it was working on radio. So part of what TV has historically done is take a look at successful people in radio because they have exposure, experience, and a built-in audience. Sonya was somebody sitting there with a very successful radio program, so it just made sense that somewhere along the line somebody would try a TV show with her. And I assume that Alan had listened to her show."

Dr. Sonya Friedman: "I had been a guest on a number of shows in town. My background as a psychologist and a newspaper columnist got me into being a guest on a number of programs, including *Kelly & Company*. I found myself on *Kelly & Company* on a weekly basis, and I started doing a number of other guest spots around the country, which were just fun and gave me an opportunity to be in this arena. I had then gone on and been a special correspondent for ABC News in the area of psychology. I was also doing radio, and I was writing. It was just a host of wonderful things that were happening at a peak in my career. I was then approached by Alan Frank at WDIV and offered an opportunity to do this particular program."

Teri Knapp: "In the early days of the show, there really weren't many others like it. There was Phil Donahue as far as one topic per hour, which was more substantive than a variety or magazine or entertainment-based talk show. Having Sonya as the host of that, to me, it really separated us from all the other shows because she had so much credibility. Just her academic background, her professional credentials, and what she was doing at the time . . . She had her local radio show, she was writing a column for *Ladies Home Journal* and one for the *Detroit Free Press,* [and] she was publishing *Men Are Just Desserts*, which became a *New York Times* bestseller. So she really had a following and a lot of respect."

Henry Maldonado: "The show was basically built around her radio show. She had a call-in show similar to *Dr. Laura,* where people would call in and she would give them advice. The TV show by its nature was a little bit different in that it was a talk show where you bring in guests, but the guests were in the self-help area. People like William Dyer who were writing self-help books at the time would be guests, and Sonya would take questions from the audience. The format was a traditional talk show format, but the theme was based on issues for women: their lives and relationships. And Sonya has always been an advocate for women having control over their destiny. In some ways, she was ahead of the curve we're seeing now, which is not just for women but for all of us to be responsible for our own actions, taking responsibility and owning up to our own destiny. That was the intent of the show, and Sonya was very good at it."

Dr. Sonya Friedman: "On radio, I was one of the first psychologists on the air. I think there were two other people who were prior to me. On television, *Sonya* was one of the first to use a psychologist in a way to get to the underpinnings of people's problems. And there was a time on the show where I used the last segment, especially when it came to first-person, personal stories, to really tell people how I felt about some of the things that they were saying and some of the issues they had brought up."

Smart Cookies Don't Crumble

Dr. Sonya Friedman: "Everybody was nervous about whether or not I would be able to do the show, including me. I remember Alan telling me at the end of the first show that when he saw me walking down the center aisle, engaging the audience and the guests, it was the first time he had taken a breath in a while and he thought that it would work."

Once the jitters on both sides of the camera subsided, Sonya mastered the art of pulling the viewers in by relating the show's topic directly to them on a very personal level. Dr. Friedman gives an example of how she typically opened the program.

Dr. Sonya Friedman: "Very often the show began with my speaking to the camera and saying something like, 'What could be a worse tragedy than losing a teenager in a drunk-driving accident? Well, what if it was your teenager who was a drunk driver? How would you feel about that as a mother? And do you feel the kind of unconditional love for your child that would allow you to feel it's my child right or wrong . . . or whatever my child did I can love him and forgive him and ask others to do the same. Today we have with us 'Mary Carter.' Mary's son 'Jack' was involved in a drunk-driving accident in which four other teenagers were killed. Jack is 16 and now in the Oakland County Jail. Mary, how did you find out that your son was involved in this accident?' And that's how the show would usually open."

Tackling sensitive domestic issues such as drunk driving and spousal abuse was one of Sonya's fortes. In the 1980s, Vicki LaMotta, the ex-wife of middleweight boxing champ Jake LaMotta, was reinventing herself as a 50-something woman. After posing nude in *Playboy* magazine and launching the 60-Second Face Lift cosmetic product, she became a symbol of sensuality for middle-aged women. And while women everywhere

Sonya prepares to take questions from the audience. (Courtesy Dr. Sonya Friedman.)

marveled at Ms. LaMotta's outer beauty Sonya probed beyond the glamour back to the days when she was an abused housewife. Dr. Friedman explains.

Dr. Sonya Friedman: "Vicki LaMotta was on, and she was quite something to behold. I have to tell you, she was just extraordinary, and I think the women in the audience were enraptured hearing what she did to keep herself together. Besides her being a centerfold, as a psychologist I found out that she always saw Jake LaMotta as family, even though he was a very abusive husband. So I was interested in why she kept inviting him to her family events. It was to recognize that there are bonds that people have and even sometimes under the worst of circumstances they're still maintained. I always, in my role as a psychologist, look to go past the journalistic side of it . . . to try to understand what makes people tick and why they do a variety of things that they do."

Even though Sonya, like John and Marilyn, enjoyed the variety of dabbling in the occasional cooking segments and gossip and welcoming celebrity guests such as Patty Duke and Shirley Temple, all of which appealed to the morning female audience . . . it was the championing of women's causes that became her program's primary focus. Henry Maldonado examines her platform and the effect it had on the public.

Henry Maldonado: "Anything that got in the way of a woman's ability to make her own decisions Sonya was very, very strong about. That was the theme of her life, that women had to get out of the stereotypes. For example, she didn't think that women should use crying as a way of getting something. She believed in strong, tough women, and she always stood up for them. And she was one of the first women to have that kind of a forum and a message that was consistent with the support women needed at the time.

"As tough as her message was, it wasn't necessarily popular [with everyone]. She was telling women to stand up for themselves, she was telling men to stop abusing women, [and] she was telling men that in some ways they've caused harm to women and that women cause harm to themselves. So you didn't have this easy message going out over the airwaves that was warmly embraced by the total population. Sonya, in some circles, was considered a bitch, an arrogant uppity woman, and the press for a long time was not kind to her. In many ways, she was the precursor of a lot of what women's [TV] networks like Lifetime became."

Sonya USA

In the 1970s, a new form of subscription television was coming into view called cable TV. It started with uncut movies and gradually worked its way up to programming regular shows by the early 1980s. With new cable networks emerging at a rapid pace, the opportunity for local programs to be nationally syndicated was greatly enhanced. The idea of taking *Sonya* national was one of the main goals of Alan Frank, who poured a lot of money and ambition into the production from the start. By 1982, after only one year on the air, Frank's investment paid off and *Sonya* became the first Detroit program to be nationally syndicated on cable television. Henry Maldonado and Teri Knapp recall how the acquisition gave a real boost to Channel 4.

Henry Maldonado: "*Kelly & Company* was very, very dominant. People loved John and Marilyn, and in many ways I don't think a time ever came when *Sonya* beat *Kelly & Company* in the ratings. So we went through a period of discovery, a period of how do we turn this into something that works, and we did okay. What did happen was when cable started to surface and started to look for product, they considered both shows. *Kelly & Company* and *Sonya* were both considered by cable because what we did with radio they were doing with television: looking around the country for programming. And in the instance with the USA Channel they chose *Sonya* to take into the national market. So, while we were not necessarily the leader in Detroit, we became the program of choice to escalate from local status to national status without any changes . . . The show they put on the air was exactly the same show we produced for Detroit."

Teri Knapp: "We still aired the shows locally, and then I believe there was a week's delay before we would send the shows off to the USA network. Going national made the criteria of what we did that much more intense. The expectations were much stricter, and it was like having the bar raised regarding the type of stories we would do and how we would execute them."

Henry Maldonado: "We made some adjustments; we got a bigger budget so we could get more national guests. The show didn't change in its philosophy, but it evolved as far as guests were concerned. Detroit has always been one of those touring points for people pushing books or whatever. The national show gave us the money, not a tremendous amount because cable didn't have a lot of money, but we did have a budget to where we didn't have to depend on these tours anymore and we could say, 'Okay, let's fly someone in from New York or Los Angeles to appear on the show.' That was the main difference between the local show and the national one; we were going for more guests with a national footprint."

Not only did cable attract a larger audience and more prestigious guests, but it also brought *Sonya* a distinct accolade that no other talk show, local or national, can claim.

Henry Maldonado: "Unbeknownst to a lot of people, *Sonya* was the first talk show to win a CableACE award. Before the cable industry was included in the Emmys, it had the ACE [Award for Cablecasting Excellence] awards; the CableACE awards were the Emmys for cable. The first cable awards ceremony was in Los Angeles, and I flew out there with Sonya for the honor of having the very first talk show to win cable's Emmy."

A Day in the Life of Sonya Friedman

Teri Knapp: "Sonya was just an incredible role model for women in general—just to follow her lead of what it was like to be a working woman in the media. At the time, I was in my mid-twenties and single, but she was married with a family, and I remember really being in awe of her; of everything she was doing and how easy she made it look!"

Dr. Sonya Friedman: "I would be at a 6:00 a.m. exercise class every morning. My makeup lady, Nancy, would come to pick me up at my house at a quarter to six, and the two of us together would take a class at the Vic Tanny on Maple and Telegraph. At the end of that class, we would drive down to WDIV, and I'd work there already showered, hair washed, exercised, and fully awake! I would read my notes in the car on the way down there, which is why it was important to have somebody drive. Reviewing my notes was just a continuation of homework started the night before.

"At the station, I had my hair and makeup done, and I had a wardrobe of clothes that I kept there. Whatever I wore on the show that day would go to the end of the line then work its way up so that I rotated the clothes, not wearing anything more than once every two weeks. There was a production staff of about four or five producers, and we would have a meeting. They would give me their points of view on what we were doing that day. I would go down and meet the guests, then it was lights, camera, action—the show was on.

"When the show was over, I would usually say goodbye to all of the guests. I would go upstairs and change back into my casual clothes before our meeting about the next day's show. You basically learned a very important lesson in life, which was about focus. And what I learned to do was completely clear out that day's show and open myself up to new material: what we were going to do the next day, what the focus was going to be, the background, etcetera. I would then take home my homework, which would often consist of books I would have to skim through. I preferred never to go on the air if I had not read through the material that was given. I never saw it in a cavalier way, I always thought I had the responsibility to do my homework . . . and I always did my homework. When that would end, I would leave to do my radio show for three hours in the afternoon, so I had very full days. And at the end of that I would go home to my family, a husband and two children, then prepare dinner for them. Afterward I would oversee my kids' homework, and then I would sit down and do my homework. I'd usually start about nine o'clock at night and go till maybe eleven; then I would get up and start the routine all over again—five days a week!"

Bookings

One of the greatest challenges in maintaining freshness in talk television lies in the booking of guests. Whether it be *Donahue, Geraldo, Montel,* or *Oprah,* the talk show circuit (past and present) has always been in dire need of topical guests that are of human interest, especially when it's on every day, Monday through Friday! Teri Knapp reflects on her days as a busy talk show producer in search of guests.

Teri Knapp: "We would get our guests, and this was in the days before computers and the Internet, by being ferocious readers! I remember reading, reading, reading, just reading all the time: self-help books, nonfiction, and sometimes fiction. There were a couple bibles that we would have: one was the ABA, the *American Booksellers Association Newsletter,* which would document all the books that were going to be published in the upcoming months. The other was the trade magazine *Publisher's Weekly,* which was also a review of books to be published. So a lot of our subject matter came from authors.

"On top of that we read countless newspapers, *People* magazine, and we all had relationships with publicists. I would go to New York a couple times a year, primarily to meet with publicists and see what was coming up and to cement and solidify the relationships. Obviously, the more solid the relationship was, the more scoop you would get, the more lead time you would get . . . so a lot of guests came that way."

Considering that there were only two talk shows in the Detroit market and they both aired at the same time in the morning, competition between them was intense, especially for *Sonya.* Always trailing *Kelly & Company,* the pressure for Sonya to surpass John and Marilyn was staggering, particularly for the producers.

Teri Knapp: "There was incredible competition with *Kelly & Company.* I can't even begin to explain the amount of mail we would get and the amount of press kits and books. Every time a book was published, their publicist would send them out mass mail. On Mondays everything would come in, all the magazines and the majority of the books from all the weekend buildup; it would be stacks and stacks and stacks of mail.

"So while we were on the air live, *Kelly & Company* would also be on live. A few producers would stay in the office, and the first thing they did was rip open the mail as fast as they could. The reason was because in the beginning, before the publicists were aware of the competition between the two shows, it was first come first served. So, just like kids at Christmas, we would rip open all this stuff and run the books or the press kits down to the executive producer, who would be monitoring the show live. And the executive producer would say, 'Yes, yes, yes' or 'No, no, no.' And we would just work the phones as fast as we could to get our requests in first, hoping that by being the first call we would get the booking . . . and this was also in the days before voice mail.

"The whole planning process was very labor intensive. I remember we used to sit for hours on end just developing the copy that would go into the *TV Guide* listing, just to make sure it was phrased properly to tease and promote the show."

Familiar Faces

Dr. Sonya Friedman: "We had a lot of celebrities: Suzanne Somers, Harry Belafonte, Alex Haley, a number of the soap stars—people really enjoyed seeing the soap stars when they came around—and a lot of other actors."

Although *Sonya* didn't necessarily draw the volume of celebrities that *Kelly & Company* did, it managed to hold its own when famous guests dropped by . . . or did it?

Dr. Sonya Friedman: "I remember one of the first shows was with a guest who took total control of the show and I really didn't know how to get it back without wrestling him to the floor. It was Richard Simmons, and if you've ever been around him he's both hysterically funny and totally out of control at the same time. You're certainly aware of the fact that you're supposed to be an elegant host or a polite host, so it's a little tough to go up and try to muscle the microphone from him; he had just taken it and walked away. We were on live, and every time I approached him to try to take the microphone he would jump off the stage into the audience and jump over seats and go down aisles. It was in one of the first few weeks I was on the air and I was very tenuous about everything I was doing and Alan [Frank] gave me hell for that, but there was nothing I could do about it unless I took him by the throat."

As difficult as Richard Simmons was to control, Dr. Friedman recalls another disastrous big-name guest, who was the complete opposite of the tightly wound weight-loss guru. This one barely uttered a word.

Dr. Sonya Friedman: "Cybill Shepherd was a bad experience. Prior to her appearance, we had Hollywood director Peter Bogdanovich on, who had a long-standing relationship with Cybill Shepherd. And there was that terrible killing of *Playboy* Playmate Dorothy Stratten, with whom he had a relationship as well. I had a terse interview with Peter Bogdanovich because of his encouraging Dorothy Stratten to maintain her position with *Playboy*. It apparently seriously antagonized her husband, who ended up murdering her. Peter had not given her good advice, and I questioned him about that.

"So when Cybill Shepherd came in, I had a sense that she knew about that interview and was very unhappy with me about it. I understand that there are loyalties that people have, so you're caught sometimes on the air between doing your job, which is to ask questions that can make people uncomfortable, and trying to do it artfully but not always succeeding. Cybill Shepherd was the master of giving 'yes or no' answers. And there's nothing more deadly to a host than someone saying, 'Yes . . . no . . . maybe . . . perhaps,' not amplifying on any of their answers."

Teri Knapp: "Cybill Shepherd was just weird. She was in town appearing at the Birmingham Theater to do a play, so we booked her. This was before her comeback in *Moonlighting* and after the whole Peter Bogdanovich affair. I remember going to the greenroom; she was there with her publicist, and I was the only staff person who went in to talk to her. She was flipping this coin, and she never looked me in the eye. I said, 'Ms. Shepherd . . .' and she responded, 'I'm not Cybill Shepherd, I'm . . .' whoever her character was in the play. So it was like talking to this split personality; it was very weird."

Good, bad, or ugly, Henry Maldonado never forgot New York City's forerunner to Howard Stern and why this "character" appeared on *Sonya*.

Henry Maldonado: "One of the things going on at the time was the success of smut, especially in New York. I'm not even sure the rest of the country's ever had local smut like they do in New York. New York had its own local 'dirty' shows, and one of them was called *Ugly George*. Ugly George was one of the first self-contained media weirdos. He had a backpack with a tape recorder in it and a harness with a camera attached to it. His whole show was to run into women on the streets of New York and you would watch the process, which was half of his gag, of him convincing women to take their tops off. That was the whole show! And 75 percent of the time they would go into an office or an alley and take their tops off for this guy. What was interesting about it to Sonya, because these were real, ordinary women, is what did this guy have that would make them want to strip for him?"

Not every famed guest left as poor an impression as the ones just mentioned. Many of Hollywood's elite, such as Janet Leigh, were a pleasure for Sonya to interview. However, there was one person in particular, before he became famous, whose emotional appearance in August 1981 personally touched Teri Knapp.

Teri Knapp: "My most memorable show was with John Walsh. If you remember the whole Adam Walsh [kidnapping] tragedy, this was right before he found out his son was dead. He and his wife were in our greenroom because they were making every appeal that they could. I was the one who booked him, and when I went to meet with him, his wife was so understandably distraught she couldn't even speak. I remember that as just gut-wrenching! And in the greenroom at the same time was Jesse Jackson. It was such a contrast in personalities. But it was the next day they learned that their son was dead. So between the time I booked John Walsh and when he came on the show and in the aftermath, I kind of felt connected with him.

"I ran into him ten years later, and as fate would have it his publicist was someone I went to high school with. John was now living in LA with his own show, *America's Most Wanted*. I told his publicist, who I haven't seen since high school, that I did a show with John that still makes me cry to this day. So then I went over to John Walsh to say hello and figured he probably wouldn't remember me because he had done so much in the past 10 years. When I walked up to him, he remembered exactly who I was . . . I think because it was such a horrible day for him."

There's Nothing Like the Theater

Henry Maldonado: "What was really memorable and special about that show was that we used to produce it in the old WWJ building. Even though by the time I got there in 1981 it was suffering from the urban decay that all buildings do, it still had those signs of some art deco history. It had some great stuff, and I loved that building. And the one thing it had that I have never seen in a TV station before, because it went back to the days of radio, it had a theater . . . a legitimate theater, with seats, a stage, a backstage, and everything. It was just a wonderful experience because it wasn't like a studio today: flats, with folding chairs, you literally walked into a theater from backstage. And in many ways for a guy like me to be doing a talk show in a theater instead of a studio, the whole thing felt very, very nice."

Take It from Here

Dr. Sonya Friedman: "After *Sonya* ended, for one season there was an attempt to evolve the show into one of the first sex shows on the air. Henry and Alan approached me about doing something that would have a little more provocative, seductive content. I think the title was *Secrets Revealed with Sonya Friedman*. They thought they weren't going to see an increase in their numbers, and I'm sure they believed cable was looking for something maybe a little different. And they thought something with sex would sell."

Teri Knapp: "That was also around the time when all the talk shows were crossing over, to me, from substance to just trash. But that was kind of the trend the genre was going in, more *National Enquirer* type of stories. Donahue was doing it, Sally Jesse Raphael was definitely doing it, so, since the national shows were going down that path, I think in order for the local shows to compete with that we had to start following suit. But I don't believe we were as blatant about those subjects as the syndicated shows were; we still added some purpose and merit to those bookings."

The year 1985 would be pivotal for local television. As Dr. Friedman watched her ratings decline, television stations all over the country were gearing up for a major programming overhaul that ultimately phased out much of their locally produced shows. Amazingly, while the programming revolution helped curtail the show, Sonya's celebrity was on the rise. Henry Maldonado analyzes the scenario.

Henry Maldonado: "Two things were going on; one of them was positive, and the other was eventually what became the demise of a lot of local shows. On the negative side, it became more efficient and more profitable to buy a show like *Oprah* than it was to produce a show. The problem with producing a show wasn't just in the expense; it was also the energy, the time, and the facilities that it took every day to do the show, most of the time live. It took a staff of producers and then a team of engineers; so all of a sudden it was draining the station of resources that really belong to news because that became the bread and butter and the primary mission of local television.

"On the other hand, Sonya herself was getting national recognition. So it was a combination of a demise of a genre, but at the same time it wasn't a demise of a talent. All of a sudden you had a talent with a national footprint who was being courted by the CNNs [Cable News Networks] of the world, so she was having opportunities that were more desirable to her career than to keep struggling with a local show. And for a long time she had a national presence after *Sonya*."

On a Clear Day, You Can See Yourself

After a mere four-year run, three of which were on cable, Dr. Sonya Friedman's television career in Motown came to a close. Two years later, in 1987, she resurfaced on cable as the host of *Sonya Live,* an informational news show on CNN that ran for the next eight years. In the wake of her Detroit TV program, she has continued to prosper both as a media professional and an inspiration to women in America. So in retrospect . . . .

Linda Lanci: "Seeing any woman on television, especially locally, has had an influence on me. When I started out in radio, my first job was in 1981, there were no women on TV unless they were doing weather or traffic . . . Sonya was way ahead of her time."

Dr. Sonya Friedman: "It was not in general a confrontational show. It's true, as I look back, that there were some interviews, like the Bogdanovich one, where I recognize that I pushed somebody, clearly beyond their comfort level . . . and perhaps I shouldn't have done it in that format. But I think my role on the show was more to bring out the best of the guest, as opposed to being informative myself, which is a different role you see in talk shows today. Sean Hannity and many of the others in the talk show business today are full of information, which they divulge instead of using it to enhance their guests. I was to be very well informed, but I was background; it was all about the guest. If the guest said something that wasn't accurate, I would try to finesse that: 'Are you sure you mean . . .' or 'Didn't this happen . . . ?' It was never, 'Wait a minute, on page 29 you said . . .' or 'I have somebody who says that what you said is absolutely not true.' Those kinds of disputes would not occur. I did everything possible to bring out the best in the guest. So for me it was just a delightful experience, and I loved it!"

Henry Maldonado: "It was kind of the tip of what *Dr. Phil* and *Oprah* became, different from *Kelly & Company*, which was a fun magazine kind of show. This was actually what eventually became the kind of talk show we're familiar with today, only we didn't know it at the time, we just did it. It was fun, and Sonya was fun to work with . . . she's a very smart woman and sometimes a very tough woman. She had a national TV show, she had a radio show, and she had books that were bestsellers. So what you got here is someone that you have to look at very strongly, not just as a part of TV history but a part of American social history!"

Lou Gordon

His commentaries, I thought, were sharp and biting, and I think in many respects he forced change that needed to be changed. He was a voice that kept a lot of people honest in this town.
  —ERIK SMITH, news anchor, WXYZ-TV

Before hard-hitting political talk shows jammed the cable news channels . . . before there was a program called *60 Minutes* . . . before anybody heard of Bill O'Reilly or saw Mike Wallace giving someone a bad day . . . or for that matter, before Bill Bonds cut loose with his "in your face" style of commentating, local audiences tuned in to WKBD-TV every weekend at 10:00 p.m. to hear Lou Gordon say, "Welcome to the pro-

Hard-hitting journalist Lou Gordon in 1968. (Courtesy Walter
P. Reuther Library, Wayne State University.)

gram, where there's no cue cards, no teleprompters, no idiot boards, just
ad-lib conversation where we tell it like it is!"

Those famous words, which frequently followed the instrumental
break of the song "MacArthur Park," launched the most tense 90 minutes of political talk ever witnessed on television from 1965 to 1977. Controversial Detroit journalist Lou Gordon created the first nationally recognized news discussion program that did more than just debate the
news—it became the news. Syndicated in seven U.S. markets from the
studios of Motown's brand new UHF station, Channel 50, *The Lou Gordon Program* aired exclusively on Saturday nights for the Motor City to
discuss local issues before tackling the national political scene of the rest
of America on Sunday nights. And at the heart of every show, regardless
of the topic, was the electrifying persona of the very opinionated Lou

Gordon. Fans Greg Russell and Dan Weaver express their views about the man and his program.

Greg Russell: "*The Lou Gordon Program* was probably the first of the type of shows where the host would get on the guest's case and not let go until he got an answer. If he were alive today, he'd have the chairman of Enron on and grill him about, 'Why did you steal all those people's money?'"

Dan Weaver: "It was kind of newsy, but it was very full of Lou. I remember on Sunday nights they ran the show in Cleveland, and I would catch it from this little town in Pennsylvania where I'm from. I would watch it religiously because it was an alternative . . . it was *The Tomorrow Show* pre-*Tomorrow*. Lou was probably the guy that gave Tom Snyder the inspiration for *The Tomorrow Show*."

The People's Advocate

After graduating from the University of Michigan and serving his country during World War II in the air force, Detroit native Lou Gordon pursued a career in journalism. Moving to Washington, DC, he landed a job with General Newspapers as a publisher's assistant and political writer. Working closely with postwar muckraking reporters whetted Lou's appetite for dangerous assignments dealing with organized crime and political corruption. When Estes Kefauver challenged the Crump political machine in Memphis in 1947, Gordon volunteered to cover the story despite jail and death threats from "Boss" Crump. His determination to uncover the truth was the focus of a *Time* magazine article, "Maintaining the Public Welfare."

Upon his return to the Motor City in the 1950s, Lou went to work as a manufacturing representative for his father's White Stag clothing distribution company. While selling the sportswear collection to top-of-the-line stores by day, Gordon never lost his ambition to speak out against social injustice on behalf of the common man. At the suggestion of a friend, he used his free time to broadcast commentaries on WXYZ radio every day at 6:25 p.m. Former WXYZ director Ron David, who directed Gordon's first TV show, explains Lou's transition from radio to television.

Ron David: "His interest in politics is what got him into television, and *Detroit Deadline* was his first toe in the water. It was on Channel 7 from 10:45 to 11:00 p.m. five nights a week, and he'd have one guest a night, usually somebody involved in politics. That became so popular so quickly that Channel 50 hired him away. He was a man who in his day did some very inflammatory programming, and he said things about people that nobody else had the nerve to say, but yet he was never successfully sued for anything he ever said because it was the truth. It was hard to sue a guy for telling the truth! He knew his stuff, and he wasn't afraid to tell it like it was."

After accessing the power of television, Lou Gordon decided to use the medium as a platform to champion the cause of the "little guy"—John Q. Public—who was intimidated by big businesses and government. In doing so, he became an original in electronic muckraking. Gordon's children, Deborah and Scott, elaborate.

Deborah Gordon: "His theme was going after the power structure and exposing abuses of power at both the local and national levels. His attempt to get the information out to people is why they loved the show. It was a way to cut through all the BS and say what was really happening, what people were really thinking and feeling."

Scott Gordon: "An interviewer once asked my dad if he was the last angry man. My dad said, 'No . . . but I've been given this position in life and I intend to use it for those who can't speak for themselves, the voiceless, the people without the clout, the powerless, and this is why I'm here . . . to speak for those folks.' One of his big thrills was that he rallied thousands of people to the Michigan Public Service Hearings when the phone company wanted to start charging for information calls. At the time, 411 calls were free, and the phone company wanted to impose a charge. Of course, now there is a charge, but back then there wasn't, and my father made sure that stayed true until long after his death."

And when it came to partisan politics, Scott Gordon describes how his dad usually favored one side of the spectrum, but not always . . .

Scott Gordon: "Though his stance was that of a liberal Democrat, he was the kind of person that would vote for the right man, not necessarily a Democrat but the guy who had the right answers on the right issues."

Dear Lou . . .

After switching stations from WXYZ to WKBD in the fall of 1965, Lou Gordon was given an hour and a half to confront and comment on any issue he desired. Seated behind a desk in front of the "hot seat" on a closed two-camera set supported by a riser and surrounded by colorful stage flats, Lou and his wife Jackie opened the program with a very innovative segment that's become a benchmark for political talk shows.

Deborah Gordon: "The show opened up with a Q&A segment that was mainly about local politics and issues."

Scott Gordon: "Viewers would write in questions during the week such as, 'Lou, what do you think of the current Detroit teachers' strike [in 1973]?' My mom would read the questions to my dad, and then he would give his opinion."

Deborah Gordon: "My stepmother, Jackie, wasn't part of the show originally. There was some other woman, an attractive woman, whose role was to come on and read these questions. But early on we got a call at the house one Saturday; this woman was ill and she wasn't going to be able to make it. So my dad talked Jackie into doing it. She had been a model. At first, she didn't want to do it, but he twisted her arm and so she did it and loved it. She was on the show every night from that night forward."

Scott Gordon: "My mother was also an instrumental part of the show behind the scenes. On a number of levels, she was Dad's right arm."

After the Q&A segment, Jackie would exit the set, leaving Lou to conduct his interviews for the duration of the show.

The Weekend Massacre

Whether it was three guests per show or three guests per segment, *The Lou Gordon Program* carried an "enter at your own risk" warning label for anyone looking to use the show as an outlet for exposure, especially when it came to the legitimacy of any social or political issue in which Lou detected what he commonly called "an element of phoniness." Former WKBD director Bill Murray recalls how the sting of the show forced the station to change the way it produced the program.

Bill Murray: "Initially the show was live, and we very quickly found out that was a bad idea. Lou was prone to spouting on the air, and it got close to being a little slanderous a couple of times. I don't remember specific topics, but I do know that we began to expect two things on Monday mornings: one was phone calls from lawyers representing the people he was talking about and the other was bomb threats. They both got to be fairly routine. The way they headed off the lawyer problem was to put the show on tape. And we wound up taping it the same evening it aired about two, three, or four hours before the broadcast. Channel 50 had an attorney who the program manager called if he saw or heard something during the taping that was worrisome."

So what exactly did Lou Gordon present each week that was so infuriating to his guests and yet so appealing to his loyal audience?

Deborah Gordon: "He loved to play 'gotcha!' He acted like a trial lawyer. He would have the guest on, and he'd ask him or her a question and kind of lead them down the path, and when the guest would say 'I never said that' he'd say, 'Well, I've got it right here,' and he'd pull out an old clip."

Scott Gordon: "He really got Dick Cavett riled up, and of course the big thing at that time was you couldn't really rile up Dick Cavett. But Dad managed to get a rise out of him based on a quote he said he didn't make. What happened was Cavett had written a book in which he plagiarized himself from a *Playboy* article he had written years before and he denied it. Of course, Dad had the evidence and got Dick in a twist."

In order for Gordon to execute his gotcha tactic without a hitch, he often had to look for a needle in a haystack. One of the many researchers Lou employed to find that needle was Joe Babiarz. Nicknamed "Joe Baby" because Lou couldn't pronounce Baa-bee-arz, he began as a research coordinator in 1976 and eventually became the last person to produce *The Lou Gordon Program.* Babiarz recounts Gordon's modus operandi for interview selection and preparation.

Joe Babiarz: "There were three categories of interviews: the politicians, the book tour people, and all others. A political interview required a tremendous amount of research, particularly if Lou disliked the interviewee and it was going to be an attack interview. Lou started his day by reading the *Detroit News,* the *Detroit Free Press,* the *New York Times,* the *Washington Post* . . . and he'd mark every article he read either with a *P* or an *F.* A *P* meant that it was a program idea, and an *F* meant 'file'—for the clip file. So we had quite a large data bank, and in 1976 computers weren't around, so research was quite different. Lou was quite a stickler for details and extremely demanding. He was very big on doing your homework and having the facts straight; he didn't want to go off half-cocked when he was butting heads with an influential politician. I would go through our own clip files, and I also relied a lot on the Farmington Hills Public Library. Lou also had a lot of political connections that I would get information from; sometimes I got help from the attorney general's office and law enforcement agencies."

One of the best examples of Lou in action flogging a local heavyweight happened on February 20, 1977, when he challenged the validity of then Oakland County prosecutor L. Brooks Patterson's stance on Proposition D.

Joe Babiarz: "Lou did not like Brooks Patterson at all. At the time Proposition D was a ballot proposal to do away with time off for good behavior for convicted felons. Patterson was very much in favor of this. We also invited Paul Rosenbaum, who at the time was the chairman of the Michigan House Judiciary Committee and opposed Proposition D. So the premise was going to be a debate between Rosenbaum and Patterson over the issue. If I may say [so], Mr. Rosenbaum was basically a pot-ted plant during that interview because it was pretty much Lou going one on one with Patterson.

"I uncovered a letter in the Oakland County Court file, which one of my sources told me to look into. The letter was written to Perry Johnson, the director of the Michigan Department of Corrections, by Brooks Patterson, requesting parole for a convicted murderer. Once I found that letter, Lou looked like a little kid who'd just gotten a birthday present. He set Patterson up very nicely as I recall. He said, 'Mr. Patterson, would it be fair to say that you are unalterably opposed to any form of parole for anyone convicted of a violent felony? Is that a fair statement?' Patterson said, 'Yes, that's a fair statement.' We had prearranged with the director to go to a split screen. On one side of the screen was an extremely tight shot of Patterson's face, while on the other half was a blowup of the letter signed by Patterson.

"So after he took the bait Lou said, 'Now, Mr. Patterson, you just told me that you are unalterably opposed to any form of parole for anyone convicted of a violent felony. Yet you wrote a letter requesting parole for a convicted murderer! Which is it?' Well, Patterson got redder than a beet, and he replied, 'I wrote that letter in exchange for this person's testimony that would convict somebody who was more guilty.' And Lou shot back very quickly, 'But Mr. Patterson, under your own plan you wouldn't be able to do that, sir.'"

Controversy

Deborah Gordon: "He was actually suspended from the show at one point. It was during the Q&A segment when he used the analogy of a 'pregnant nun.' Back in those days, that was enough to get you suspended because it was considered very inappropriate."

It comes as no surprise that any person who repeatedly speaks their mind very candidly is not only going to ruffle a few feathers but is likely to be permanently branded as controversial. Long before Oliver Stone made a movie career out of Vietnam War issues and presidential conspiracies, Gordon stirred the political pot by being one of the first journalists to speak out against the Vietnam War; to believe in the conspiracy theory on the assassination of John F. Kennedy; and to publicly point the finger at Richard Nixon in the Watergate scandal. News anchor Erik Smith of WXYZ describes the controversy that surrounded his friend and colleague, Lou Gordon.

Erik Smith: "Lou was a very tough guy, and I felt that he didn't always see both sides of a question. I think he tended to see the side he was comfortable with, and that's not a criticism, just an observation. I was uncomfortable with some of the things he did. We didn't work together on a day-to-day basis; we did talk a lot, and we met quite often. I have respect for many of the things he did, and I lacked respect for some of the others. And that's difficult to square, but he was a dynamic guy. If he were here today, a lot of people would be running for cover. Everything isn't black and white, and Lou found a lot of the gray areas."

Deborah Gordon: "Over time, as people became more aware of him, especially local people, they became apprehensive to appear on his show. Sometimes on the air he would say, 'I tried to get so-and-so, but they declined to appear on the show.' But in general there weren't that many outlets [in talk TV], so anybody that had a book or an issue and wanted the television exposure came on the show. Now what did happen a lot of times is that people would not come back as a repeat guest."

Joe Babiarz: "His critics often said his questions were unfair and insulting, but Lou once told me, 'All I do is confront a man with his own words. Now what could be more fair than that?' And that's what he did."

Scott Gordon: "I think one of his greatest thrills was to get somebody to walk off the show."

Joe Babiarz: "When George Wallace was running for president in 1968, Lou said, 'Mr. Wallace, I don't want to embarrass you, sir, but I have to ask this question . . . Do you really think that someone who has a mental discharge from the air force is qualified to run for president?' George Wallace reacted very negatively and stormed off the show.

"I can also recall when he had Erica Jong, the author of *Fear of Flying*, on the program. During the course of the interview, she was bragging about her writing ability; she was comparing herself to Henry James and Ernest Hemingway and other noted writers. Lou said, 'Ms. Jong, I really must tell you, I detect an element of phoniness here.' That went over like a lead balloon. She got up and stormed off the set and walked right out of the building. The amusing thing is that wherever she was going next on the book tour she got back at Lou. She said, 'The other day I was interviewed in a cornfield in some suburb of Detroit, and this hostile interviewer, whose toupee looked like a pork chop, was insulting me!'"

Likes and Dislikes

Joe Babiarz: "Lou liked Attorney General Frank Kelly. He would bring him on to talk about new developments in consumer protection law. He respected Henry Ford II and had him on the show now and then. He liked Senator Don Riegle; they got along well. He was friends with Governor William Milliken . . . and he respected working journalists, so they were never attacked."

Deborah Gordon: "He couldn't stand Richard Nixon. He called him 'Tricky Dick' and he just hated him, so that was always a favorite topic. At one point, he found out he was on the Nixon enemies list and was absolutely delighted! That was a real thrill for him. Then there was Detroit mayor Jerry Cavanagh . . . they had started off as friends; my dad supported him when he initially ran for office. But over time my father began to feel that he [Cavanagh] had lost his dedication to the average citizen and that the power had gone to his head. And later he couldn't stand Coleman Young. As time went on, he thought that Young was engaging in all kinds of things unbecoming of a mayor."

Joe Babiarz: "Because Lou viewed himself as the people's advocate, he saw it as his duty to really give politicians a rough way to travel . . . and he did."

Expect the Unexpected

Dan Weaver: "What I loved about *Lou Gordon* was you just never knew who you were gonna see on that show. I remember he had a transsexual whose name was Rachel Harlow. And for whatever reason this is stuck in my head; she was one of the most beautiful 'women' that I could imagine, and there was Lou sitting there talking with this transsexual. I was probably 10 or 12 years old when I saw the show, and it was the first time I ever saw something like that on TV."

Unlike the news, but very much like the talk shows of today, Lou Gordon had his share of "sensational" guests. Whether it was an interview with Miss Nude America, a psychic, or an exotic animal trainer, subjects relating to sex, the occult, or the outright weird were frequently showcased on the program. However, this was not necessarily Lou's preference.

Deborah Gordon: "He had those people on for one reason: the sweeps ratings. It was strictly because it was the sweeps rating period, and audiences tuned in to see the bizarre, so that's what he gave them. My father was very much a political junkie, so some of these kinds of interviews became a bore for him, but he also, like everybody else, had a fascination with some of these guests. I remember Joey the Hitman fascinated him, and he also had this woman on named Christine Jorgensen, who had previously been a man [the first successful sex change], which was unheard of back in those days and it became a fascinating thing for him, too. But in general he just wanted the political people on the show."

No matter who it was that came on *The Lou Gordon Program,* one thing viewers could always count on was the bold rawness of Lou's questions and comments. What would Lou ask or say today? Who could have predicted that he would ask consumer advocate Ralph Nader if he was a homosexual? He asked Billy Hayes, the author of *Midnight Express,* which was later made into a movie by Columbia Pictures in 1978, if he had repaid his parents all of the money they spent trying to buy his freedom from the Turkish prison he ultimately escaped from. He lambasted porn king Larry Flynt to his face, but in the same breath he stood up for his constitutional right to free speech against the Cincinnati prosecutor seated next to him. Their lively, no-holds-barred debate was one of the few times Gordon was ever outshouted on his own program.

In Lou's eyes, everybody was fair game . . . even beloved Hollywood celebrity Bob Hope. Hope made two appearances on the show, the first in 1973 and the second in 1975. When the comedian was in the hot seat for the first time, he vigorously defended his friendship with ousted vice president Spiro Agnew in response to Gordon's relentless questions regarding Agnew's alleged corruption along with an attack on the integrity of President Nixon. When Hope returned again two years later during the Ford administration, Lou continued to take shots at Nixon, asking, "Who do you like better, Nixon or Ford?" Hope dodged the bullet by answering, "I never met a president I didn't like."

Brainwashed

Perhaps no guest on *The Lou Gordon Program* regretted his or her appearance more than Michigan governor George Romney. Gordon viewer Larry Dlusky, former WKBD (and WXYZ) stage manager Chuck Derry, Bill Murray, and Scott Gordon reflect on that critical interview in 1968, which resulted in national headlines.

Larry Dlusky: "I recall they were talking about the Vietnam War and Romney made a statement that he had been brainwashed about Vietnam. Well, being a politician, especially the governor of a state, and going on a popular TV show in your state and saying that you believed you were brainwashed, that's not going to do a whole lot for your political career. George Romney was somebody who had presidential aspirations, and I think that moment was a big setback in his career."

Chuck Derry: "I remember being about five feet away from George Romney when he said he was brainwashed, and they just kept going on with the show. Nobody said anything about it until after the show was over, and then they nailed him to the wall. I thought it was unjust to ride

Gordon with Michigan governor George Romney on the day of the historic "brainwashed" interview. (Courtesy Joe Babiarz.)

Romney like that. He was being frank with Lou in that he was duped about Vietnam. He could have said 'I was duped' or any number of different things, so in context what he said was fine. To me, it was not a big deal because it was somebody being very candid with the audience. It was the governor being real honest with people, and the media blew it up."

Bill Murray: "No one at the station thought it was a significant remark when it aired. A week or two after the show, a columnist picked up the quote from a WKBD press release and called for confirmation. As it happened, we had not yet erased the tape, which was usually done soon after airing because the station could not afford enough videotape to library any show, and so someone at the station confirmed the quote. The story was eventually given national prominence, and Romney was tagged as not being smart enough to see through [Lyndon] Johnson's tactic [regarding Vietnam]. He soon ended his race for the White House as a direct result and was the butt of 'brainwash' jokes for many years thereafter."

Scott Gordon: "It wasn't my father's intention to ruin Romney's chances for the presidency; it was simply to interview the man to see what he was all about."

Beyond Detroit

Scott Gordon: "My dad didn't own the show outright at all; he was an employee of WKBD. But the way he negotiated his deal was that he could do whatever he wanted. So he wasn't a hired host doing what the producers wanted; he was the executive producer of the show."

In 1966, the Kaiser Broadcasting Company, which owned Channel 50, decided to capitalize on Gordon's Motown popularity by syndicating him nationally across all seven of their stations. For the next 11 years, Lou's controversy reached the eyes and ears of households in Boston, Philadelphia, Cleveland, Chicago, San Francisco, and Los Angeles. Without the satellite technology of today, exactly how did Kaiser broadcast the program from Detroit?

Scott Gordon: "The way the syndicated cities received the show was my brother and I would go down to the Detroit Post Office and put 20, 30, 40 stamps on the tape boxes. We had to mail them out because there was no other form of distribution back then."

As archaic of a concept as mailing tapes sounds, the results far outweighed the cost of the postage. The Motor City's own Lou Gordon caught the attention of the rich and famous.

Joe Babiarz: "We had a fella on whose name was James Phelan, who'd written a book about Howard Hughes, and he had a couple of Hughes's aides with him. So when he came on to talk about his book with Lou I met with the aides, and one of them, Gordon Margulis, said Howard Hughes was a big fan of *The Lou Gordon Program* and never missed it. We had a lot of fan mail from Hollywood people, too. I remember distinctly that Burt Reynolds wrote in once to say he enjoyed the show. Rod McKuen, the poet, also liked Lou Gordon."

A True Workaholic

Scott Gordon: "He read seven newspapers a day . . . and this was before FedEx and UPS Overnight. He would have, one paper I remember specifically, the *Miami Herald* flown in every day on an aircraft and then a taxicab would deliver it from the airport to our house. We had four telephone lines at home, and this was when people still had rotary dial phones with party lines, but we had these advanced key phone setups. He would routinely work from home in the morning before rolling into the office at Channel 50 in the afternoon.

"When we would vacation in Florida once or twice a year . . . he was consumed with work. He was constantly reading newspapers, always on

On the set with Jackie in the 1970s. (Courtesy Scott Gordon.)

the phone with his staff, so as a child it drove me nuts because I wanted him in the swimming pool with me. He had a difficult time disconnecting himself from his work."

Deborah Gordon: "All he ever really wanted to do was discuss politics. He couldn't have cared less about going to a movie or to see a play or going out to socialize. He really didn't care about those things; he didn't have an interest in them. He wanted to be home watching the news, reading the paper, making phone calls to figure out what was going on in the news, making contacts, talking to the politicians . . . that's really what he did 24/7."

Death Threats

Erik Smith: "Lou and I shared a period of time together with a common source. We were both looking into organized crime here in the Detroit area, and we both had access to a mobster who was ratting on some of the higher-ups in organized crime that were connected to people in local politics—politicians who had their palms greased by underworld figures."

Deborah Gordon: "He had this idea about going after the Mafia, which was another one of his pet topics, and he would name names. It was very nerve-racking, and I was worried about it. When I was going to school in

Ann Arbor with my sister, apparently unbeknown to us my dad actually had the State Police trailing us at some point. You can imagine that I wasn't too happy about that, being a college student at U of M back in that era. There had been some sort of threat, and he kept it quiet because he didn't want to scare us. But I know those kinds of threats were out there somewhere; a lot of people hated him—there's no doubt about that."

Scott Gordon: "Many, many, many times his life was threatened by many different types of people. Our entire family was under surveillance by the FBI because we had Mafia threats. There were a few times my mom and dad had to be escorted to and from the television station. But let's face it, he made people mad, and there was plenty of angry mail and angry everything; whether it was from the bad guys or from the mayors, he upset a lot of people. In my opinion, he felt that this was his calling in life, this was his duty, this is why he was put on this earth . . . and if he got killed doing so, well then that's the way it's going to be. I really believe that."

The Silent Farewell

Joe Babiarz: "I remember what became the last show I produced; [it] was with Mickey Mantle and Whitey Ford—they had written a book called *Mickey and Whitey*. When I got into work that morning, I was told that Lou had died early that morning. That was quite stunning news, and that was the end of the program."

On the morning of May 24, 1977, the people's advocate died peacefully in his sleep exactly one week after his sixtieth birthday. The suddenness of his passing came as the result of a condition caused by rheumatic fever, which he had suffered from in his childhood. In the mid-1970s, Gordon underwent surgery for an aortic valve replacement, which at the time was still a very new and risky procedure. But, despite the success of the operation, the scar tissue that had built up from the damage of his boyhood illness was so extensive that the valve replacement gave way after two years.

In the wake of Lou's death, an attempt was made to continue the show under a new name, *Crossfire*. After trying a number of guest hosts, including Lou's widow Jackie and *Free Press* columnist Bob Talbert, the WKBD management hired New York talk radio host Barry Farber. The ratings for *Crossfire* were dismal compared to *The Lou Gordon Program*, and consequently the first real talk show to play hardball with the news makers pitched its final inning. And, though the game may have been over for Lou in 1977, the playbook he wrote years before set the standard for today's news talk shows.

And Let's Not Forget . . .

7

The Lady of Charm

I was little when my mother was watching that show. I remember I just loved the cooking part of it, the way she would talk through a recipe and seeing all those bowls of chopped up things . . . and of course the mess would always disappear. I've long joked that my aspiration was to grow up and be the Lady of Charm.
  —PEGGY TIBBITS, Detroit TV fan

Once we lived in a society in which everyone understood the meaning of common courtesy. Decades before Martha Stewart became a household name, Edythe Fern Melrose taught the housewives of Detroit the finer points of proper etiquette. As one of the first programs on WXYZ-TV, the Lady of Charm began her small-screen life in November 1948. Home-based topics for women such as cooking, table settings, manners, and fashion were addressed every afternoon by Motown's own seasoned veteran of social grace. The Lady of Charm's grandson, Steve Southard, can personally attest to his grandmother's mannerisms.

Steve Southard: "The public persona, the gracious giving individual, wasn't an act. That *was* my grandmother . . . that was the same thing we saw with her at home. She was charming and warm and a real doer!"

Although the Lady of Charm epitomized the image of the dutiful wife that was so prevalent on television in the 1950s, behind the camera Edythe Fern Melrose was far from being the traditional "little woman." She was in fact a brilliant self-made businesswoman who carried a tremendous amount of clout at WXYZ.

The Lady of Charm, Edythe Fern Melrose. (Courtesy Carol Marenko.)

Farmer's Daughter

The Lady of Charm was born Edythe Fern Culp on November 18, 1897, on a farm in West Mansfield, Ohio. While growing up in the rural Midwest, Edythe discovered she had a natural talent for home decorating. Whether it was a table setting or fine needlework, she always found creative ways to make things in the home look "prettier." In school, she excelled in writing, literature, and mathematics.

In her late teens, she married a 38-year-old widower named Will

Carleton Southard, whose farmhouse in the neighboring town of York Center was the first in the state to have electricity. The couple produced two sons, Harold and Warren. When Harold was nine, Warren died of leukemia at the young age of seven. Edythe's husband had come from a wealthy family that lost its fortune due to bad investments. Having been affluent, Southard rarely ever worked a "regular" job and subsequently made little effort to find employment, which strained the marriage. Eventually the couple divorced, and the responsibility of raising Harold was split between both parents: summers with Mom and winters with Dad.

Radio Days

After completing a nursing curriculum and attending a charm school, Edythe traveled to Cleveland in the early 1930s to start a new life. Fascinated with the glamour of radio, she accepted a receptionist position at one of the city's stations. In order to get her voice on the air, she volunteered to read poetry for free. During this time, she caught the eye of the station owner, Grant Melrose. The two fell in love and were married. Edythe became the manager of the station in 1934, making her the first and only woman radio station manager in the United States!

While her newfound career was prospering, Edythe's personal life suffered another tragic loss. Less than a year after her wedding day, Grant Melrose died unexpectedly of a massive heart attack. In the wake of her husband's death, Edythe Fern Melrose left Cleveland to pursue a career in a larger radio market—Detroit.

Once she arrived in the Motor City, Edythe approached WXYZ radio with a "charm" program she had conceived that would showcase her lifelong love of feminine hospitality. The Lady of Charm, as Melrose called herself, was based on the premise that a woman's charm depends on three things: the way she acts, the way she looks, and the way she cooks.

Upon submission to the station, the show was rejected. As disappointing as that was initially, it didn't stop the woman who had previously managed a radio station in Cleveland—no sir. If WXYZ wasn't going to financially support the program, she knew she'd have to find someone who would . . . and that's exactly what she did. After securing an impressive list of sponsors, there was no way WXYZ could refuse her program a second time. From that day forth Edythe Fern Melrose continued to attract major sponsors for the station while portraying herself as the happy homemaker to housewives all over Metro Detroit.

A Cup o' Hospitality

In October 1948, WXYZ-TV signed on the air, and a month later the radio institution known as the Lady of Charm was making regular appearances three days a week (Wednesday through Friday) on a televised version of *The Charm Kitchen*. Retired WXYZ director Mason Weaver recalls how the opening incorporated one of Melrose's many poetic gestures.

Mason Weaver: "Her show would start with a slide and harp, and the announcer [Larry McCann] would say . . .

Breathes there a man with soul so dead,
Who never to himself hath said,
We-l-l, if she can COOK, I think we'll WED!
Now, here's your very own Lady of Charm . . .

We'd dissolve to her, and every day she said the same thing: 'Greetings to you and to everyone.'"

With the new visual media at her disposal, the Lady of Charm was afforded the luxury of showing Motor City housewives what she could only discuss on the radio. *Charm* fan Maurine Robinson summarizes many of the topics depicted on the show.

Maurine Robinson: "She was into a lot of feminine stuff. Cooking, setting tables, and doing place settings with the fancy place mats, positioning the goblets at the tip of the knife with the silverware in the right places. She was into making things pretty—like a centerpiece with the candles in different places—and arranging furniture to make rooms look nice, things to be here and there, a bowl of flowers here . . . things like that.

"And of course kitchen things . . . she was into cooking, so she gave out many, many recipes. She showed everybody how to do the food, every aspect of it, whether it be an apple pie or a custard. How to cut this or slice that . . . how to grate something, what temperature to set the oven; it was shown very clearly for beginners and newlyweds.

"She would also say things like, 'You have to cook these popovers so they'll be ready right when the man of the house sits down at the table; otherwise, they'll collapse.' Saying things like that made me think she was telling new brides that they should have dinner ready when their husbands came home."

The Charm Kitchen

Much of the action on the program centered around the kitchen. To create an atmosphere of authenticity, Melrose insisted that a fully functional

Assisted by Mattie Mack (*left*), the Lady of Charm whips up another delicious meal for Motor City housewives. (Courtesy Carol Marenko.)

replica of her own home kitchen be constructed in the studio at the Maccabees Building. Retired WXYZ art director Jack Flechsig remembers the outcome.

Jack Flechsig: "When she came to TV, we had a smaller studio next to the big studio, so we made that her kitchen. And it was very nicely done, with all the latest appliances."

Fashionably dressed in fine clothes, Melrose prepared a variety of dishes cooked and/or baked with name brand appliances and utensils she always called by name. When a supper tray was ready to come out of the oven after the timer bell rang, she would say, "Thank you (brand name)." Her strategic use of product names to identify appliances proved to be a very effective method for advertising her sponsors' products, as Jack Flechsig notes.

Jack Flechsig: "John Pival used to tell us in the early days, 'I don't know what we got here . . . TV might catch on or it might fall flat . . . we don't know. But if you want to stick it out and see what happens—fine.'

We realized what we had when the Lady of Charm casually mentioned on her show one time, 'I'm cooking on my Sears double-oven stove.' Sales skyrocketed at Sears! And Sears called to say, 'Stop mentioning the stove . . . [we] can't make them fast enough.' They sold out overnight. Anything she said, people did."

Because appliances and decor changed so frequently, the Charm Kitchen was subject to annual updates. Last year's colors are out, now these colors are in; this pattern of wallpaper was fashionable, now it's gaudy; the dials on this appliance now have push buttons . . . and the list goes on. For every update that was made in the kitchen, a lucky station employee was awarded the "obsolete" item.

If a dinner plate was to be featured, Edythe displayed it in the kitchen, but when desserts were presented they would appear on a beautifully decorated dining table. The Lady of Charm's motto was, "Cook for a man so he loves it, then he'll love the cook." Melrose prided herself on knowing the tastes of men. And to exploit that notion her son Harold appeared on the show as Justimere Mann—in plain English, "Just a mere man." On the rare occasion when the man of the house didn't make it home on time for dinner, a stagehand would substitute. Retired WXYZ stage manager Art Runyon recounts one of the times he appeared and threw a wrench into Edythe's theory about male preferences.

Art Runyon: "When I was stage manager, she'd always give me a sample. 'What do you think of that, Art?' 'Oh, that's delicious, Edythe.' One time she was doing a cake, and she said, 'We can do it this way . . .' It was first with a plain chocolate frosting, and then she did one that was fancy, with curlicues and things like that. She said, 'Now, I know men prefer the plainer, simpler, chocolate one. How about you, Art? What do you like?' I said, 'I like the curlicues.' She replied, 'Well, nothing for you after the show.'"

Though Art may not have gotten anything to eat after the show, the men who usually did were the directors. Former WXYZ director Ron David walks us over to the "Captain's Table."

Ron David: "For a period of time, I directed her show. There were many directors during the time she was on, but one of the fun things was if you directed her show you were invited to have lunch in the studio at what she called the Captain's Table. It was a little folding card table with a red and white checkered tablecloth. You'd sit there with Edythe Fern Melrose and have the lunch that she had prepared on live TV. It was a great honor. Not everybody sat at the Captain's Table with Edythe, so when you were invited you were happy to do it."

Kitchen Prep

Preparing the entrées as well as the scripts for the cooking show was an enormous undertaking, much too time consuming for the Lady of Charm to execute single-handedly. Edythe's granddaughter, Carol Marenko, takes us behind the scenes with the on-air kitchen staff.

Carol Marenko: "Grandma, my mother, Gretchen, and [their assistant] Dorothy wrote and typed on carbon paper all of the scripts. There was also a wonderful lady, Mattie Mack, who prepared all of the food trays beforehand and then she would take the trays away [on the air]. The food would be placed out at the table when it was ready to be presented. When she would do the cooking, she wasn't scooping the flour out of a canister; everything was premeasured—ready, set, go. She had samples of something fixed, something in the preparation stage, and something ready to slide into the oven."

So where, exactly, did the Lady of Charm get all her recipes?

Carol Marenko: "She had a collection of cookbooks, but she never took another recipe and copied it; she always did something [unique] to them."

Steve Southard: "After a time, folks sent her a lot of recipes, and she worked with them, tweaking them and so on."

A Word from Our Sponsor

Ron David: "She had tremendously important sponsors like Chrysler Corporation, Frigidaire, General Electric . . . manufacturers of all the major appliances were her sponsors. Whatever the Lady of Charm wanted, she got. Tough lady, but she knew her stuff and did a wonderful show. She had a big following with housewives."

Carol Marenko: "Chrysler was one of the sponsors. They had a special car made for her—a yellow convertible with an extended rear bumper."

Mason Weaver: "The biggest thing on that show was getting her at the end, sitting in the car to give you a kiss goodbye."

Carol Marenko: "Wrigley Grocery Stores was also one of her sponsors. Every week she would give them [notice of] what she was going to be making each day, and Wrigley would have flyers at the front of their stores that the shoppers could take as to what the recipes were for the upcoming week."

Fashionable Living

In the early 1950s, Melrose stepped out of the kitchen every Tuesday with the addition of a separate program called *Charm Time*. Maurine Robinson and Carol Marenko highlight some of its features.

Maurine Robinson: "She was into clothes, fashionable things, nothing too extreme in any way . . . more middle-of-the-road type of stuff. She didn't go for anything outrageous. She wanted women to look nice and very feminine."

Carol Marenko: "When she focused on fashion, she did women's fashion and children. When she did children, she got the kids from our neighborhood to come and be models. She was always pulling in what was new, what people might want to know out there in the way of fine living and improved living and what women were doing. Around 1961, I remember, contact lenses were kind of new, and so I got to be the contact lens guinea pig . . . which was cool with me."

For the fashion and lifestyle segments, the small studio normally used for the cooking show three days a week was unsuitable.

Jack Flechsig: "She needed a lot of space because she had a lot of people on, maybe 20 or 30 models modeling clothes. The models came in through an archway, which didn't match anything else on the set. The fashion set varied [with or without runways] depending on what she was doing."

Alongside the fashion set was an area with a desk and chairs so Edythe could interview guests—generally ladies with some degree of expertise in fashion or fine living—but she also welcomed women in politics such as Diane Edgecomb, the head of Detroit's Central Business District Association, and Michigan's lieutenant governor, Martha Griffiths.

The House o' Charm

One of the most impressive and grandest monuments attached to the Lady of Charm was her House o' Charm. It was the first and only time in local radio and television that an actual house was constructed for the purpose of product testing and home decorating for an audience to witness. Even during the construction phases, the first in 1948 and the second in the mid-1950s, Melrose shared every detail from the raw building materials to the interior designs with her audience. And who better to explain some of those details than Carol Marenko and Steve Southard, in whose view the House o' Charm was simply Grandma's house.

Carol Marenko: "My dad was the general contractor for the building of the house, so grandma had a direct pipeline to the contractor. The choices that were being made for what was going to be put in the house and the materials to be used, some of them were new materials on the market, so it opened up to folks what was available in materials for your home. You'd be going from tract building to custom building. Tract building had been a very big thing at the end of the war [World War II], so this went back into the customizing again, and people were starting to open up to the business of we can build our own custom home again. She was bringing back the expression of your own choices and your own personality."

Steve Southard: "It was part of the image: Lady of Charm—House o' Charm. The lady sets the mood, so the home ought to be charming. The first one was in Saint Clair Shores at Eagle Point. The second one was built in the mid- to late 1950s at 906 Lakeshore in Grosse Pointe. My dad was big on some of the Frank Lloyd Wright concepts and employed some of them in the second House o' Charm. It was a trilevel, kind of exotic, with some South Pacific influences . . . floor to ceiling glass facing the lake and a suspended spiral staircase leading from the living room upstairs with a planter in it and plants growing up toward the ceiling. It was an exciting place. Those were the two main houses . . . utilized in conjunction with the show."

Although the Houses o' Charm were highly publicized for radio and television, they did become the primary residences of Edythe and her third husband, Forrest Webster. The fact that the Lady of Charm resided in the homes constructed and decorated with all of the products she endorsed proved that she wasn't just a mouthpiece for advertisers—she truly lived by her word.

Charming Mishaps?

Like anything else that's performed live, mistakes are unavoidable! The Lady of Charm didn't have many, but as retired WXYZ director Chris Montross, Jack Flechsig, and Channel 7 news anchor Erik Smith remember, when they did happen it was anything but pretty.

Chris Montross: "In those days, there were four lenses on the front of the camera. One long lens, two medium, and one that was a real wide-angle. The only way you could get a close-up of any object was to use that wide-angle lens. The camera would have to be right in tight on it. Sometimes when the camera people were in front of these lights that were shining on an object on [The Charm Kitchen], they couldn't see through their viewfinder very well; it had an extension. So they would take off the extension and set it on top of the camera. Well, this one cameraman forgot about the extension on top of his camera when he was told to zoom in on the cake. So as he zoomed in he tiled the camera down to look at the cake and the viewfinder slid off the camera into the middle of the cake!"

Jack Flechsig: "The station opened in 1948. I was there when they opened, and I knew the Lady of Charm. I worked on her show, and my wife Connie and I got married in 1949. Edythe said, 'Oh, you have to have your wife on . . . I'll teach her how to cook.' So she had taken this occasion to do that, and it was a disaster. When the [studio] lights went on, the lemon meringue pie they made on the show just melted off the plate and ran all over the place."

Erik Smith: "We were on a remote doing some sort of beauty pageant. And in all pageants the young lady has to step forth and tell us how she's going to improve the world. Well, this one young lady, after Edythe's introduction, gets up in front of the microphone and camera and begins her dissertation on world peace. All of a sudden her eyes roll back and she falls over backward like a lead weight on the stage—KABOOM! I don't know who was running the camera, but the camera panned down as she went thump, hitting the floor. Edythe came running in from the wings, yelling, 'Cut the tape! Cut the tape! Cut the tape! Stop the videotape!' Well, it was live, so there was no stopping the tape. Here was this beautiful young lady in the beauty pageant lying unconscious on the floor and Edythe looking at the camera: 'Cut the tape!'"

Changing Times

The passing of the Fabulous Fifties marked the end of an era when courtesy was viewed with a sense of reverence. Even though the early 1960s mirrored much of the previous decade, the societal turbulence that was brewing at the time began to surface by 1964. Proper manners became something to ridicule rather than respect. The young housewives of the 1950s were older, and the new ones were less receptive to the etiquette lessons of the Lady of Charm. After 16 years on the glass screen, Edythe Fern Melrose no longer had an audience to school.

In the years following the cancellation of her show, she returned to the studio at WXYZ to appear in a commercial that was being filmed there. While backstage, she tripped over a cable wire and suffered a severe knee injury. Over the years, the affliction worsened, forcing Melrose into a wheelchair. The pain gradually took its toll, draining her both physically and emotionally. In May 1976, Edythe Fern Melrose passed away quietly in her sleep at her northern Michigan home in Grayling.

> Though her brand of charm has long since passed,
> She left an impression that will forever last.
> Edythe was a lady who settled not for less,
> So any woman that follows her lead will be a success.

George Pierrot

The big thing about George Pierrot's show was keeping George awake. You had to be sure coming out of a break that he was awake—that was usually the stage manager's job. He'd go to sleep during the film, and you'd have to shake him a little bit to keep him from snoring too loud.
  —JERRY BURKE, retired director, WWJ-TV

These days, when we think of home movies broadcast on TV, *America's Funniest Videos* comes to mind. And when we want to escape to an exotic distant land without getting off the couch we tune to the Travel Channel. For 27 years, Detroit's own George Pierrot combined travel and home movies to create small-screen expeditions that were way ahead of their time. Appearing six days a week on two channels concurrently (an amazing feat in itself), Pierrot gave local audiences a unique glimpse into our world through the eyes of travelers. Local TV fan Larry Dlusky notes how Pierrot's show was anything but a televised sightseeing brochure.

Larry Dlusky: "It was a travelogue show with people who were adventurers. They would show home movies of their travels, except their travels weren't to Atlantic City and lying down on the beach . . . their travels were going to the Swiss Alps, climbing a mountain, or going to Rome and seeing the Coliseum . . . going to Africa on a safari . . . it was those kinds of excursions that would be on *George Pierrot*."

In 1949, a gruff-voiced, grandfatherly man who resembled a clean-shaven Santa Claus introduced local viewers to the wonders of the world every Sunday afternoon on WXYZ-TV. George Pierrot's *World Adventure Series* became so popular by the early 1950s that WWJ-TV decided

Detroit's own world travel authority, George Pierrot. (Courtesy Dr. Alan Pierrot.)

to cash in on the excitement with a daily version of the program entitled *George Pierrot Presents.* Former WXYZ director Ron David, who worked on the Sunday show in the 1950s, reflects on Pierrot's audience appeal.

Ron David: "He was a wonderful man who traveled the globe eight or nine times and was in all kinds of very dramatic situations all over the world. He was best known locally for bringing [in] well-known travel lecturers. He spoke from knowledge because he had been around the world, so he was not a phony by any means. He was one of the few people who could speak to these people about anywhere they had been because he had been there, too."

Traveling Man

George Pierrot was born on January 11, 1898, in Seattle, the son of a family doctor. Looking to carve out his own path in life, he attended the University of Washington to study journalism and subsequently became the editor of the *Washington Daily*. In the early 1930s, he abandoned the local paper when an opportunity to write for a new national magazine based in Detroit called *The American Boy* came knocking at his door. And so Pierrot packed his suitcase for a new life in the Midwest. As his creative writing abilities kicked into high gear, the publication quickly promoted him to editor. Unfortunately, his days in the sun would soon be overshadowed by the harsh reality of the Great Depression. The troubled economy caused the magazine to collapse in 1934, just seven years after its first issue went on sale.

However, despite his occupational shortcoming, George became very active in civic organizations, primarily the Detroit Institute of Arts (DIA). Assigned the task of boosting the museum's poor attendance during the worst economic period of the twentieth century, Pierrot devised a promotional campaign that would affect the rest of his life. His son, Dr. Alan Pierrot, explains the concept with the assistance of Ron David.

Dr. Alan Pierrot: "He got the idea that if he put an event on in the auditorium people would come and discover the museum. He had an interest in travel and traveled a fair amount as a young person. He went around the world and wrote a book called, *The Vagabond Trail*, which recounted his trip around the world in the 1930s. And he was a member of the Circum Navigators Club, a New York based club for people who'd gone around the world. In those days, it was a bigger deal than it is now. So he started booking travelogues. There were only about four the first year, and they were very successful. He increased it the following year, and soon it became his occupation. It started out as a community service effort to improve the attendance at the museum, and it turned into his life. He formed what was called the World Adventure Series, booking speakers usually in September/October through about May every Sunday afternoon at 3:30."

Ron David: "Back in the days of the thirties, forties, and fifties, there were a number of travel lecturers. The biggest one that comes to mind is Burton Holmes; when he died, *Life* magazine did a six-page spread on him. He was one of these lecturers who'd go to China or India and shoot silent 16mm footage, then book theaters all over the country like the Masonic Temple. People flocked to go see that stuff because travel was still not that easy for the average human being. It was very exotic, dramatic, and successful for [the travelers]. Pierrot had a line on all of them, and those are the people who came to do his show."

To escape the hardships of the Depression, Detroiters were willing to sacrifice 25 cents a week to watch films of places they'd only dreamed of visiting. With the advent of a new medium in the late 1940s, Pierrot realized that television could bring his DIA travelogue show to an even greater audience. *The World Adventure Series* premiered on WXYZ in 1949.

Dr. Alan Pierrot: "It was a half-hour show on Sunday at one o'clock, and it was the same lecture that would take place later in the afternoon at the museum. So they were promoting the museum show, and the speakers liked it because they got paid twice on the same day. It was conversational, and he always tried to ask questions he thought the audience would be interested in . . . travel-related questions: How much would it be for a meal? What were the accommodations like? How does one travel to this country? What do you have to watch out for? What was your most interesting experience? [He brought up] whatever he thought would lead into a particular segment or would be of interest to the individuals watching the show.

"*The World Adventure Series* got good ratings, and that led to another show—*George Pierrot Presents*— which had the same format. But now, instead of the speakers coming Sunday to do a show on TV and then a live show at the museum, they would come for a week because he was on every day. And so it got to be where the biggest and the best booking you could get, if you were a speaker, was the one in Detroit."

Travelogues

Working as an independent producer out of his home, Pierrot assumed the responsibility of booking all the guests for his program. With the support of the DIA and two TV stations, he was very successful in drawing the attention of the travel industry's top speakers.

Dr. Alan Pierrot: "Every year he would have his World Adventure Series audience, the live one that went to the museum; he would have the season ticket holders vote on who the best speaker was. He'd give them an award and automatically book them on the show. So he kind of knew which ones sold out and were very popular. He became sort of the premier show, I mean, if you were on the George Pierrot show, you pretty much had the Good Housekeeping Seal of Approval."

Retired WWJ director Jim Breault and Dr. Pierrot briefly review the types of guests that appeared on the show.

Jim Breault: "We had an old lumberjack, Don Cooper, who would bring in his films. There were so many of them, but they were all a little different from one another. Some would specialize just in the United States, some in Europe . . . things like that."

Dr. Alan Pierrot: "The most popular guest was Stan Midgley. He was a chemist by degree, but he bicycled through the western United States and made films and did a lot of gag photos, so he was entertaining. Irving Johnson was a popular speaker. He sailed around the world on, I think, seven different year-and-a-half-long trips. He would take college kids in this great big three-mast brigantine, *Yankee,* and he'd make a film of each voyage. So kids would sign up for a year and a half and they'd go around the world by sail. He was very entertaining and adventurous.

"The [speakers] would come for a week and be on both channels. Most of them had multiple shows. So, for example, Midgley, he would have one [film] on Montana, one on Colorado . . . Kenneth Richter would have Libya for one and the Middle East for another . . . they usually had four or five shows, more material than they ever had TV time for."

Jim Breault: "We'd have the same ones every year, and they'd show the same films. It would take a long time for them to produce a new one, so they would just show excerpts. The films would be about an hour or two hours long, so we just took excerpts from them."

Not every travelogue speaker was a seasoned filmmaker. Pierrot had his share of wannabes.

Dr. Alan Pierrot: "The people who were trying to 'break into' the business would come over to our house and show their film and my dad would preview it. So, if he thought they weren't any good, he didn't hesitate to tell them. When we were kids, we'd come and watch [the films] and then we'd clear out because we got to where we could kind of tell if one wasn't as good as the others . . . and then we knew what was gonna happen. We left because we'd get embarrassed by what he'd say. He'd tell them they were pretty bad! He was very direct in his commentary because he felt that was the only way to be helpful to them."

Even though George carefully screened every movie for content prior to its airing, retired WWJ stage manager Bob Stackpoole remembers one particular piece of celluloid that didn't quite make the cutting-room floor.

Bob Stackpoole: "This gal came in, I believe it was her first time, and she had a film on Africa . . . a native village with some tribal ceremony and the women were in skirts only! It was on for five or ten seconds, and everybody in the crew was looking at each other because that was the first time we saw any nudity, particularly at five in the afternoon. But nothing ever materialized; there weren't any complaints."

Zzzzzzz . . .

Jim Breault: "We had some speakers that were quite humorous, and they were fun to watch . . . some were really well produced, and we enjoyed them . . . others were humdrum; you'd have to fight to keep from closing your eyes and dozing off with George."

And speaking of snoozing, it was those notorious catnaps of Pierrot's that audiences found humorous. Perhaps it's because so many of us can relate to the pain of having to sit through someone else's home movies—bored to tears and then having to say how much we enjoyed them for fear of hurting the filmmaker's feelings. So to see a television host doing what many of us would like to do without a care in the world, in an odd sort of way it added to the charm of the show. Channel 7 news anchor Erik Smith and Bob Stackpoole describe the effects of working with sleepy-eyed George.

Erik Smith: "I had to run the music for *The World Adventure Series* and his travelogues. We taped those, and while I would play the music behind Stan Midgley's tour of Yosemite George would be dead asleep. He would instantly go to sleep as soon as we went to the film. The problem for the crew was to keep his guest's microphone open so they could narrate the film and not hear George snoring. George snored intensely. It was the stage manager's job to wake him up. He'd wake up groggy, 'Ah . . . uh . . . we'll be right back with more of Stan Midgley and his wonderful tour of Yosemite right after these messages.'"

Bob Stackpoole: "Some of the newer [guests] that didn't know George got to be a little prickly; their egos were bruised because George would nod off. But the old-timers, the Midgleys and the Coopers, they knew George had already seen their films 20 times before."

As much as the dozing was perceived by the audience and crew as boredom, Dr. Pierrot believes an undiagnosed medical condition was at the root of his father's drowsiness.

Dr. Alan Pierrot: "I have a theory that he was Pickwickian. The Pickwickian syndrome was named after a Charles Dickens character, Mr. Pickwick, who was a very obese man. Obese people don't move their diaphragm as much [as people of more normal weight], and they tend to build up carbon dioxide because they don't move air quite as easily . . . and that tends to put them to sleep. You'll see a lot of obese people fall asleep and wake up then fall asleep and wake up again. He was overweight and he was stiff for a while, so if he wasn't speaking he nodded off. But that was sort of his appeal."

Bon Appetite!

Larry Dlusky: "George Pierrot was a rather stout man, and he loved his food. So anytime a travelogue would end up in a restaurant, you could almost sense he was salivating. He'd get real interested and ask a lot of questions about the food, especially the desserts . . . anything with whipped cream on it. Now, if it was a safari and the guy was saying, 'We chopped off the head of a monkey, and we ate its brains,' there'd be no questions about that. But if they were having Weiner schnitzel and a seven-layer torte with mounds of whipped cream on it, then there were lots of questions."

With food consistently in the forefront of the discussion, Pierrot's passion for dining was no secret. However, contrary to his "public" tastes, he had a hidden appetite for the bizarre that was unknown to his loyal audience but revealed to his crew.

Erik Smith: "He would throw a dinner for the crew at the Safari Lounge over by City Airport, which at the time prepared and served exotic wild game dishes. I only went once, but I approached it with caution. I know what a hamburger is, but I don't know what zebra tastes like and I wasn't sure that I wanted to know. I just recall that as an hors d'oeuvre they served monkey fingers . . . and that was too much for me. George ate a lot of the exotic foods from the different cultures all over the world."

King of the Limericks

Bob Stackpoole: "George was one of the best storytellers . . . limericks is what he was really known for. When word came that George was in— sometimes he'd come in a little early and sit in the studio—all the cameramen and stagehands would start filing in because you knew George was going to start telling stories and jokes. He could just keep going on and on and on."

Erik Smith: "I always looked forward to seeing George because without fail he probably had the greatest memory bank of limericks of any human who walked the face of the earth. The man could go on for hours. It was just sensational."

Dr. Alan Pierrot: "He loved limericks, he loved words, and he liked wordplay. He was a writer, and that was a big interest . . . how you put words together. Limericks were particularly of interest to him because they were funny and fun and yet they were obviously word based. Frequently there was a little stretch at the pronunciation to make it rhyme, and he just really enjoyed the puns."

The End of the Road

With all of the buzz surrounding George Pierrot in the late 1950s and early 1960s, an attempt was made to syndicate his program in other TV markets, but unfortunately the rest of the country wasn't willing to embrace the heavyset, gravely voiced, world adventurer the way Detroit had. Through the support of First Federal Bank, Pierrot's show managed to achieve a longevity in local television for an impressive 27 years, an accomplishment matched only by Bill Kennedy.

While America celebrated its bicentennial in 1976, Detroit TV said bon voyage to George. Times were changing, and so was the audience demographic.

Jim Breault: "The people that watched that show were over 30, and anybody over 30 is considered elderly in television. And of course George was quite old in those days. The younger part of his audience was quite small."

Viewer shrinkage ultimately caused First Federal Bank to withdraw its backing, and with such a narrow audience there was no way any station in town could sell the show to other sponsors. Never wanting to retire, the loss of his television program affected Pierrot very deeply on a personal level. Four years later, in 1980, the man who took Metro Detroiters to the ends of the earth for nearly three decades died on his way to the hospital after suffering a heart attack at the age of 82.

Michigan Outdoors

Oddly enough, Mort was not a hunter. So it was really odd for
somebody that really wasn't of that lifestyle to do that kind of a
show at all, and yet he could do it so well, without ruffling any
feathers. He had something that was very believable, and people
were comfortable with it.
   —MAUREEN MAYNE, widow of Mort Neff

While George Pierrot whisked Metro Detroiters to exotic destinations
around the world, Mort Neff rarely set foot outside the confines of the
Great Lakes. For more than a quarter century, *Michigan Outdoors* captured on film the best places for the outdoor enthusiast to pitch a tent or
dock a boat within the scenic boundaries of the peninsulas every Thursday evening at seven on Channel 4 and later on Channel 7. Syndicated
throughout the state, television sets from all four corners gathered
around the big stone fireplace in the middle of the hunting lodge facade
to hear Mort boast about the latest and greatest events in the world of
hunting and fishing. It's true, you know . . . just ask veteran outdoor TV
host Jerry Chiappetta or retired WWJ director Jim Breault or even
WXYZ news anchor Erik Smith, and they'll tell you how addictive that
weekly outdoors program really was.

   Jerry Chiappetta: "When I first came to Michigan as a reporter back
in the late 1950s, I used to watch Mort all the time and thought, 'What a
great program . . . to get paid to go hunting and fishing.' You can't beat
that! So I just envied the thing; I watched it religiously. You could go to
any TV sales place and every TV set would be turned on to *Michigan
Outdoors* at that time of the evening. Everybody in the state watched
that show, I mean everybody, even if you didn't hunt or fish."

   Jim Breault: "One of the neat things about *Michigan Outdoors* is that
it wasn't a commercial. Quite often, these hunting shows are all commercials in this day and age. Mort did the show for Michigan . . . and I'll
tell you, it was like a religion . . . people never missed that show!"

   Erik Smith: "I always looked forward to that show, and I don't know
why because I'm not an outdoorsman; I never did much hunting and
fishing. But Mort Neff had a way of bringing a guy like me, who's not an
avid hunter or fisherman, into that environment. He made it interesting,
along with the wildlife photography, much of which [freelance camera-
man] Gene Little shot, and there was that cozy hunting lodge set. In a lot
of ways, I think Mort was 'every guy' . . . every guy who enjoyed the out-

Michigan Outdoors host Mort Neff on the hunt in 1966. (Courtesy Maureen Mayne.)

doors and brought the outdoors inside to people who probably never ventured much beyond the cyclone fence in their own yard."

The Man with the Petoskey Stone Tie

Recognized by his string tie with a Petoskey stone cut in the shape of Michigan, Mortimer Neff was born on December 5, 1903, in Birmingham, Michigan. Fascinated by telegraphy as a boy, he studied Morse code and became a wireless radio operator. On April 15, 1912, while his family was temporarily residing in Boston, young Mort would be among the first radio operators in the country to receive word about the historic *Titanic* disaster. His pet hobby of stringing wire led to a bachelor's degree in electrical engineering from the University of Michigan. Realizing that his forte lay more in writing and reporting, he went back to U of M to major in journalism.

After his second round at the university, Neff went to work in advertising. When it came to promoting a client, Mort's second wife, Maureen Mayne, recalls one of his hidden talents.

Maureen Mayne: "At the advertising agency, he wrote jingles. One of them really stuck in my mind because I remember as a little kid I used to sing it. It was for MacDonald Coal: 'MacDonald for coal . . . MacDonald for coal . . . MacDonald for quality fuel . . . Honest weight, we guarantee more heat . . . One hundred trucks assure a service hard to beat . . . We feature black night, a fuel that's just right . . . Call Townsend-eight-three-oh-oh-oh . . . We claim 50 years of honest service . . . many warm friends, too . . . Let MacDonald make a friend of you!'"

But advertising wasn't Neff's only occupation, Jerry Chiappetta cites a few others, including the one that foreshadowed his future in television.

Jerry Chiappetta: "Mort was also a tennis coach and a ski instructor. He used to work for the state of Michigan. He did a radio report on hunting and fishing in Michigan. He wasn't a real hard-core hunter or fisherman, but he was an outdoor enthusiast and certainly a good showman."

Michigan's Action Television Show

In 1951, while Mort was filming TV commercials, an ad executive named Fran Congdon approached him to create a 15-minute program for a client that wanted to sponsor a television show. Collaborating with an outdoor magazine writer he knew, Neff packaged *Michigan Outdoors* for WWJ-TV. Never intending to host the program himself, he bestowed the honor on the writer, whom he deemed as an authority on the great outdoors. Unfortunately, the writer's publication wasn't willing to go along with the plan, and subsequently its decision changed the face of the show.

Jerry Chiappetta: "Ben East from *Outdoor Life* magazine was supposed to be the host, Mort was just the producer. And just before the show was about to air Ben East's company, *Outdoor Life,* said, 'You can't do television. We don't want our magazine writers on television.' So Mort had no host, and the show was sold to a sponsor and ready to go on the air. Mort jumped in there temporarily to host the show, and that 'temporarily' lasted the next 20-some years."

With the responsibility of hosting the show in addition to an expansion in airtime to 30 minutes, what exactly did Mr. Neff deliver to audiences every week that was so appealing?

Maureen Mayne: "*Michigan Outdoors* was generally about what was going on in the state—what the special attractions were, so people going away on the weekend could make their plans. So it was a combination of information about the special events in the state and then he chose a couple of them to do a story on. He never took any kickbacks in advertising, so they had to be very reputable places so that nobody would come back and say, 'You steered us wrong!' He covered all the openings of the game seasons. And then there were things like the AuSable canoe race, which people expected to see every year, and other annual events of one kind or another.

"It always aired on Thursday nights, so there was filming from Friday morning until Sunday. The film went in on Monday [for editing] and was finished by Tuesday. Then the script was written on Wednesday, and everything was all set to go by Thursday night. And it never changed time slots or its format."

Jerry Chiappetta: "Mort's program was more of an entertaining show; you didn't have to think too hard. It was fun to watch. He had pets and wildlife, and he'd bring animals into the studio. There were some hilarious things because in the days when it was live he'd have a pet raccoon running around the set knocking over the flats in the background."

Despite the occasional unexpected animal mishaps on the set, the remainder of the program was carefully rehearsed. Given the complexity of the production, Neff asked that rehearsals begin as early as four o'clock in the afternoon, especially since he would lose the studio staff when it was time for the evening news. Erik Smith recounts from his days as an electrical transcription operator just how intense Mort was about the show.

Erik Smith: "When he came in, he was prepared, he was ready . . . very few things ever went haywire on a Mort Neff show. He just had a great grasp of who he was, what message he wanted to convey, and how to convey it. He was the host, the writer, the producer . . . He really was, in a nutshell, the complete package."

As the producer, Neff sold sponsorships to pay for the program and in turn purchased the airtime from the television station, thereby making him the sole owner of *Michigan Outdoors*. As such, he was free to hire his own film crew for the location shoots. Maureen Mayne, Jerry Chiappetta, Jim Breault, and retired WXYZ director Mason Weaver collectively summarize the production of the outdoor segments.

Maureen Mayne: "In the beginning, it was just Mort himself, and I was 'Girl Friday,' doing all of the schlepping and note taking, and [I] also acted as a second cameraman if need be. The show was owned by Neff Productions, Inc. And as it got going Howard Shelley [from Pontiac] became our first employee. From the time we took Howard on, he was with us until the end. We had other photographers as time went by that submitted stories, but not too often. Mostly our two or three cameramen covered the area."

Jerry Chiappetta: "Mort had a couple of other guys that worked for him for a number of years, Eb Warren from Gaylord [and] Dick Black from western Michigan. They covered their parts of the state, [and along with Shelley] they had it geographically divided up."

Jim Breault: "The regulars on the show who would go out with their film cameras and film segments would write a script and Mort would narrate it or sometimes they would narrate it. The film segments were narrated live."

Maureen Mayne: "The whole production was up to Mort. We had some 'spotters' who kept us informed as to what was going on around the state, and then he would decide what sounded interesting. There was always a chamber of commerce in those places that would help organize our time frame for production."

Mason Weaver: "Mort flew everywhere, so I was able to fly with him all over the state. When we'd go somewhere on a hunting story or a fishing story, the guys were there and everything was set up for you—they practically drove the deer right by you."

Outdoor Gurus

Jerry Chiappetta: "Mort Neff was a legend in television, particularly outdoor television, nationally as well as in Michigan."

Much of the success of *Michigan Outdoors* hinged on the credibility of Mort Neff. Although he wasn't much of a hunter or fisherman, his excitement and appreciation for nature in the Great Lakes State spoke volumes, especially since he had the power of television in his corner.

Maureen Mayne: "Mort was a rather unique person . . . because of his knowledge and ability to identify [with everyone] without ever being condescending or controversial nobody ever got angry with him. Basically he was a reporter, and that's what he considered himself, not a performer but a reporter. He got along with the Conservation Department, and it was always a nonadversarial role that he took. At that time, Arthur Godfrey was big on radio, and he was very opinionated. I thought that was great because he changed a lot of things, and I thought Mort should do that, too, but Mort said, 'No, I won't do that . . . I'm a reporter.'"

In spite of Neff's efforts to refrain from controversy, celebrity status pegged him as an "outdoor guru" whose advice was taken as gospel by his plaid-shirted followers. The word of Mort could sometimes create a frenzy, as Jerry Chiappetta describes.

Jerry Chiappetta: "A lot of people just absolutely loved Mort; he couldn't do any wrong. And a lot of people, maybe not an equal amount, didn't like him because Mort had a habit of telling people where to go fishing and where the hunting was good. He would just devastate an area with people. If he mentioned that 'Cold Fanny Lake' [figuratively speaking] had good fishing . . . Cold Fanny Lake was swamped the next weekend because the people would go there for the good fishing. And telling people when the fish are going to bite is the most asinine thing you can tell them because nobody except God and the fish know when they're going to bite."

By the mid-1960s, color was edging its way into television, and what better program to display in living color than the very picturesque *Michigan Outdoors?* Since Neff bought his airtime at WWJ, he was essentially under no obligation to stay there for any length of time. His use of the studio and production crew were bought and paid for by Neff Productions, Inc. Therefore, he was free to produce the show at any television station he desired.

Noticing the immense popularity of *Michigan Outdoors*, WXYZ general manager John Pival sought to capitalize on Neff's profitability. The opportunity to steal the program from WWJ arose with the allure of a newer facility and, more importantly, color. Mason Weaver recalls those times.

Mason Weaver: "John Pival only got Mort to come over from [Channel] 4 to 7 because we were going to get color cameras, and he promised Mort he'd be the first show in color on Channel 7. And as a guy that likes to hunt and fish, this was right down my alley. When John Pival said, 'I've got Neff coming over here, and you're gonna direct it,' I said, 'Wow!' I was as happy as could be. That was a thrill and a half."

Feeling the loss of revenue generated by *Michigan Outdoors*, WWJ succeeded in countering WXYZ's offer to draw Neff back to the home base he had established in 1951. After a short stint at Channel 7, Neff's hunting lodge was reassembled in the Downtown studio on Lafayette Boulevard. Unable to stop Mort from straying back to his native hut, John Pival went on the prowl to capture another outdoor guru to go head to head with WWJ. On the recommendation of sports director and anchor Dave Diles, Pival hired the outdoor editor of the *Detroit Free Press*.

A graduate from the University of Pittsburgh with a B.A. in Journalism, Jerry Chiappetta, an avid hunter and fisherman by nature, transferred to Michigan in 1957 to embark on a career as a hard news reporter. During his transitional years with *United Press International*, the *Lansing State Journal*, and the *Detroit Times*, he regularly contributed an extra column reflecting his love of the outdoors. When the longtime outdoor editor at the *Detroit Free Press* retired, Chiappetta was asked by the paper to fill the vacancy. Given his newfound status at the *Free Press* coupled with an accumulation of journalism awards, Chiappetta was a shoo-in to produce and host Pival's new weekly syndicated outdoor series in 1968.

Jerry Chiappetta: "My show, to compete with *Michigan Outdoors,* was called *Michigan Sportsman.* It was the first 'all color' show in the state. The video was color, the films were color, and the commercials were color. We had two outdoor shows running in prime time throughout the state of Michigan at the same time, which was a real testament to the quality of our shows—they were different kinds of shows, but they both catered to the interest in the outdoors in the state of Michigan. My show was always based on outdoor news, while Mort's was more entertainment."

By 1971, the management at WXYZ had changed. The man who championed Chiappetta's television debut was long gone, and after a three-year run, *Michigan Sportsman* was about to be squeezed out in favor of a show that had graced the cameras at Broadcast House years before. Chiappetta relives the day he received the alarming news.

Jerry Chiappetta: "The income was falling and the expenses were rising and they called me in the office one day and said, 'We're gonna bring Mort Neff and *Michigan Outdoors* to Channel 7. And you're gonna work for Mort.' I was floored! Here was my friendly competitor . . . and he was friendly; we were friends. I said, 'I don't want to work for Mort.' That was like General Motors buying Ford Motor Company and everybody at Ford now works for General Motors. So I said, 'I don't want to do that. I think I'll leave.'"

Refusing to work for the man who he'd been a fan of, Chiappetta took his production, lock, stock and barrel, across the river to CKLW, Channel 9. Operating under the title *All Outdoors,* the program broadened its appeal to a younger audience with the inclusion of sporting events such as snowmobile racing. In the meantime, Channel 7 had successfully acquired the unchanged *Michigan Outdoors* for the long haul.

In the following year, while Jerry Chiappetta was experiencing a high level of frustration in having to lug film equipment across the border under the constant scrutiny of customs officials, the aging Neff was getting itchy to retire. Another surprise awaited Chiappetta . . . only this time it would be for the better.

Jerry Chiappetta: "Mort called me one day and said, 'Let's have lunch.' I said, 'Why, what's up?' He said, 'I'm gonna make you an offer you can't refuse.' You know, that kind of a deal. What it was: he wanted to retire, and he knew that the minute he retired his income ended. There wouldn't be anymore *Michigan Outdoors* show, and the only way he would ever make any money would be for Jerry Chiappetta to produce the *Michigan Outdoors* show back at Channel 7 and syndicate it throughout Michigan. And I would give up *All Outdoors* over in Windsor and drop my network.

"So it was a pretty good offer, and Mort said he would stay around for about the next 10 or 11 months . . . then he would quietly go off into the sunset and I would own the show, but I would pay him a royalty every week till hell freezes over. I said, 'That's no problem.' It was like retirement money for Mort. I took over the show in 1972 . . . Mort retired eventually, and then I ran the show."

Special Features

Jerry Chiappetta: "One of the stories that Mort had a lot of fun with was: there was this farmer up by Gaylord, and he had cows in a pasture. They were fenced in the barnyard, and a big bull elk jumped the fence. It was in love with one of the cows, and Mort had a big story going about this on his show. It was like an ongoing soap opera for animals. This bull elk was pursuing this cow all to hell. So Mort went over there to interview the farmer, and in the background you had this elk chasing this cow around the barnyard. He got a lot of mileage out of that . . . it was kind of a cute story."

Touted as "Michigan's Action Television Show!" with the slogan painted on the *Michigan Outdoors* station wagon, the action wasn't always restricted to the road. Sometimes it wandered into the studio.

Jim Breault: "It was all live, and at times it was a tough show to do. He would have the biggest deer racks, antlered racks on the deer, or the biggest fish day, where all the people who caught the biggest fish for the year would come in and win prizes. And it was a wild show to do. We'd have all these people with smelly fish in the studio or with the racks from the deer. It was very busy to direct. It was a three-camera show. Most of our shows were two cameras, but as I recall that was a three-camera show."

Maureen Mayne: "There would always be some great way to cook whatever game was in season. There was also once a year a big cooking contest for game. The recipes went into an annual cookbook, and so all the winners went in there . . . I don't ever remember money being given away."

The hunting lodge didn't just open its doors for dead prey; live animals were welcomed, too. Wild pets were often brought in, some of which belonged to Mort himself. The most notable was a raccoon, which frequently hung from his shoulder.

Maureen Mayne: "The first raccoon, which is the one we had the longest, was Goldie. She was named after the sponsor at that time—Altes Golden Lager Beer. She was a pet that was never quite intended to be that, but [she] turned out to be an important part of the show. She used to be on quite a bit; we used to have a lot of people on with animals. At one point, we had a baby porcupine that we called Cuddles. And I remember a baby skunk running around the kitchen for a while. I never knew what was going to show up. Mort didn't acquire them by choice; he got them as a result of rescues. They never could be housebroken, which was a real disaster most of the time."

When animals weren't scurrying around the set, Neff would interview guests seated on the couch in front of that grand stone fireplace. Most of the visitors were related to the outdoors in some capacity, whether they were hunters or a game commissioner. But every now and then there would be an oddball who would be a big hit with the audience.

One of them happened to be a leathery-looking "snake charmer," Paul Allen, whose famous bit revolved around a first-aid kit he developed to treat poisonous snakebites. This impressive fellow would allow a snake to bite his arm live on the air, after which he would proceed to demonstrate how to extract the venom using the items from his kit. Not surprisingly, Allen died some years later while attempting to retrieve a loose cobra that had slithered underneath a car. It proved to be one chomp too many.

Aye, Calypso

Jerry Chiappetta: "When Mort and I were in the overlap period, Channel 7 told us that we were going to have Captain Jacques Cousteau on our show for an interview. Cousteau had done a series for the ABC network [which owned WXYZ at that time] called *Under Fire and Ice,* which was about diving in Antarctica. Captain Cousteau was in town with his entourage doing some interviews with the Detroit papers. Since ABC was carrying the network show, [the station] thought we could interview him for our *Michigan Outdoors* show. He was free for about an hour or two in the afternoon. I was kind of against it, but Mort was always the gentleman: 'Oh, let's accommodate him; he's a big name.' This was live on tape . . . [so there'd be] no editing.

"So we're sitting there sort of chatting and having some coffee at our little stump table. I said to Mort, 'What the hell are we going talk to this guy about?' He said, 'We'll ask him about Great Lakes salmon fishing.' We started with 'This is our guest tonight, Captain Jacques Cousteau, the

Neff interviews an audience favorite, snake man Paul Allen.
Note the bandage on Allen's arm. (Courtesy Maureen Mayne.)

famous underwater explorer and the man who invented scuba equipment. Captain Cousteau, what brings you to Detroit?' He says, 'I'm here to promote *Under Fire and Ice*.' I said, 'What do you think about our salmon program in the Great Lakes?' 'I know nothing of your salmon program in the Great Lakes.' I look at Mort, and Mort's false teeth almost fell out. I said, 'Well, Captain Cousteau, what about capturing the currents of the Great Lakes and turning them into energy?' That was in the news at that time. 'I know nothing of your Great Lakes currents. I only know about *Under Fire and Ice*.' He kept going back to promoting his feature. I said to Mort on the side, 'This is deadly. Our viewers are going to kill us.'

"Then I said, 'Captain Cousteau, maybe you could recommend a good seafood restaurant in Paris.' He said, 'I don't eat seafood.' I said, 'I watch your guys on the *Calypso;* I watch your documentaries and I see them eating fish.' He said, 'That's only because they have to. I don't fish.' And I said, 'We have about 72 million anglers in America who fish and enjoy it for the sport, and they eat their catch.' He says, 'If you enjoy eating fish that you catch, you are suffering from a perversion.' Now Mort's sitting there like, 'I don't want to be a part of this . . . this is between Chiappetta and Cousteau.' He [Cousteau] said, 'If you enjoy catching the fish, even though that animal is mute and can't cry out, you are suffering from a perversion.' I said, 'There are 72 million perverts in America!?' And he said, 'If they enjoy catching their fish, yes, they are perverts!'

"The mail came pouring in on us . . . and this made the national news. It was the talk of the National Outdoor Writer's Association . . . I was getting calls from writers all over America, asking, 'Did this really happen?' That was our famous Jacques Cousteau interview."

The Soggy River Rats

Once in a blue moon, *Michigan Outdoors* stretched beyond the state's borders into northern Ohio and parts of Ontario. It was on one of those rare excursions into a desolate region of Canada that Jerry Chiappetta and company experienced the canoe ride of their lives!

Jerry Chiappetta: "We almost died on that show, literally, the whole crew! We had three canoes, and there were six of us going up into northern Ontario. There are waterfalls up there named after us now because we were some of the only non-Indians to ever go down some of these rivers. This friend of mine named Ed Chruscz lived in Canada about six months out of the year, and he was our guide. He didn't know these rivers as well as we thought he did. So we took Mason Weaver, Gene Little, and a couple of guys from the staging department at Channel 7. There were three canoes with two guys in each.

"We started off going downstream, and it was high water, fast water, and rapids. It turns out that most of the people in our group weren't good canoeists. We were flipping over, spilling our food, and dumping our equipment. Fortunately, Gene Little had plastic garbage bags and had his camera wrapped up. We got into water over our heads; we were lining our canoes down the rapids. Lining means you walk the shoreline or shallows among the rocks with a rope or a stick in your hand so you don't break your neck or a leg. And you hold the canoe back to let the current walk it down and you use the stick to keep the canoe from smashing into the rocks. So, we didn't know what was around the bend—we were back in the wilderness. Right off the bat, when we flipped our canoes we lost most of our food. That's always tough. This was virgin country, and we really didn't know if we were going to make it. If you got off on the side, you were fighting blackflies and mosquitoes that eat you alive. There are coyotes, bears, and moose and all kinds of small critters like lynx and porcupines.

Jerry Chiappetta sets up a shot on location. (Courtesy Jerry Chiappetta.)

"Miraculously, we managed to finally make it! It took us a week, and we barely got back in one piece. That was the toughest story we ever did. We called it 'The Saga of the Soggy River Rats,' and it was one of the most memorable programs ever. Through it all, I'm talking of being in danger of dying—drowning. Gene Little, God bless him, was able to continue to film on these occasions. It was quite an epic!"

Out of Season

Jerry Chiappetta: "I thought, 'I'm getting burned out and I'm quitting.' Nobody quits a successful show that's fully sponsored, but I did. It is very, very difficult to produce a good outdoors show 52 weeks a year . . . very difficult and very expensive! It takes a lot of people with a lot of different talents, editors, and expensive equipment. I used to run around in the woods with a $65,000 video camera on my shoulder and climb a tree like a red squirrel to wait for a deer to pass underneath so I could film it. And you're fighting weather, you're fighting mosquitoes, you're fighting the elements, and you're fighting hunger."

Thus, five years after purchasing the show from Mort Neff, Jerry Chiappetta put an end to the original *Michigan Outdoors* in 1977. After taking some well-deserved time off in Florida, Chiappetta returned to produce and host a string of syndicated outdoor programs as well as a series of independent videos related to hunting and fishing. And when he's not in front of the camera he's behind the desk writing magazine articles and books about, what else, the outdoors. As for the man who started it all, Mort Neff spent his retirement years with his family up north in Harbor Springs until a stroke ended his life on August 15, 1990. His widow, Maureen, leaves us with a personal glimpse into the love and dedication her husband had for *Michigan Outdoors*.

Maureen Mayne: "He was such a true showman that he could leave the house feeling absolutely dreadful and you wondered how in the world he could possibly get through the rehearsals and the show. The children used to say when they'd watch the show, 'Mom . . . Dad looks fine! He's not sick anymore!' And nobody would ever know."

Bowling for Dollars

I was the one who would call the house and say, "You've been selected to be on *Bowling for Dollars.*" People would put down the phone and just start screaming! It was like winning a million dollars. At the time, the show was very popular. It was a show that let everybody be a star for a minute.
    —LAURIE OBERMAN, program director, WDIV-TV

When you look at all the local programs that gave away prizes, none of them epitomized the core of the Motor City like *Bowling for Dollars.* Confused? At the center of the community stands its people, ordinary folks who work regular jobs five days a week, far from the glamorous world of television. That was true until a game show franchise rolled into town and struck the jackpot with viewers five nights a week on WWJ-TV, Channel 4. Just listen to what Detroiters Mark Nowotarski and George Young have to say about *Bowling for Dollars* and you'll undoubtedly see why it was such a big hit in Motown.

Mark Nowotarski: "*Bowling for Dollars,* I used to get a kick out of. It was just common people going on there having a good time bowling and trying to win some money."

George Young: "*Bowling for Dollars* with Bob Allison was the hottest program on Channel 4. Why was it so hot? Because when Bob interviewed these people they talked about local things. 'Where do you work at?' 'I work at the Ford Motor plant in Highland Park.' 'Really?' 'I bowl at the so-and-so lanes at Gratiot and Eight Mile . . .' They're talking about local streets, local things, what's happening locally, a little gossip . . . and that's what people watched that program for . . . The local stuff is so important because it's the life of the city!"

From the Thunderbowl Lanes in Allen Park, seven Motor City hopefuls would take their best shot each night at one frame of bowling for cash and prizes on local TV while their family and friends rooted from the alley's grandstand. Whether it was the cash jackpot, the hot new Corvette, or the five-dollar consolation prize that bowlers pursued, they all, without a doubt, looked forward to their brief moment in front of the television camera when Bob Allison asked them about their hobbies, the guests they had brought with them, and who they'd like to give a quick "hello" to at home. Anyone appearing on *Bowling for Dollars* was guaranteed to walk away with at least a few extra dollars in their pocket and a second of fame to their name!

Bowling for Dollars host Bob Allison. (Courtesy *Detroit News.*)

Detroit Joins the League

Claster Productions, the creators and franchisers of the highly successful children's program *Romper Room,* devised a new bowling-oriented game show called *Bowling for Dollars* in the late 1960s. The Baltimore-based producer's concept was simple: contestants win money based on the number of pins they knock down in a single frame of bowling. The difference between this program and previous bowling shows such as *Beat the Champ* was the competition factor—none. What? *Beat the Champ* pitted contestants against professionals, resulting in winners and losers. *Bowling for Dollars* eliminated losers from its competition, thereby making everyone who played a winner.

Using special lanes built into the studio of WBAL-TV in Maryland, Claster prepared a video package to present their revolutionary program to other television markets, giving them the green light to produce their own localized version of the Claster format. In 1973, Detroit was ranked as one of the top cities in the country for bowling. Some sources even had it listed at number one. There were more registered members in the National Bowling Association in Motown than in any other city in America. With that in mind, it was only natural for WWJ-TV to buy into this new game show franchise. Host Bob Allison recalls another strategy employed by the station.

Bob Allison: "They decided to do *Bowling for Dollars* as a lead-in to the six o'clock news. They signed the contract with Claster Productions for 13 weeks to see whether or not they could attract a larger audience to feed into the six o'clock newscast to see if they would get a better rating."

The Object of the Game

So, with all of the chatter about *Bowling for Dollars* coming to the Motor City, how was the game played? Were there any rules? Bob Allison, along with WDIV program director, Laurie Oberman, who produced the show, outline the game plan.

Bob Allison: "You bowl two balls: if you throw a spare, you get dinner for two someplace [usually the Roostertail] and 10 bucks. And if you didn't throw a spare you got a dollar for every pin that you knocked down . . . you knocked over eight pins, you got eight dollars. If you threw one strike but not another one, you won prizes. If you threw two strikes, you won the jackpot."

Laurie Oberman: "It was three strikes in a row to win the appliances and five strikes to win the Corvette. There was this Corvette that everybody was always dying for, and we did give a few Corvettes away in the time I was there. It wasn't unobtainable, but it was pretty hard to win."

The cash jackpot always started at 500 dollars and increased by 20 dollars for every missed opportunity. On the chance of hitting less than five pins total or back-to-back gutter balls, there was a five-dollar minimum, so even the worst bowlers could win some money. Additionally, the prizes won from a single strike were selected from the "pin board," which hung on the wall in the shape of a triangle. A formation of bowling pins was attached to the board, with small prizes, such as dishware, listed on the back. Laurie Oberman briefly explains the more coveted high-end prizes.

Laurie Oberman: "I would sometimes call advertisers to get them to sign up for a package. I remember Highland Appliance; they were one of the sponsors who provided TVs and other miscellaneous prizes. Obviously, the more strikes you got the bigger the prizes were."

However, the contestants who bowled on the show weren't the only winners. People at home had the chance to win the same prize as the bowlers by sending in a postcard. Huh? Before taking to the lane, each contestant was required to select a "Pin Pal" from a lottery barrel on the set. The clear container was filled with postcards from viewers. The Pin Pal's name was announced on the air, and his or her prize matched that of the bowler with the exception of the jackpot—the cash would always be split between the two of them.

Throughout the years, *Bowling for Dollars* was often viewed as a bowling show. As Bob Allison points out, the program paid very little attention to the sport itself. So, for the record . . .

Bob Allison: "It's a game show; it's not a bowling show. We were giving away money and prizes; bowling was just the way you won. People weren't competing against each other as bowlers, they were competing for prizes."

Kingpin Bob

Long before the word *kingpin* had criminal implications, Bob Allison was routinely introduced at the start of the program as the Kingpin. Following an animated sequence of a man bowling a strike, Allison entered the lanes from a sliding door (in later years the single door was reconfigured into double doors shaped like a bowling pin) adjacent to a bleacher section of cheering fans, who adored him. The Kingpin describes how he went from being the pick of the litter to carrying the mother lode.

Bob Allison: "They had several prospects of people who could be the host. I was the number-one choice for Channel 4 to be the host. I never knew this because the management at Channel 4 said, 'He's got a big show on radio. He's already kind of a celebrity, and we should maybe promote one of our own.' So they had a fellow who was a wonderful performer—the weekend weatherman—but this wasn't *his* type of show . . . he couldn't do it.

"This guy went for five weeks and bombed like a lead balloon. This was a hard show to do, and it took somebody with a particular kind of attitude or experience to do it. At the end of the fifth week, I got a call to go to the general manager's office at Channel 4. I didn't work for Channel 4; I worked for WWJ radio, both of which were owned by the *Detroit News*. I knew everyone at Channel 4, so I go over there and [the general manager] says, 'We want you to do this television show. It's not doing well, and we need to make a change to see if we can save it. We've got eight weeks to do it.'"

Although Allison was promised by the station that he wouldn't be publicly blamed for the demise of the show if it failed, it wasn't enough . . . he needed more assurance. Taking no chances, he appealed to the listeners of his successful morning radio program, *Ask Your Neighbor*.

Bob Allison: "What I did was say, 'Hey gang, you've always wondered what the heck do I look like . . .' I never had pictures in my ads because I was a radio guy; I wanted to be a voice. I said, 'I'm going to do a television show; it's called *Bowling for Dollars,* a game show. We're gonna do a little bowling and have a lot of fun. It'll be on at 5:30 tonight, [so] tune in to Channel 4!' Everyday, I would tell them that. So over the period of two months I was able to bring in a great number of people from *Ask Your Neighbor* and that, to me, was the reason the show made it."

Laurie Oberman amplifies Allison's "neighborly" persona.

Laurie Oberman: "One of the reasons he was so popular was [because] he had a radio show going on for years, and it was [still] going on during *Bowling for Dollars*. It was a very chatty radio show. Ladies would call in for recipes; it was very homespun . . . very different from the way things are today. So he had a huge following before he was even doing *Bowling for Dollars*. People would be like, 'Oh, there he is . . . there he is . . .' And he would sign autographs like crazy between shows; he was very gracious to everyone. He was definitely a star . . . people were so excited to see him."

Before Motown's favorite neighbor could announce his induction into local television, he had to meet with John Claster, the president of Claster Productions, to learn the ropes. After their discussion, Allison concluded that the cookie-cutter template concocted on the East Coast was not appropriate for the Midwest. He didn't hesitate to speak his mind to Claster, even if it meant termination from his TV gig.

Bob Allison: "I did not like the format of the show. Before I started, one of the things I had to do was fly out to Baltimore and talk to John Claster and see how they did the show. He gave me the indoctrination thing, telling me exactly how to do it, and I said, 'John, all of that is kind of wrong; that's not what ought to happen.' He said, 'Well, that's the way we do it.' I said, 'Okay, but I'm going to make some changes. I'm going to do what feels right when I'm out there.' That's what a good performer does. He was showing me the Baltimore show, and I think the Los Angeles show; those were the [programs] they showed the prospective talent from a new market."

Much of what bothered Allison was the time spent on the "hellos." It was way too much! Contestants in the other markets were reading long lists of names as well as acknowledging every person they knew in the live audience. Detroit's new host believed that was time wasted and the show would suffer for it. He felt each contestant should briefly name a few of the folks seated in the audience, then say a quick hello to the people at home. That way contestants could spend a little more time talking about themselves and it helped to increase the pace of the show.

Firm in his conviction, Bob Allison told John Claster that in a year the Detroit version of the show would set the standard to which all other markets would aspire. His instinct was right. A year later Claster showcased the Motown edition to all of the markets. Ultimately there were more than 25 cities across the country producing *Bowling for Dollars*.

Fridays at the Thunderbowl

Unlike WBAL in Baltimore, WWJ did not build a bowling alley in its studio to accommodate the program. This meant that *Bowling for Dollars* had to be a "remote" production on location. But where? With alleys all over the Metro area, which one could best accommodate all of the props, the studio flats, the cameras, the remote truck, and, most important of all, the live audience. The Thunderbowl Lanes in Allen Park became the prime choice. Former Thunderbowl owner George Prybyla remembers why.

George Prybyla: "At the time, [the Thunderbowl] was the most popular alley in the [area], the largest one also. As a matter of fact, it was the largest bowling alley in the state. We were approached by the station, WWJ. They wanted to put on a bowling show, and they laid out their program to me. The station said to me, 'We'll run the show there, and you'll get all the publicity; people will know your place.' And I agreed to it, saying, 'What the hell, why not?' There's a section here called the Arena; it has 20 lanes there and grandstands. The main section has 54 and the north section has 20 . . . for a total of 94. They used the ones in the Arena for the show. The bowling was always played on two lanes."

Although the program aired five nights a week at various times over the years, a week's worth of episodes were taped on Friday afternoons beginning at one o'clock. Each show was recorded at the top of the hour, with half-hour breaks at the bottom. Laurie Oberman relives a typical day of production.

Laurie Oberman: "The contestants would show up, and I would check them in and get them all set up. There was that peanut gallery where their family and friends sat, so their family and friends would go sit in the audience. While the bowlers were practicing, I would go warm up the audience and let the family and friends know when they could wave. Then I prepped the bowlers, letting them know how the game worked and exactly what was going to happen during the show. Once we started taping, I was there keeping score and keeping it all under control.

"It was quite a setup. We had one side of the bowling alley set up with cameras, and it was back in the days when we did credits with flip cards. They were literally still graphics where the camera guy would shoot it, then you flip it, then shoot the next one . . . In between shows, when one show was over the crew would take a break, but I was still working [because] I had the whole next group, who'd just arrived for the next show. Bob would go and change into his next outfit and about 15 or 20 minutes later we were back on doing the same thing all over again. The crew used to bowl during the in-between time. They'd be bowling just for fun."

Because *Bowling for Dollars* attracted so many viewers every night, Fridays at the Thunderbowl evolved into a ritual that nobody could disrupt . . . not even Mother Nature.

Laurie Oberman: "There was a 'show must go on' mentality [at the station]; that show could not be missed. Once there was a horrible, horrible snowstorm, and literally they were canceling everything else that was scheduled for the next day because we had to do *Bowling for Dollars*. It was a Thursday night, and they took our crew and kept us all here at work, booking us into a hotel just to make sure that we could get to Allen Park the next day. Nothing stopped that show!

"Every Friday there I was, for years, and what would happen at the end of the day, you'd go home and hear the pins falling in your head! But it was a fun time because we all had a blast doing it."

Who Did You Bring with You?

Bob Allison: "The charm of the show was [that] it was local. People were talking about things that we knew about in Detroit . . . and they had people they knew in the audience. I had a cue card set up behind [the contestants]. You couldn't see it from the camera angle, but I'm looking at them and talking with them, looking over their shoulders, and here's this cue card that I had written pasted on the wall. It told me their names, where they were from—their city—and then I'd say, 'Who did you bring with you?' Then I'd turn around, and the camera would take an audience shot while [the contestant] started naming his or her friends and family in the audience. [They] would stand up, and everybody would applaud. Then I would say, 'Who do you want to say hello to at home?'"

Without question, it was those quick interview segments that mattered more to the viewers than the actual events. The chance that you might see somebody from your locale on TV had massive appeal. The opportunity to see yourself on television simply by sitting in the bleachers was enough to draw a crowd. On one of the many celebrity bowls, local entertainer George Young, whose horseshoed bald head has become a trademark, couldn't resist using the popular audience shot as bait for a joke.

George Young: "I did a funny bit. I was about to bowl, and Bob says, 'Who have you brought with you to watch you bowl for dollars for your favorite charity?' So I said, 'Well, Bob, I brought my brother and all my relatives.' Then they took a shot of the audience, of my brother, and I had brought everybody a 'bald' wig. So, everybody in the audience had a bald wig on! Bob died at that bit—it was cute."

Laurie Oberman: "George was on quite often; he was always willing to come on the show. I did have to book celebrity bowls, which was not the easiest thing to do. Radio personalities were key people . . . I booked people playing at the Fisher . . . like I remember Eartha Kitt, who was a nationally known performer, and it was interesting because in some ways the people liked the local celebrities better than the national ones."

With all of the hype about audiences, what about the bowlers? How were the contestants chosen? What were the odds of getting picked to be on the show? Laurie? Bob?

Laurie Oberman: "Every week in the mail I would get a list of names of people who had been selected. The way they were selected was they mailed in postcards to be on the show. The postcards went to the [Claster] production company. Once they were selected randomly, I'd get a list of people to book on the show. I had more names than you'd need for a given week, so if you didn't reach them you'd move on to another name."

Bob Allison: "We used to get the big canvas mailbags; two of them every week would come into the station—full! This was the number-one [local] television show of all time. It was a strip show [meaning the same program ran Monday through Friday] five nights a week, and it carried a

50 share in a 30 to 35 rating. This meant, very simply, that of every television set that was turned on in our area, half of them were watching *Bowling for Dollars.*"

Bob's Bankrupt Ball

Bob Allison: "I was identified with bowling as a result of being on *Bowling for Dollars*. Things used to come to me, [for example,] I used to go and hand out trophies to junior leagues. The kids just loved that Bob Allison was there from *Bowling for Dollars* to hand them their trophies.

"One time I was asked to throw out the first ball for the Masters League, the very good amateur bowlers; you had to be at least a 190 or 195 average, and they bowled at the Thunderbowl in the Arena. So I come out with this big introduction; there are a couple of hundred people in the stands watching, and I wasn't a bad bowler. I was fairly proficient and bowled in three leagues. So, I walk up, thinking, 'Just throw a good shot.' I went out there and threw the ball right over the second arrow, just like I wanted to, with just the lift I wanted in my fingers . . . and I thought, 'Oh boy, this is gonna be good!' I'm watching the ball go down, and it's not hooking because they *really* oiled the lanes. I thought, 'Well, at least I'm gonna hit the three pin and get a nice pin count.' And I'm watching it go down farther and thought, 'I'm going to hit the four pin.' By the time the ball got down there, I said, 'At least give me the ten pin . . .' It rolled right into the gutter! Everybody was, 'Awww . . .' I turned around and said, 'You've just seen my best shot!' Everybody broke up laughing. The next week in the *Bowler's News* on the front page was this little article that says, 'Allison throws bankrupt ball!'"

The Tenth Frame

Although *Bowling for Dollars* was a top-rated show for most of its television tenure, in 1979 the ratings began to decline. With a new decade on the horizon, the local bowling show began to fade like every other piece of pop culture from the 1970s. After an ownership change the previous year, WWJ was renamed WDIV by the new proprietor, the *Washington Post*. The new management attempted a kids' version of *Bowling for Dollars* hosted by Chuck Springer, which was short-lived. As for its predecessor, the cost of production in proportion to its ratings slump motivated the station to cancel what had been the highest-rated game show ever on local television. The six-year tournament may be over, but it still remains as one of Detroit TV's crown jewels.

George Prybyla: "*Bowling for Dollars* was a real good show for bowling as far as I was concerned. It attracted a lot of attention."

Bob Allison: "We struck a nerve . . . it was a locally produced show that was very homey and folksy. I think *Bowling for Dollars* was very good for Detroit and for bowling; it was a positive thing. Being a part of it was a very big plus in my life."

At the Zoo

I was definitely a fan of the show. I saw a lot of animals that I didn't know existed, and it piqued my interest in zoology. I thought, that's a cool place to work.
—MARTY MITTON, project manager, Detroit Zoo

When Paul Simon and Art Garfunkel sang, "Someone told me it's all happening at the zoo," that someone just might have been Detroit's own Sonny Eliot. The wisecracking weatherman known for such antics as creative weather conditions—"snain," a mix of snow and rain or the playful butchering of small towns such as Engadine (translation: "Enga-ringa-ding-enga-dinga-dine")—showed home audiences all of the awesome happenings at the Detroit Zoo. The weekly small-screen safaris served up "Eliot-style" on WWJ-TV, Channel 4, would often leave viewers puzzled as to which was cuter, the animals or Sonny.

The story begins in the spring of 1962, when WWJ had acquired a brand-new, highly sophisticated mobile unit. The station's news director envisioned the Detroit Zoo's annual grand opening in the spring as the perfect vehicle to break in the new mobile unit. The idea was to produce a half-hour special highlighting the zoo's season opener to be called simply *At the Zoo*. And who better to host the "family-friendly" program than the lovable weather guy who, in his early forties at the time, was preparing to walk down the aisle of matrimony. As a wedding present from the station, Sonny was given the program. What an opportunity it would be for Eliot to escape his "supporting role" on the evening news and be the star of the show!

Sonny Eliot befriending a chimp at the Detroit Zoo. (Courtesy Sonny Eliot.)

In the days that followed *At the Zoo*'s debut, WWJ received such an overwhelmingly positive response from viewers that it forced the program director, Ian Harrower, to think, why not do another half hour? If it does well, then maybe another half hour the following week and so forth until it busts. It would take 17 years for that bust to finally happen! So, with Sonny and the Channel 4 production crew making weekly visits to the zoo, exactly what would audiences see on the show that they couldn't see when visiting the grounds? Sonny Eliot outlines the premise.

Sonny Eliot: "The show was slated to be just an informational show, but it became an entertainment show because, since I didn't have a great background with animals at the time, [we thought,] 'What would an ordinary person, meaning me—very ordinary—want to know about an animal? How fast can he run? How much does he eat? Where does he go to the toilet?' And that's the kind of show it was . . . it was very, very down to the level of the ordinary person rather than someone with a background in zoology."

For an "ordinary" person, Sonny managed to accumulate a fair amount of knowledge about the animals, enough to intelligently discuss them on the program. Was it cue cards? Coaching from zoo curators? Or was it because he was there so much that he picked things up? Eliot reveals his secret.

Sonny Eliot: "I became involved with the animals in that I started reading all the zoological books, all the biology I could get. I became kind of, excuse the expression, a half-assed expert on animals and their habits, their speed and their evolution, whether they're ungulate or non-ungulate, cloven and not cloven in the hoof—there are many, many animals."

And with such a complex assortment of animals on the grounds the format in which to showcase them was kept quite simple. Marty Mitton, project manager at the Detroit Zoo and a fan of the show, along with Sonny Eliot, walks us through a typical episode.

Marty Mitton: "I can recall him being in all parts of the zoo: in buildings, in exhibits and talking with some of the curators at the time. Sonny highlighted different animals and different kinds of species every week, whether it was chimps or gorillas or what we call our megavertebrates—elephants, hippos and so on . . ."

Sonny Eliot: "It was a half-hour show with three segments: 10 minutes each, theoretically, which in television time comes out to eight minutes and some seconds. There are several hundred kinds of snakes; you do a segment on snakes. Or we'd do one whole segment on a lion or one whole segment on a seal. And there's always something to talk about; regardless of how many times you do an animal, there's something you don't know about it.

"The show ran for 17 years, and no matter where [WWJ] put it [on the schedule] people found it and liked it. It was just a simple show, and it had great, great appeal because of its simplicity. It just spoke of birds and bees . . . and feathers and fins . . ."

Grizzly Eliot

The Life and Times of Grizzly Adams depicted a mountain man's "special way with animals" to quote the 1970s movie and television show. And one of the things that made *At the Zoo* so wonderful for audiences of all ages was Sonny's "special way with animals"—minus the grizzly bear.

Sonny Eliot: "I became a part of it by getting in with the animals when I could. The dangerous animals I would not get in with, but I would get on the South American Pampas with the llamas and other animals. I would get in the water with the seals, I would go in with the elephants, I would go close enough to the gorillas to make friends with them, and I would handle the snakes if they were not toxic."

Just like Adams's Native American friend Nakuma, who helped Grizzly scout the wilderness, Eliot had his own veteran guide on hand within the man-made compound.

Sonny Eliot: "The fellow who was as responsible for the success of the show as anybody else was Bill Austin, who was curator of the reptiles and curator of education. He wrote a book called *Fifty Years at the Zoo*. He would put together the show. I would call him and say, 'What do we want to talk about?' He'd say, 'Well we've got some new snow leopards in, so let's talk about snow leopards.' And I go to the books and read up on snow leopards . . . then Bill and I would talk."

Shooting Season

Whether at the zoo in Royal Oak or the aquarium on Belle Isle, each week the WWJ production crew and host would arrive early in the morning prior to the park's opening to set up for the day's shoot. While shows produced in the summer were often videotaped, some were live. Retired WWJ director Jerry Burke notes the difference in the visual medium employed for the winter months.

Jerry Burke: "In the wintertime, we switched over to 16mm film and shot film shows, just with a film crew. We were usually inside in the wintertime, though we did some outside shows . . . we did some nighttime film shows [too]. We'd go to the zoo at night and shoot at night in the winter."

Regardless of the type of camera used, film or videotape, only one thing mattered to the viewers . . . the animals.

Sonny Eliot: "We talked about the animals and did not dwell on personalities other than [those of] the animals themselves. While we talked about them with the various curators, the cameras just roamed freely; there was no plan. We did a half hour a week. Sometimes we would go out and tape two half hours at a time. Every week we would go out and do a different portion of the zoo. People at the zoo were most, most cooperative."

While the zoo staff may have been cooperative, that wasn't always the case with the crew. Retired WWJ/WDIV stage manager Bob Stackpoole recalls a "traveling shot" fiasco that made Sonny and Bill Austin's day.

Bob Stackpoole: "I remember once, now this is with the big studio cameras and a big remote truck, we had a traveling shot through the park. We had two cameras on the big truck: we put one on the roof and one shooting out the side door. Then there was a generator to supply power for all of us, and then behind that was the stagehands' truck [a Ford Econoline van] with another camera shooting out the back door. And behind that was a golf cart with Sonny and Bill [Austin]. We didn't have wireless mics back in those days, so I'm back there next to the camera feeding the mic, picking up the slack so [the cables] don't get caught under the tires. And so there was a miscommunication and the stagehand driving the truck didn't understand and all of a sudden—BOOM—I fell out of the back end of the truck! Sonny and Bill thought it was the biggest joke of the year."

Monkey Business

As lighthearted and full of fun as *At the Zoo* appeared, there was an era in zoo history when respect for the animals was less dignified. It came in the form of entertainment for humans. With the aid of retired WWJ director Jim Breault and Marty Mitton, Eliot recalls an act that was perhaps the most popular of all the animal shows.

Sonny Eliot: "The chimpanzee was a half-hour show in and of itself. Every time you showed that, it was just fun for the people . . . but not for the animals."

Jim Breault: "They would train the chimps all winter long in the routine they had to do, so the first people they saw in the spring were us. We were out there getting ready to do the show, and we were standing there watching them. The chimps were riding these motorcycles in a circle, and they were so shocked to see people that they ran right into a wall."

Marty Mitton: "The chimps would dress up in little costumes and so on . . . And that was kind of an entertainment philosophy that fell nicely into the program, even though you would still get some educational information. But zoos have evolved over time to get away from the entertainment or exploitation of animals, and the zoo business has gotten into really purely education and conservation now. If there was a Sonny Eliot program today, it would be, in my estimation, a totally different format than what was done 40 years ago."

Sonny Eliot: "You don't see many animal shows anymore because they lack dignity and people have changed their minds about what is and what isn't [appropriate]."

Animal Planet

Certainly one thing that isn't common on the part of the animals is predictability! It's a world where anything can happen . . . and usually does! Take it away guys . . .

Jerry Burke: "You'd be setting up out there, pulling cables and moving cameras, setting up a monitor, moving a truck . . . and the animals would be right there with their faces over the fence looking at you, everything that was going on, all the excitement . . . And [when] you rolled the tape and looked at the first shot all you'd have were 'hind' shots—they'd moved to the other end of the exhibit looking the other way. It would happen time after time after time! You'd have to sit there and beg them with bread to get them to come back."

Bob Stackpoole: "I remember the rhinoceros, when we were shooting back there, and that thing would charge the bars. He just bashed into it."

Sonny Eliot: "Rhinos pee with a curved penis and they pee 20 feet and you'd get peed on by a rhino. Or [you're standing] in front of a gorilla cage and the gorilla poops on his hands and throws it at you."

Jim Breault: "I remember that on the shows I did out there the gorillas would come out when they'd see us and put the hand below, [poop], and just throw it at us. Oh yeah, I remember that!"

Sonny Eliot: "Once when I went into the South American Pampas where they had wild geese; one of them came up and bit me on the back of the leg and tore through the pants."

Jerry Burke: "One time Sonny was doing a thing with a goat, and the goat chewed the audio cable in two—the one connected to his microphone."

But, not every mishap was the fault of an animal. The stagehands caused their share of mischief as well . . . right, Sonny?

Sonny Eliot: "They would sometimes fill my pockets with small snakes!"

Talking to the Animals

"If we could talk to the animals . . . what a neat achievement that would be . . ." Well, he may not have been as successful in conversing with the animals as Dr. Doolittle, but Sonny Eliot created a piece of memorabilia that did the next best thing . . . it let "them" talk to us.

Sonny Eliot: "I made a record. We went out there with a microphone and got into the cage with the lions and into the pen with the elephants to record the natural sounds and put them on a record. Then I wrote a script. They were 45 [rpm]; we sold them for a dollar apiece. And we sold thousands of those records—*A Trip to the Zoo with Sonny Eliot*. Every sound on it was a legitimate sound that we taped . . . that made it believable."

The Children's Zoo

At the Zoo excelled at piquing children's natural curiosity about animals. For fans such as Mark Nowotarski and Greg Russell, those childhood memories of "Sonny" days have never stopped shining.

Mark Nowotarski: When *At the Zoo* was on, I was a child. Sonny pointed out things I never knew about the animals. I used to want to go to the zoo after I'd see his programs. I haven't been to the zoo in 20 years. There's a person I was talking to [who said], 'I'd like to go to the zoo,' and right away I started talking about Sonny Eliot's program. Even now, so many years after the fact, when somebody happens to mention the zoo I happen to bring up [the show] because it clicked—they were parallel."

Greg Russell: "I remember one time there was this kid named Clifton who lived down the street from me and was on the show. I was so bummed because it was like, 'He's on TV . . . I'm not . . . put me on with the giraffes!' It was such a good show—a nice family show. You always knew you could tune in, enjoy it, and it was local, which made it even more special!"

And for those kids, like Clifton, fortunate enough to be there on the day of a show taping, there was a little added bonus.

Sonny Eliot: "I would hand out pictures to the kids when the zoo finally opened and we had crowds around. Everybody liked it."

Closing the Gates

In 1979, after a healthy 17-year run, Sonny made his last televised trip to the zoo. Having undergone a change in ownership the previous year, the

WWJ call letters were now WDIV. Along with all the restructuring at the station, management felt that *At the Zoo* had run its course and closed the gates on the show. With some final thoughts on what may have been his most treasured wedding gift . . . once again here's Detroit TV legend and *At the Zoo* host, Sonny Eliot.

Sonny Eliot: "Surveys show that there are three things [you should do] if you want to gain attention: do a show with travel in it, children in it, or animals in it. So we incorporated it all. And we had nothing but great fun out there. It was a show that developed in and of itself and became of great interest because of the great interest in animals that people have. It would be a good show even today, I think. It could not compete with animal shows that are on Animal Planet—no way it could compete. But it could compete with a popular show if you said, 'Come on kids, be on-camera, and we'll talk about the alligators today . . . ' and get them all around and let them ask questions . . . it'd still be a good show."

The End of an Era

8

Where Have All the Good Times Gone?

It's hard to imagine that the creative spirit behind the golden age of Detroit TV fizzled after only 32 years. Even though local television in the Motor City dates back to 1947 and continues on a very small scale today, there's no official gauge for determining exactly when the golden age began or ended. Perhaps the best way to calculate the period would be to start with the arrival of Soupy Sales in 1953. *Lunch with Soupy* was the first really big show on the local airwaves to attract an audience of all ages. Some people may dispute this claim, but it's derived using the same formula that defines other golden or classic periods in the media.

For example, Hollywood's golden age is often connected to the "studio system" that arose in the 1920s and collapsed in the 1960s. Classic rock coincides with the Beatles' landing at Kennedy Airport in New York on February 7, 1964, and ends sometime in the late 1970s with the rise of disco. Television's golden age is commonly referred to as the 1950s and 1960s, though some may believe differently. Regardless of the precise dates, it's safe to commence Detroit's golden age of television in 1953, when Soupy Sales ate his first lunch on the air, and end it about 1985. By that time, the vast majority of local productions had been replaced with prepackaged syndicated programs that were more cost effective for stations to air.

327

Syndication and Infomercials Reign Death

Former WDIV-TV program director Henry Maldonado explained it best in his discussion of *Sonya* when he outlined the philosophy behind the local stations' purchase of syndicated shows—money and resources. By the early to mid-1980s, syndication distributors such as KingWorld offered hometown stations strip programs (meaning that the same show airs at the same time Monday through Friday) such as *Wheel of Fortune, Jeopardy,* and *Oprah,* which were more profitable to run. The syndicated shows are already produced, packaged, and audience tested; the stations pay for the licensing to air them and consequently almost all the revenue generated from commercial spots is sheer profit. And, as Maldonado noted, the overhead in personnel and facilities it took to produce the entertainment programs could now be redirected toward a more efficient execution of the news—the stations' new primary focus.

Another animal that began to show its colors on the local dial sometime around the late 1980s or early 1990s—and still lurks in our living rooms today—is the dreaded infomercial. Whether anybody truly watches them in their entirety is debatable, but what's not in dispute is their presence on the tube. Originally they were aired during the night after stations decided to run programming 24 hours a day and blocs of airtime needed to be filled. Soon they spread like a virus into the weekends and then the early morning hours during the week. They were long, paid advertisements for everything under the sun, from cooking utensils to exercise equipment, music collections, vitamins, and get-rich-quick schemes. With 24 hours of airtime to fill seven days a week, the infomercial has become a gift horse to local stations. The sponsor pays for the entire time slot, and all the station has to do is air it. Why spend the money to produce programming to be seen at odd hours when a sponsor is willing to pay?

Local television is first and foremost a business, just like any other entity that produces, manufactures, and distributes a product or service. And because the stations are in the business of making money, just like any other corporation, they will always opt for the most cost-efficient productions to maximize their profits. Some might say television has forgotten how to cater to the community it serves. Others believe that trends and changes in public tastes are responsible for the demise of local shows. How about the increased demand for more and better local news coverage? Blame it on the 1980s, the decade of greed, yuppies, and corporate mergers. Regardless of the reasoning behind the change in programming, one conclusion is obvious: the days of locally produced entertainment shows reminiscent of the golden age are gone forever.

So What's Left? Anything?

Actually there is but to a lesser degree. Other than the newscasts, sports and public affairs have never stopped. Tigers baseball, Pistons basketball, Lions football, and Red Wings hockey continue to be covered by the local channels, complete with pre- and postgame shows. Sunday nights after the 10:00 and 11:00 p.m. newscasts, Channels 2, 4, and 7 run their own weekly sports update program. Weekly public affairs and interview discussion shows, particularly on WTVS-TV, Channel 56, haven't fallen to the wayside, either. However, the difference between these types of programs and the ones depicted throughout this book, other than the content, lies in their production and promotion.

Sports and public affairs programs are produced by the news departments as extensions of them. Very often the on-camera talent is the stations' sports anchor for the sports show and a news anchor for public affairs. The same staff responsible for delivering the news provides these weekly discussions about sports and political issues. And while promos for these programs do run on the air you won't find the talent endorsing advertised products or signing autographs or posing for pictures at an appearance like you used to see with Jingles, Johnny Ginger, and Sir Graves Ghastly. The only local media folks carrying on that tradition are on the radio.

Very few local entertainment programs remained in existence in the 1990s. The last decade of the twentieth century in many ways saw the end of entertainment-based shows. After *Kelly & Company* ended in 1995, the only station-produced shows appeared weekly, none of which was built around the talent. Many of them contained stylized formats in which anyone could carry the show. For instance, WDIV created a Saturday evening game show, *Mega Bucks Giveaway* (later renamed *The Road to Riches*), hosted by weatherman Chuck Gaidica; WKBD dished out *Straight Talk* with news anchor Amyre Makupson; and WTVS sent us a *Backstage Pass* with radio air personality Ann Delisi. Documentary specials of local interest prospered in the 1990s, as did special events such as the Freedom Festival Fireworks, the Thanksgiving Day Parade, the North American International Auto Show, and the Woodward Dream Cruise, all of which continue to be favorites today.

Although these original productions occasionally pop up, they fall short of the glory days when local programming was plentiful and the stations were home to the stars—our stars! There were television celebrities that the public, especially kids, could aspire to meet, whether it be at an organized appearance or a random sighting in public. Yes, those old shows reached out and connected with the community on an intimate level by catering to the preferences of its people. We grew up with them, they made us laugh, they taught us lessons, they eased our fears, they inspired us, and, most important of all, they entertained us by emphasizing all that is positive about the city of Detroit. They may be gone, but they're certainly not forgotten!

Text design by Mary H. Sexton
Typesetting by Delmastype, Ann Arbor, Michigan
Text font: Sabon
Display font: Franklin Gothic Medium

"Sabon was designed by Jan Tschichold in 1964 and jointly
released by Stempel, Linotype, and Monotype foundries."
  —Courtesy www.adobe.com

Franklin Gothic, named after Benjamin Franklin, was
designed between 1903 and 1912 by Morris Fuller Benton
for the American Type Founders Company.
  —Courtesy www.myfonts.com